14 AUGUSTINE'S LAWS
17 "ASSUMPTION OF THE RISK"
28 2010
42 THE DEATH OF COMMON SENSE
  * CHILD - TOKYO - PUBLIC TAXES FUNDED
59-60 EPA

1.8 TRILLION
BUDGET

A = 721/.4

1802S
.4 ⟩ 7210

The Case

AGAINST

Lawyers

The Case AGAINST Lawyers

How Lawyers, Politicians, and Bureaucrats Have Turned the Law into an Instrument of Tyranny—and What We as Citizens Have to Do About It

CATHERINE CRIER

BROADWAY BOOKS

New York

BROADWAY

THE CASE AGAINST LAWYERS. Copyright © 2002 by Catherine
Crier. All rights reserved. No part of this book may be reproduced
or transmitted in any form or by any means, electronic or
mechanical, including photocopying, recording, or by any
information storage and retrieval system, without written
permission from the publisher. For information, address
Broadway Books, a division of Random House, Inc.,
1540 Broadway, New York, NY 10036.

Broadway Books titles may be purchased for business or
promotional use or for special sales. For information, please write to:
Special Markets Department, Random House, Inc.,
280 Park Avenue, New York, NY 10017.

PRINTED IN THE UNITED STATES OF AMERICA

BROADWAY BOOKS and its logo, a letter B bisected on the
diagonal, are trademarks of Broadway Books, a division of
Random House, Inc.

Visit our website at www.broadwaybooks.com

First edition published 2002.

Library of Congress Cataloging-in-Publication Data

Crier, Catherine.
    The case against lawyers: how lawyers, politicians, and
    bureaucrats have turned the law into an instrument of tyranny—
    and what we as citizens have to do about it / Catherine Crier.
    1st ed.
        p.   cm.
    Includes bibliographical references and index.
    —1. Law—United States.   I. Title.

KF384.C75 2002
349.73—dc21

                                                    2002074563

ISBN 0-7679-0504-0

10   9   8   7   6   5   4   3   2   1

FOR

Henry Drummond

and

Atticus Finch

Contents

Lawyers in the United States

form a power that , , ,

envelops society as a whole,

penetrates into each of the

classes that compose it, works

in secret, acts constantly on it

without its knowing, and in

the end models it to its own

desires.

—Alexis de Tocqueville,
Democracy in America (1840)

From the time I was a little girl, I wanted to be a lawyer. I was obsessed by the notion of justice. Like the boy who became a marine biologist after witnessing his goldfish being flushed down the toilet, I had my reasons. My heroes were the great trial lawyers of our time, like Clarence Darrow, as portrayed by Spencer Tracy in *Inherit the Wind*, and Atticus Finch, as portrayed by Gregory Peck in *To Kill a Mockingbird*. These were the fellows who, in Texas terms, could charm the socks off a rooster or, better yet, could change the course of human destiny with the force of their words. These were the characters who convinced me I wanted a career in the law. Now, if you'd asked my mother, she'd tell you I'd argue with a post and had to find a profession that would pay me to do that. Nevertheless, I like my story, and I'm sticking to it.

As a youngster, I believed our founders had divined a bit of heaven on earth. They believed that the rule of law could defeat tyranny. Remember, the first immigrants came to this new world to escape arbitrary decrees. A king could, for example, pronounce a tax on wheat and immediately begin collecting revenues. If he chose, the law would affect only certain segments of the population, while his cohorts remained immune. The favored grew wealthy while others starved. Witnessing this injustice, our founders gave such authority instead to the people. Tempered by their representatives and restrained by the Constitution, Americans would make and administer the rules for our new society. Lawyers, pledged to justice and democracy, would be the guardians at the gate. No one man, no single group, could arbitrarily or selfishly direct our lives.

But there was a catch, as Benjamin Franklin forewarned. As he left the Constitutional Convention, a woman asked, "What sort of government have we, Mr. Franklin?" He replied, "A Republic, Madam, if you can keep it." Thomas Jefferson, ever the idealist, believed our countrymen would live up to the challenges of a self-governing society. The pragmatist Franklin had his doubts.

An ingenious fellow, Alexis de Tocqueville, described our challenge over a century ago in his monumental work, *Democracy in America*. So clearly did he see the strength of a democracy and the weakness of human character, his words might have been written today. He said, in summary, that our real power as a people came through voluntary associations. Our personal freedoms would be protected if we could voluntarily resolve the problems of society rather than permit the heavy hand of government to do it for us. But he recognized our great weakness—the willingness to live "as strangers apart from the rest." If we lost our communal bond, then authority and social control would arise elsewhere. "Man would yield his sovereignty to an immense power," he predicted, "one that does not destroy, or even tyrannize, but one that serves to stupefy a people, reducing them to nothing better than a flock of timid and industrious sheep."

Over the years, as a student of history, politics, and the law, I have concluded that Tocqueville's prediction was correct. While the Constitution and Bill of Rights provided an extraordinary blueprint, the plan required appropriate execution. Unfortunately, we Americans have failed to shoulder our responsibilities. The qualities of active citizenship that Jefferson ascribed to us have not been realized, nor have our appointed leaders lived up to their noble assignment.

The rule of law was never meant to be a substitute for community standards. Tocqueville rests his entire case for democracy on our shared values and ideals when he says, "I am convinced that the happiest situation and the best laws cannot maintain a constitution despite mores, whereas the latter turn even the most unfavorable positions and the worst laws to good account." He believed that you and I would actively perform as citizens and express our principles and concerns. Communities, not some distant government, would define the rules and laws for society. Members of those local groups were likely to agree on those enactments and obey them accordingly. This shared acceptance is one characteristic our laws should reflect. There are others.

Most obviously, the law must be known. It is not. Today IRS agents cannot give us consistent advice at tax time. They don't know what the tax laws say any more than we do. Contractors and manufacturers have thousands of rules to follow governing the smallest activity under our Occupational Safety and Health Administration regulations. No one can possibly know them all. Police officers can't even rely on a rule book. They don't know from case to case whether their judgment is good or bad until some court reviews their conduct.

The law must be fair. It is not. A cigarette smoker gets cancer then collects billions of dollars because he can't kick the habit while some pathetic drug addict goes to prison. White-collar shysters scam millions and get probation or a stint in Club Fed while a petty thief does serious time. The death penalty is administered to poor and often minority defendants while celebrity murderers go free.

The law must be reasonable. It is not. Labels now warn us against the most absurd events. A thirteen-inch wheel on a wheelbarrow warns "not intended for highway use" while an electric router for carpenters says "This product not intended for use as a dental drill." These warnings are not a corporate attempt at humor but are the result of litigation. Rules of due process can keep a bad teacher in the classroom for years or forestall a federal mandate, like seat belts, for decades.

The law should compensate only for legitimate injury caused by another. It does not. If you were exposed to asbestos at some point but have never taken ill, that doesn't stop you from collecting. Some hacker decides there's a flaw in computer software and sues, although no one has experienced any problems. Never mind. You can collect. Why not testify to what your loved one *may* have felt as the car or plane crashed? This is compensable.

The law should provide for just compensation. It should not unfairly enrich the players. Punitive damages have rocketed into the stratosphere for the lucky plaintiff with the right jury. Virtually every lawsuit can be handled on a contingency fee, making the attorney a financial partner in the outcome. Class actions are accepted under the flimsiest of filings, and the lawyers pocket millions of dollars while winning discount coupons for their clients. States hire private firms to bankroll and litigate against unpopular defendants, such as the tobacco industry. This practice has created an entire class of billionaire lawyers paid outrageous fees from public money.

The law should address the concerns of our citizens. Yet it is often created and enforced for political reasons. The tax code is the greatest source of corruption on Capitol Hill as tax breaks and favors are delivered to big campaign supporters. Lax enforcement and exemption from regulations can be just as valuable to these groups. Just ask Enron.

The law must emerge from our legislative process. Often it does not. Lawyers and judges now preempt policy areas that legislatures are not addressing. Entire industries now operate under judicial fiat rather than statues and regulations thanks to legal settlements and consent decrees. The big-tort lawyers brag on their ability to legislate as they use a court case to rewrite the laws on tobacco, guns, or HMOs.

The law should be pragmatic. It is not. Despite forty years and billions of dollars, the war against drugs goes on. Statistics show that neither supply nor demand has changed a wit during this battle. Yet we respond with more laws and tougher enforcement in the face of failure. The same holds true for the death penalty. Study after study demonstrates the inequity and injustice that accompanies this punishment. Given the fallible nature of human beings, there is no way to guarantee that only the guilty will die.

We have come to expect everything from the law and very little from ourselves. We do not trust one another to be honest or fair. Subjective decisions are suspect. We want things measured objectively and reduced to writing. The most minute decisions or tasks are governed by rules that conveniently replace judgment, reason, and innovation. Yet all the statutes in the world cannot insure we have good cops or teachers or politicians.

Not everyone loses in this trade-off. In barely a generation, lawyers, politicians, and bureaucrats have taken the palace without firing a shot. These groups control the creation and enforcement of law. Their ability to write rules and manipulate them at will has established a new tyranny in America. The rest of us, sometimes willingly, other times selfishly or in ignorance, succumb to their false promises. Believing that mere words can guarantee security and equality, we have traded away our liberties. Abdicating personal responsibility, we now expect the government and courts to compensate for the vagaries of life. Succumbing to divisive rhetoric, we support intrusive laws that unsuccessfully target social and moral behaviors. Finally, we permit the selective enforcement of rules and the legal giveaway of tax dollars as political favors for those big contributors who feather the political nests.

Our great cornerstone of democracy, the rule of law, has become a source of power and influence, not liberty and justice. I resent the insidious manipulations by those entrusted with such authority, but even more, I despise our deliberate ignorance and passive acceptance of these shackles on the American spirit. We have abdicated our freedom, literally our democracy, to the rule makers. Our institutions now serve these masters. They are the ones clearly winning the game. The rest of us are their timid and industrious sheep. It is time for a citizens' revolt. It is time to break the rules!

ONE | We Love Our Rules

Sports have always been a favorite metaphor in American life. It is hard to have a conversation with an American male that doesn't include some reference to goals, yard lines, home runs, Hail Marys, you name it. I find an amazing correlation between the way we play our games and the way we live our lives.

Compare many European sporting events with American games. In soccer or rugby, the play is virtually nonstop. There is only one referee on the field. When infractions occur, the ref approximates the site of the foul, the ball is replaced, and play immediately resumes.

In American football, the field is covered with officials on top of every play. Yellow flags fly constantly. Chain markers carefully measure every inch the ball progresses. There are constant timeouts for consultation, even video review of contested plays. The rules are endless. Arguments abound and controversial calls will be examined for years. Thank God there's not a level of appeal beyond the head referee. As it is, a game with sixty playing minutes takes three times as long to finish.

But we love our rules. We think they make a game safer, fairer, and more just. If someone gets injured, it is time to sue the other player, the equipment manufacturer, or the school. If a ref makes a bad call, we need more cameras for the instant replay. We seem unwilling to accept that there will be times when chance, accident, bias, or corruption will defeat the best rules and regulations.

I say, get a life. Let's get on with the game. I find it amazing that people who profess to be so rugged, independent, and free want even our roughest sport to be predictable and safe. The rugby players I know scoff at our wimpy version of football. "Imagine," they say, "if we put those guys on our field and made them play without pads essentially nonstop for an hour. They'd all be dead!"

This is more than a metaphor. This is now the American way of life. Name one thing you did today—after rolling off that mattress (bearing the label "Do not remove under punishment of law"), showering in water with the temperature preset by a boiler manufacturer to prevent scalding, using the hairdryer that warns against electrocution in the bathtub, eating breakfast properly labeled for the allergy or calorie conscious, getting into your car as the seat-belt warning dings, then heading down the road with traffic signs and lights everywhere you turn—that isn't somehow regulated. It's hard to do.

Take a gander at ten of my favorite examples from the annual Wacky Warning Label contest sponsored by Michigan Lawsuit Abuse Watch. Remember, these are all legitimate labels to protect you from yourself:

NUMBER TEN: The label on a handheld massager advises "Do not use while sleeping or unconscious."

NUMBER NINE: A label on a public toilet reads "Recycled flush water unsafe for drinking."

NUMBER EIGHT: A can of self-protection pepper spray warns users "May irritate eyes."

NUMBER SEVEN: No matter how slow the print out, please heed the warning on a laser printer cartridge: "Do not eat toner."

NUMBER SIX: A thirteen-inch wheel on a wheelbarrow warns "Not intended for highway use."

NUMBER FIVE: A label on prescription sleeping pills warns that they "may cause drowsiness."

NUMBER FOUR: A cardboard car sunshield that keeps sun off the dashboard warns "Do not drive with sunshield in place."

NUMBER THREE: Bicycle shin guards warn "Shin pads cannot protect any part of the body they do not cover."

NUMBER TWO: A household iron warns "Never iron clothes while they are being worn" (and don't steam yourself either; I've tried). And finally, my favorite, and 1999's big winner:

NUMBER ONE: Parents, please read the baby stroller label that cautions "Remove child before folding."

These labels are more than superfluous "information." Most are a response to some lawsuit as courts have expanded the right to be an idiot. Company lawyers, fearing liability, are madly composing such moronic disclaimers while Washington bureaucrats are codifying them as laws. These are our taxpayer dollars at work.

Once two or more people are involved, things only get worse. Whether at work, at school, or in the marketplace, everything is regulated. We have more protective employment laws on the books than ever, yet complaints are at an all-time high. (If you write it, they will sue!) Discrimination and disability rulings now cover every conceivable human variable, exacerbating our differences rather than insuring a specious "equality." Our educational process is monitored by an endless litany of rules for teaching and discipline, yet student performance is abysmal and the kids are out of control. Government regulates our nutrition and foods, while the national girth and associated health problems explode. Every aspect of workplace safety is regulated, yet the number of workplace deaths has been static for years. The safer cars get, the more auto insurers are hit for bodily injuries. Even worse, we have developed a plethora of excuses to justify the most aberrant or plainly stupid behavior. Speed down an icy roadway without your seat belt and relatives still can sue the automaker and hospital when you crash and burn. There is no personal responsibility for asinine conduct.

Litigation is no longer a crapshoot, it is becoming a sure thing. If you can't get a satisfactory nuisance settlement, then try your case; the awards are phenomenal! Human life is now quantified in astronomical terms. In 1999 the ten biggest jury awards to individual plaintiffs totaled almost $9 billion—three times the amount in 1998. One verdict delivered $1.2 billion to the family of thirty-two-year-old Jennifer Cowart. She died of burn injuries after a go-cart accident at an amusement park apparently due to a defective gas cap. The accident was horrific to be sure, but $1.2 billion?

Many of these huge verdicts are reduced on appeal, but it wasn't until 1996 that the U.S. Supreme Court first overturned *any* punitive damage award for being excessive. The case was against BMW of North America. A fellow bought a new car in 1990 only to discover months later that its surface had been damaged and refinished before sale. The automaker's policy at the time was not to reveal repairs that were less than 3 percent of a car's retail price. In this case, the resurfacing cost $601. The jury, however, awarded $4,000 in compensatory damages and $4 million as punishment for the practice. The Alabama appeals court kindly cut the punitive award to $2 million.

BMW appealed to the U.S. Supreme Court. In his majority opinion, Justice John Paul Stevens found the "damage" to the car had no effect on its performance, safety, or appearance. He then ruled that there should be some fair ratio between the actual and punitive damages. Even at the reduced rate of $2 million, this sum was still 500 times the so-called damage to the car. The case was sent back to the lower court for review with this admonishment: "We are not prepared to draw a bright line marking the limits of a constitutionally acceptable punitive damage award . . . however, we are fully convinced that the grossly excessive award in this case transcends the constitutional limit." (I guess it's sort of like pornography. You know it when you see it.) Ultimately the punitive award was cut to $50,000.

By 2000 these sums were merely peanuts. One fifty-seven-year-old smoker who testified (with a straight face) that he didn't know the dangers of smoking until 1994 was awarded $3 billion against Philip Morris. Upon judicial review, smoker Richard Boeken saw his $3 billion fizzle to a mere $100 million. In March 2002 a jury awarded $150 million to the estate of Michele Schwartz after finding that a tobacco company falsely represented low-tar cigarettes as less dangerous than regular cigarettes. Although Philip Morris argued the company only promised the brands were "milder," the plaintiffs asserted that Schwartz had switched from regular cigarettes because she believed the low-tar version would be better for her health. By the way, Schwartz worked for years for her husband, who just happened to be a doctor. I'm no fan of cigarette manufacturers, but people have certainly known since 1964 when the Surgeon General slapped a warning on smokes that this was a ba-a-ad habit.

In 2000 the $246 billion settlement of state tobacco suits toppled the scales. It has been called the largest redistribution of wealth to the smallest number of people in the history of the world. This payout does not refer to the monies awarded to the sick but the billions that went to a cluster of attorneys for their work on the cases. As much as I hate the product, the lawsuits are ridiculous. We have known for almost forty years what smoking does to the body. Quitting is hard, but we tell illegal drug users to stop or go to prison. Cigarette addicts get money instead! Tobacco litigation has opened the floodgates for creative lawyers now targeting the gun industry. HMOs, nursing homes, and paint companies are on their radar screens. Get ready for the alcohol and fatty foods litigation. It is coming.

This type of litigation has also put dreams of riches into the minds of governors and attorneys general around the country. An incestuous relationship between these officials and private attorneys is growing. Here's how it works. The government decides to attack some "dangerous" industry to protect its citizens. Instead of calling on lawyers already on the state payroll, the officials hire big outside firms—often the same firms that are major contributors to the political campaigns that put and keep the officials in office. These state executives get bragging rights with the voters for lawsuit awards that pump up the general revenue fund, the private attorneys get huge contingency fees, and often some of those fees recycle right back into the campaign coffers for the next election.

But as long as the appellate courts are reducing most excessive verdicts, is there a problem? Yes. These remittances coming long after the awards make headlines do not correct the broader damage to our justice system. Back in 1998 Mark E. Dapier, general counsel to Mercury Finance Company, testified before the Senate Judiciary Committee about these other effects. His company had been sued for "fraudulent suppression" of material information to a consumer. Mercury sold a car loan at a discount to a subsidiary that would collect on the note (a very common practice). When the original car buyer defaulted on the $6,000 note, he sued Mercury, alleging that the failure to reveal this discount was fraud. The initial jury found $90,000 in actual damages and $50 million in punitive damages in a case where the plaintiff suffered no harm!

While the trial judge ultimately reduced the punitive award to $2 million, the defendant's headaches were far from over. When the initial verdict was reported, more suits, some as class actions, cropped up in other states. The original plaintiff's attorney immediately filed nine more identical suits. Fearing more huge awards, Mercury settled many of these cases. Others went through protracted litigation and appeals. Finally, after Mercury obtained several state and federal court rulings that this discounting practice was perfectly legal, the suits stopped. Of course, no one compensated the company for the millions it had spent on legal fees and settlements or the enormous amount of time and energy it had devoted to dozens of lawsuits.

Insurance companies don't wait for any rebate before upping their fees. In 1999 the Oregon Supreme Court refused to put a $500,000 cap on pain and suffering awards in malpractice cases. Almost immediately, juries came back with three multimillion-dollar awards. Insurance rates went up. Mississippi's *Hattiesburg American* reported in 2002 that a group of emergency doctors "paid $140,000 for malpractice insurance" two years ago. "Last year, the premium went to $250,000." Doctors have been warned that "the next annual premium would be $437,500 or $475,000." An Associated Press article in March reported the immediate result. "The Mississippi Trauma Advisory Committee has suspended re-inspection of its hospitals for a year to give health officials time to address the growing problem of surgeons leaving the system." The hospitals are losing so many specialists that they cannot meet state trauma standards, so the enforcement agency must simply look the other way. "We're in a crisis," said State Health Officer Ed Thompson. This development is being replicated across the country.

Damages for pain and suffering are also soaring, as is our expectation of large payoffs for every tragedy that befalls us. These sums are rarely reduced on appeal. In a *U.S. News and World Report* piece entitled "How Lawyers Abuse the System," the authors discussed various trial tactics designed to elicit the most melodramatic statements possible. Using the power of suggestion, one attorney asked his client, "Did a false arrest and imprisonment bring back memories of the Holocaust?" People who merely witness an event will line up to recover.

After the terror attack of September 11, the government made a determination, whether right or wrong, that it was necessary to protect the airlines from repeated lawsuits. While we may be able to survive without asbestos or lead paint companies, bankrupting the airlines to satisfy thousands of judgments would not be in the best interests of the nation. Unfortunately, that big-picture consideration has never stopped attorneys and their clients before, so the government legislated limits on those industry suits while trying to fairly compensate victims and their families with taxpayer dollars.

As politically incorrect as this may seem, the families from September 11 who object to the government fund that specifies a set $250,000 in emotional damages and $50,000 for each additional survivor need to ask themselves: Just what would compensate for the psychic loss? If you can name any number, you're way ahead of me. In a February *Time* magazine piece in 2002, one family objected to these sums by saying "Have you ever seen a twelve-year-old have a nervous breakdown?" Therapy would be covered under actual damages so again, my question is "How much cash will make the pain better?" because for most people, no amount of money will excise the hurt. The sad truth is that thousands of people are killed every year in myriad tragedies, from accidents, to crimes, to terrorist horrors. The shooting victim's family rarely recovers from the robber's attack. The suicide doesn't leave his or her loved ones much room to recover. Which victim is worth hundreds of thousands for suffering relatives and which one is worth absolutely nothing . . . and why?

Moving on, plaintiffs no longer have to show any actual damage to be included in class action suits. One example is the asbestos litigation, where the courts have expanded the right to sue to the point that plaintiffs with only a "likelihood" of becoming ill are collecting. You've heard the commercials: "If you have ever been exposed [not necessarily made ill by] to X, Y or Z call now!" Many people truly suffering from asbestos exposure may never recover a dime as company after company goes belly up paying plaintiffs with no apparent injury. It is interesting to note that plaintiffs' lawyers are now recognizing the need to keep these companies on life support. They try to pace their attacks and awards against certain industries so that they don't destroy them completely. If you hear a plaintiff's lawyer say "We're going to put big tobacco or gun companies out of business," that's just for show. Since there is no notion of double jeopardy in these civil actions, the attorneys can return to feed on these defendants as long as they remain financially viable.

Attorneys now sue for "potential" problems certain products may display. In 1999 Ford was a defendant in a mass product defect class action that ended in a mistrial. Ominously, the judge had allowed plaintiffs to go to trial after pleading only the "prospect that an alleged stalling defect might someday manifest itself," although none had ever occurred. The greatest scam in these big class actions is the recovery of those discounts or coupons for the plaintiffs while the attorneys pocket the actual cash.

Lawyers are making out like bandits as we litigate the most inane conflicts. Billable hours now dwarf any social contribution by the profession. In 1999 the top 100 law firms had annual gross revenues approaching $27 billion. One Manhattan shop actually topped the $1 billion mark. Accompanying these astronomical receivables was a footnote. The pro bono work by this group was down 35 percent, to an average of eight minutes a day.

Norman Augustine, the former CEO of Martin Marietta, obviously wrote from personal experience when he penned his amusing book, *Augustine's Laws*. He made an excellent case for the proposition that the more lawyers per capita a country has, the bigger the drain on its economic growth. He carefully charted the annual productivity increases from 1960 to 1982 for ten industrialized nations against the incidence of lawyers in those populations. In ninth place for productivity increases, trailed only by the United Kingdom, was the United States. With three lawyers per thousand citizens, we led all other countries in lawyerly output. So on target was this correlation that Augustine was able to predict that France had 17,000 lawyers working from that country's productivity figures alone. He was right on the money. All in all, this is dramatic confirmation of John Naisbitt's assertion in *Megatrends* that "Lawyers are like beavers. They get in the mainstream and dam it up."

In 1989 Stephen P. Magee concluded that the optimum number of lawyers in our society was 60 percent fewer than those then practicing. He presented his findings to the White House and again in his book, *Black Hole, Tariffs and Endogenous Policy Theory.* This economist estimated that every additional lawyer over that number reduced our gross domestic product by about $2.5 million. That was over a decade ago! Today lawsuits are filed in state courts at the rate of one every few seconds. These suits add a tremendous amount to everything we purchase. Eight of every eleven dollars spent to purchase a vaccine, one-fourth the price of a tonsillectomy, about one-third of the cost of a pacemaker: All of these costs are attributable to litigation expenses. But the social price tag is much greater than the inevitable rise in the cost of goods and services.

Just look around. Schools and public parks are eliminating playground equipment as fast as they can cart if off. When the Connecticut Supreme Court struck down a city's protection against lawsuits resulting from the free use of recreational facilities, seesaws and merry-go-rounds began to vanish. Even donations of parkland, particularly containing "water hazards" (translation—ponds) become suspect. When South Windsor bucked this trend and spent $50,000 for an "injury-proof playground" built to federal specifications, it thought it had done the right thing. Not so, said the litigious parents of a little girl who fell and broke her wrist.

Recess is rapidly disappearing. Dodge ball is now considered a serious threat to a child's welfare. Educators in several states are fighting to ban the game, also known (horrors) as war ball, sniper, and bombardment. They describe it as "litigation waiting to happen." A spokeswoman for the National Association for Sport and Physical Education says, "The game encourages the strong to pick on the weak"! A seventh grader in Ohio was the voice of reason, however, saying "It's just a game, and you don't have to be very good at it to have fun."

Tommy Norman and I had quite a round of dodge ball in the fourth grade. It became a daily war to get the other out. The grudge match ended when Norman downed me with a football tackle after I sent him to the sidelines. We were both sporting black eyes at school the next day and were quite the topic of conversation, but lo and behold, we survived. Not days after, my class gathered excitedly around Jimmy Pennington, ogling his broken arm, the result of some recess high jinks. Our principal, Mr. Stuart, drove him to the hospital. Similarly Karla Hendricks climbed our backyard fence and attempted a tightrope act, only to fall and fracture her arm. I remember my father rushing out, bundling the little girl gently in his arms, and striding down the alley to her waiting mother. A few days later she reappeared, proudly displaying a cast and gathering signatures. No one ever contemplated lawsuits for what were seen as the normal hazards of childhood.

How times have changed. A touch football game between two buddies, Joe Smith, Jr., eight, and Kyle Grzechowiak, six, back in 1999 resulted in a broken arm for Joe. The facts are in dispute as to whether the eight-year-old tripped or was the victim of a "late tackle" by the six-year-old. As of July 2001, a pending lawsuit alleged an "intentional battery." Joe's father said, "[Kyle] has gotten away with something. It's a matter of fairness." According to the pleadings, the jury should award actual and punitive damages "as a warning to other aggressive children and their parents and to provide a lesson Kyle will not soon forget." One psychologist summed up the real lesson nicely: "The boys will learn that the place to resolve a dispute is in court. . . . We're really using a bat to kill a fly."

This trend is even crossing the Atlantic, where some British schools have now forbidden skipping and other "potentially hazardous" activities. A survey of English parents in 2000 revealed that 57 percent would sue if their child were injured at school. One headmaster was quoted as saying he would prefer to "ban all playtimes, as they are a nightmare." Oh, goody. Our hyperactive overweight children can vegetate twenty-four hours a day.

I will detail disability laws a bit later, but for now, just note that our morass of rules is often at cross-purposes. For example, while some parents seem terrified their kids might get hurt in the simplest activities, others are demanding that obvious risks be ignored in an effort to "accommodate" their children. The parents of a nine-year-old boy with cerebral palsy successfully sued a soccer league after it denied him the right to play. He could do so only by balancing on a metal walker as other children crashed around him. The league reasoned it was much too dangerous. Wrong decision! Now he stands about ten feet from the goal while the other players try to play a vigorous game without injuring him. If he gets hurt, who wants to bet there will be a lawsuit?

In a wonderful piece a few years ago, *Reason* magazine contributor Nick Gillespie summed up my reaction to this new world. He told of an encounter with a young neighbor who was preparing to ride his bike. Gillespie said, "I waved hello and stared transfixed at the boy's elaborate preparations. First, he shimmied a set of hard plastic and soft cushion pads over his sneakers . . . and positioned them carefully over his knees for maximum protection. He did the same with a pair of elbow pads . . . then came the gloves, thickly padded on the palms and across the knuckles. Finally, he picked up the helmet, adjusted it on his head [and] strapped it down across his chin. As he peddled off in his body armor, his father appeared, coffee mug in hand. 'You be careful,' he called . . . then turned to me and added sheepishly, 'I remember riding my bike barefoot in the rain. Things sure are different nowadays with the kids.' " If any of that equipment doesn't work as promised, the manufacturers better watch out!

When I moved to New York from down south and began riding the horse trails behind my house in Westchester, I was amazed at the equestrian outfits I witnessed in the woods. The only thing some people lacked was a safety belt. I have yet to encounter another lone rider; everyone is in pairs. I guess the safety of the buddy system is more important than the wonderful solitude of just you and a horse.

At home in Texas, I began riding as a child, bareback, in tennis shoes. We learned to vault over the horse's rear end or swing topside clutching a handful of mane. My father once boosted me up with such vigor he propelled me right over the horse. I landed headfirst. I shook myself off and we tried it again, with a bit more finesse. Over the years I've been thrown over fences and have been trampled, kicked, and stepped on. Temperamental colts have taken me on many a wild ride over hill and dale, and I even had a mare fall on me in the middle of a show ring. Thank goodness there hasn't been a single serious injury. Sadly, however, I will not take friends out to ride with me now, even if they allege proficiency. The potential liability is just too great.

Not long ago I tried to rent some horses to trailer up to my ranch in Wyoming for a few days, but every outfitter I called feared litigation and had simply ceased the practice. I now have a friend who will accommodate when I'm up for a week or so, but he's relying on good old-fashioned trust and friendship when he leaves his horses with us. If I get hurt, it is what used to be known as "assumption of the risk." I will bear the responsibility.

I better not tell my friend about the strict liability laws in New York, Rhode Island, Connecticut, Maine, and Iowa. Don't lend your car (horse?) to other people no matter how good their driving record, or you might get sued for the favor. In July 1998 a road rage incident in upstate New York left a passenger in one of the vehicles with severe brain damage. Both drivers involved in the fracas were found to be criminally liable and received jail time. The victim's family was awarded $47 million in damages for the injuries, but not from the drivers involved. Enterprise Rent-A-Car had rented a vehicle to one of the operators and was hit with the entire judgment.

The five states just mentioned have enacted vicarious liability laws that allow trial lawyers to sue completely innocent car owners, whether an individual or rental company, for the actions of those using their car. Other jurisdictions look for actual fault or negligent conduct by the car owner, such as lending an auto to an uninsured motorist or to a person known to drive recklessly.

On top of this absurd liability standard, some states, such as New York, make it almost impossible for a rental company to reject a customer. Even age cannot be a reason to refuse to rent as long as the person has a valid license. (Age may have been a factor in the road rage incident.) I think that is what's called putting Enterprise between a rock and a hard place. Of course, you and I ultimately pay. Small companies hesitate to do business in these states, which leaves the markets prey to a few large businesses and higher prices.

Then there is this little conundrum. As reported in the *National Law Journal,* "A Florida jury has awarded $5.2 million to the family of a slain tourist after finding that Alamo Rent-A-Car failed to warn the victim and her husband about a high-crime area near Miami." A Dutch couple "rented an Alamo car in Tampa and planned to drop it off in Miami." While stopping for directions in a bad Miami neighborhood, the tourists were robbed at gunpoint and the woman was killed. Her family sued Alamo, alleging negligence for not warning customers about that particular neighborhood where other similar attacks had occurred. This case proceeded despite the fact that this rental company was located hundreds of miles from the shooting. The judge instructed the jurors on the duty to warn customers of *foreseeable* criminal conduct, and they promptly tagged Alamo with millions in damages. What would have happened had the company issued the warning? Other service and delivery businesses have been sued for discriminating against certain parts of a city known to be dangerous. You can't win, but the lawyers will.

The concept of personal responsibility and truly foreseeable conduct has all but disappeared as case law moves from the ridiculous to the downright outrageous. Remember the multimillion-dollar lawsuit against Sea World? A drifter wandered in one night, jumped in the killer whale's fifty-degree pool, and was found quite dead the next morning. The family's lawyer said the park was negligent for not warning visitors to stay out of the water and for portraying the whales as "huggable" when in fact they are "extremely dangerous." The family ultimately dropped their suit (Sea World denies a settlement), but given recent trends, they might have recovered.

If you think whales are dangerous, try gophers! Tucson resident Michele Nations sprained her ankle in 1996 when she tripped in a hole at a municipal park. In April 2001 a jury awarded her $450,000. No, that's not a misprint. Her attorney said, "The case hinged on the city's responsibility to post adequate warnings about burrowing animals [such as squirrels and gophers] and to provide a safe alternative to dodging holes and caved-in tunnels." The city's attorney was far too rational when he responded, "You would think in a park—a natural space—people should have to watch where they're going." Apparently not.

That theory may have encouraged the Manhattan orthopedic surgeon who sued Nike in April 2000 for $10 million after her running shoes became untied and she tripped, causing a wrist injury. A company spokeswoman responded to the filing by saying "Sometimes [people] don't tie their shoes properly." Apparently dancing can be hazardous as well. In Atlanta, a forty-one-year-old dental hygienist, Linda Powers, was spinning with her partner when her thumb failed to turn quickly enough . . . and broke. She sued the poor fellow. The jury awarded her $220,000! I'll bet his disco days are over.

All the precautions in the world may not save you from suit. Countless danger signs and barricades weren't enough to protect the Chicago Transit Authority against a $3 million jury verdict. A drunken man who couldn't read English climbed around the notices to relieve himself on the train tracks, only to spray the electrified third rail. The trial judge reduced the award by half after assigning the deceased some (!) responsibility, but his wife still recovered a bundle.

In Atlanta, police officer Gordon Garner warned the department's psychologist, Anthony Stone, that he'd had visions of killing his captain, the chief, and several other officials. A lawyer from the Georgia Psychological Association told the doctor that he had a duty to warn those who had been threatened. Guess what happened? The doctor was hit with a breach of confidentiality suit that netted the cop $280,000.

In Maine a woman hit an errant golf shot that landed near a set of railroad tracks. Her second shot hit the tracks, and the ball ricocheted back into her face. She sued the country club despite the fact there was a warning sign posted on the tee box and the obstacle was clearly visible from there. Her initial award of $250,000 was later reduced to $40,000 in recognition of her "partial" fault in the accident. While these cases may sound absurd to the intelligent reader, law books are increasingly filled with such nonsense.

Thank God Congress came to its senses over the home ergonomics rules. In January 2000 the Occupational Safety and Health Administration (OSHA) asserted jurisdiction over home workplaces. The agency proposed to regulate some 20 million telecommuters who worked at least part time from their houses. Businesses that hired these people would become responsible for their safety at home. One wonderful exchange occurred during a congressional hearing on the proposal. Pat Geary, vice president for human resources for the National Association of Manufacturers, delivered this report: "I woke up yesterday and tripped over my border collie, Riley. . . . I was O.K. until I realized he is now an OSHA hazard. I've either got to take him back to the pound or paint him yellow."

Good Samaritans are disappearing as the beneficiaries of their efforts turn to the courts when dissatisfied with the results. Doctors drive right by accident sites even if they could help. Last year an eighty-four-year-old Florida woman made the news after surviving in an overturned car for three days, only to have her attorney threaten the rescuers with suit for not finding her sooner. In the fall of 2000 police officers stopped a young Hispanic man in Gainesville, Florida, who was "committing mischief." You might think here's another case of profiling or harassment. No, the officers actually were trying to be good guys. Although Richard Garcia had been drinking, the officers did not charge him with public intoxication but instead told him to go home. He wandered away, found his car, and some time later had a wreck. His resulting injuries produced $100,000 in medical bills. He sued the police officers and department for failing to arrest him and thus prevent the accident.

In Norwalk, Connecticut, officials said that state regulations prevented volunteers from feeding the needy unless food preparation occurred in a specific fashion. The Community Advent Christian Church was not permitted to donate pies to the city's emergency shelter last Thanksgiving because they were not "commercially baked" or prepared in the kitchen's own ovens. The church members were told any home-baked goodies would be tossed out. One parishioner said it was "ridiculous" that she should cook in the shelter's kitchen, saying "Do you think their oven is cleaner than my own?"

I had more than my share of frivolous lawsuits while on the bench. Here are two of my favorites, both in the malpractice arena. One plaintiff sued his urologist after surgically acquiring a much-desired penile implant to aid his erections. The complaint? It wasn't as big as before. Interestingly, on appeal, the plaintiff asserted that all those women (twelve on the jury and one on the bench) couldn't possibly understand his dismay. I must confess that no lawyer would take his case, and he represented himself in the matter. In the second suit, a woman could not be administered much anesthesia at the time of childbirth because of her hypertension. She filed against her obstetrician—because the delivery hurt. Thankfully, neither case produced a recovery. Just remember, even if these cases ultimately are thrown out by the judge or laughed out by a jury, there is a cost attached to each one. Courts, clerks, process servers, defense attorneys, the parties themselves: All have to commit time and effort to pushing these papers around.

The list of absurdities goes on and on: wrongful birth versus wrongful death; protect people and risk discrimination or allow access and face liability; admit a problem and actually fix it, then sit back as lawyers use your remedy as an admission to justify their lawsuits. Forget the word "accident"; apparently there's no such thing. Better yet, family members can now sue each other and collect on the insurance. Assumption of the risk has all but disappeared. Contributory negligence is waning. Joint and several liability insures that the deepest pockets will be brought into any lawsuit, no matter how tenuous their connection to an event.

The omnipotence of the rule of law has altered our very mind-set. The image of ourselves that we export, that of the frontier-minded, self-reliant, and free-spirited American, is all show. For every problem there is someone or something else responsible. For any loss, no matter how nebulous, there is a deep pocket out there from which to collect. For every complaint, no matter how worthless, there is an advocate. Our self-worth has been inflated to the point that Fort Knox could not compensate for the loss of a single life. Our psyches are so fragile; the mere mention of pain and anguish brings tears to the collective eye and dollar signs to the mind of the attending attorney.

Beyond the destruction of the American character, we have been suckered into extraordinary trade-offs for an allegedly risk-free world. Do you really prefer a padded room to the open range? A free society necessarily has dangers that more autocratic systems do not. The more liberties people have, the more varied the choices and the chancier the environment. However, the reverse is not true. More rules do *not* guarantee our security. They may afford a legal venue for redress, but they won't save our skins or our souls. Words on a page will not prevent babies from drowning in the bath or some hiker from diving in your pond. We must understand the false exchange as we seek more protection from unpredictable or dangerous behavior.

Finally, reliance on endless rules proved disastrous in the former Soviet Union. People were subjected to numbing regulations while innovation, reason, and personal judgment were not allowed. Ronald Reagan would credit the buildup of U.S. arms and the ensuing cost to the Soviet government, but it was the strangulation of the people that ultimately doomed that nation. This same fate can still be ours.

Freedom is a messy thing. It permits the development of an elite society, albeit one defined by merit, ability, intellect, even craft and cunning. We profess to love liberty yet rebel against natural differences by passing laws that pretend to eliminate them. Having abdicated personal responsibility to the law, we now expect it to homogenize the world. Our legislatures and courts are manufacturing new rights by the bushel, ostensibly in pursuit of human equality. However, just as all the rules in the world cannot insure our survival, neither can they create the impossible. These rules can however operate as legal weapons, sufficient to bring an independent, competitive nation to its knees. In his book *Sovereign Virtue: The Theory and Practice of Equality*, Ronald Dworkin recognized this very real possibility when he said, "Any genuine contest between liberty and equality is a contest liberty must lose."

In fact, our nation is fracturing under the weight of this absurdity. Equality is a wonderful sounding word, but the Constitution has been misinterpreted beyond belief. True equality is best described as "of the soul" or in religious terms. The Englishman Auberon Waugh described it thusly: "equality is not some crude fairy tale about all men being equally tall or equally tricky; which we not only cannot believe but cannot believe in anybody believing. It is an absolute of morals by which all men have a value invariable and indestructible and a dignity as intangible as death."

Ben Franklin said, "The gifts of the intellect proceed directly from God, and man cannot prevent their *unequal* distribution.... The means that Americans find for putting them to use are equal." As a people we recognize that everyone, whether born of riches or in poverty, with status or without, can elevate him- or herself by hard work and determination. Only opportunity is guaranteed at birth, not outcome. The law cannot inject ability or correct infirmity, but it can pervert itself trying.

That is exactly what is happening. Instead of focusing on an equal place at the starting gate, our laws attempt to rig the finish by mandating an equal outcome for everyone. This is unachievable. Even more, it is a truly stultifying thought. In the classroom, we spend enormous sums to deliver an "equal" education to each student. That sounds good, doesn't it? Unfortunately, this doesn't mean giving each child the same instruction. Instead, teachers are expected to discriminate with every pupil by giving *unequal* attention to each one. Instruction must now accommodate every mental, physical, and emotional variable, often at the same time and in the same classroom. We have redefined equal education to mean equal output from our students. The only way we come close to achieving this is by lowering all standards. Accomplishment has been rejected in favor of a bland commonality at best. At its worst, no child gets a competent education.

Whether in business, education, or government, we have elevated this skewed notion of equality over increased opportunity, improved qualifications, and real, meaningful achievement. If we do not alter our present course, this pseudoequality will have been won, but the bigger goal will be lost.

When this nation was founded, one phrase represented our ideals and intentions: *E Pluribus Unum,* "from many, one." Our Statue of Liberty describes this land as a haven for the multitudes "yearning to be free." Regardless of race, national origin, or religion, there would be a place for liberty, self-expression, and the opportunity to pursue one's dreams. Some will argue that a bunch of white guys were simply protecting their own. After all, our founders failed to abolish slavery or grant equal access to women and minorities. I judge them, however, by their time and circumstance. In doing so, I remain in awe of the principles they devised. Over time, our modern democracy emerged from those prescient words.

The Bill of Rights was designed to protect people *against* intrusion by the government. As Justice Oliver Wendell Holmes said, "Rights mark the limits of interference with individual freedom." In barely a generation, this definition has been turned on its head. Instead of political rights that belong to the people, we have created affirmative obligations that are imposed on government, businesses, and individuals. These two concepts couldn't be more different. Said simply, we now assert a "right to" rather than a "freedom from." This notion has become our national mantra.

From public accommodations to private companies, from voting rights to employment rights, a plethora of rules and laws are supposed to eliminate discrimination in America. We have moved well beyond the pedestrian distinctions of race, color, religion, sex, or national origin. Protected classes now include pregnancy, age, and disability. Some states now include sexual orientation, smokers, and overweight individuals. Students' rights, taxpayers' rights, patients' rights, passengers' rights, parents' rights, and more emerge fully formed from the minds of lawyers and politicians. They require layers of bureaucracy to regulate and implement. Employers and institutions must record and report statistics, post notices, and form new management committees to oversee these protections. Litigation increases to enforce them. Tax dollars must sustain these efforts. Costs soar to pay awards for violations. The spiral goes on.

In the meantime, no one asks if the ultimate goal of fairness is being achieved and what is being exchanged in the process. Americans forget that they wear several hats: worker, employer, consumer, and, yes, citizen, in a so-called free society. Each new right that is legislated will affect each role differently, sometimes disastrously. We seem oblivious to the conflicts we are creating.

Look at the workplace. After thirty years of expanding rights against employment discrimination, Congress has tried to please just about everyone. According to statistician Aaron Wildavsky, if you examine all of the protected categories, they add up to *374 percent* of the population. Imagine a group of people, all hired on the same day with equal qualifications. When a layoff is required, who should go—the young black woman or the white man over fifty? The Asian with a bad back or the blind Hispanic? Careful now, each category is protected. How do you choose? Now justify your choice and prepare to defend it in court.

The workplace has become a constant battleground as employees fight each other to achieve "most protected" status. Companies are faced with impossible choices, and litigation awaits almost every decision. Many businesses simply settle cases rather than face disastrous jury verdicts. Often they allow outside groups to monitor consent judgments that result in "voluntary" quotas. Jesse Jackson has done well by threatening businesses with alleged civil rights violations. Unfortunately, the perverse result is a nation of businesses that fear the hiring of qualified women, minorities, and disabled persons, given the legal repercussions from disciplining or firing them.

I remember a disagreement I had with Roger Ailes, the CEO of Fox News Network. The substance is irrelevant; his reaction, priceless. At the appointed hour for our discussion, I entered his office to find a female lawyer sitting across from his desk. When I asked, "What is she doing here?" Roger replied, "I can't be too careful. I've been threatened with suit over private conversations with female employees." Only after repeated assurances on my part that such a tactic was not in my playbook did he call off the counselor. We were able to resolve our grievances like civilized human beings. Sadly, if I were in Roger's place today, I'd probably do the same thing.

The ultimate winner in this war may surprise you. As these so-called rights become entitlements, it is the lawyers and government that are strengthened and individual freedoms that disappear. Freedom of association, freedom of contract, freedom of speech—all of these rights have been increasingly abridged. Although the Boy Scouts of America won their Supreme Court case to ban homosexual scout leaders, the ruling was unexpected. The opposing brief summed up current legal thought: "The State has a compelling interest in eradicating invidious *private* discrimination." Yet a gay rights group filed a brief in support of the Scouts. The group didn't approve of the ban but wanted to retain their own freedom to keep unsympathetic heterosexuals out of their organization. They understood that real freedom, as Justice Oliver Wendell Holmes said, includes "freedom for the thoughts we hate."

Currently, pro-gay students in Orange, California, are litigating for the right to form a gay-straight student alliance at their public high school, and a federal judge already has indicated that they will likely win under the Equal Access Act. Ironically, that law was passed in 1984 at the behest of religious conservatives seeking to protect the ability of religious clubs to meet in public high schools. It was championed by none other than Ronald Reagan. Now the very same law has facilitated the establishment of more than 700 gay-straight organizations at public high schools. It must be the Law of Unintended Consequences. I'm sure the fundamentalists are thrilled.

The Boy Scouts supplemented their argument with this reflection:

"A society in which each and every organization must be equally diverse is a society which has destroyed diversity." Think about it. Walter Olson described the same position in his book, *The Excuse Factory*: "A nation that truly cared about diversity would allow the flourishing of both bawdy calendars at some workplaces and Bible readings at others, rather that insist on some homogenized middle ground in which no one could have either."

Take a look at the state of free speech on our school campuses. Teachers and students alike are watering down their remarks to the same muddy gray for fear of offending some sensitive soul. Liberal students are shutting down conservative speakers while the reverse became true for those delivering unpatriotic opinions after September 11. David Horowitz is blasted nationwide for objecting to the slavery reparations movement. He is threatened and censored on campuses from coast to coast. After September 11, a New Mexico professor applauds anyone who can bomb the Pentagon, and he has to run for cover. Similar comments brought dismissal for teachers and reporters alike. In May 2002, the New York Regents Exam was found to contain doctored quotations from famous authors for students to analyze. Almost every reference to race, religion, ethnicity, sex, nudity, and profanity was eliminated from the original works so as not to offend anyone reading the material. This puts a new spin on literary expression.

In our grade schools, the zero tolerance movement equates words with weapons. A frustrated youngster who says "I'll kill you" is suspended. School manuals warn against any speech that *might* offend another student as viewed through the listener's prism, the speaker's intentions be damned. In the workplace, frightened employers prohibit anything that could appear disagreeable to someone else, and again, the listener gets to define "disagreeable." Employers with multilingual workplaces are in a real bind. If they try to enforce English only so they can monitor what is being said, they may face discrimination charges. If they fail to control objectionable phrases, whatever the language, the same results apply.

As for freedom of contract, there have been many positive steps taken to level the playing field for workers who would otherwise be at tremendous bargaining disadvantages with their employers. Minimum wage laws, child labor laws, and limits on working hours have all had a benefit for employees and the nation as a whole. But how far do we take this? The notion of employment at will has become laughable. Once upon a time, the courts respected the idea that an employer had the freedom to choose employees just as workers could leave at will and go elsewhere. Then courts began to read into agreements "promises of employment" where none existed. Lawyers gleefully discovered that an oral statement like "Keep producing like that and you'll really go places here" might become evidence of a reasonable expectation of a lifelong job.

Juries began to infer such a promise from the simple fact that an employee had no bad notes in his or her file and had been promoted previously in the company. In 1990 Sun Life of Canada got hit with a $3.5 million judgment for firing a person under those very facts even though the employment agreement said that employee could be terminated without cause on thirty days' notice. Soon we had an entire area of the law known as "workplace rights." Subjective standards are unacceptable. You cannot hire or fire because you like or dislike someone. Bad work habits, slovenly appearance, even downright incompetence may no longer be just cause for dismissal. Not only can a worker recover for lost wages, but the law now permits damages for defamation and emotional distress, and can even order reinstatement with promotions or extraordinary accommodation for alleged disabilities. Don't forget that the plaintiff's costs and attorneys fees are paid as well. If a dangerous employee is dismissed, the employer better keep that characterization quiet, although the next place of employment might sue for failure to warn in the event of trouble.

How about a little historical perspective? During the New Deal, our national government took some amazing steps to ease human suffering stemming from the depression. The social safety net and countless work programs were created as statutory obligations. They became legal relationships between the government and the people, contracts (not "rights") that could be modified or eliminated as needed. This moderate approach was abandoned in the 1960s as the civil rights movement gained momentum.

In 1964, responding to the rightful demand that existing constitutional provisions against blatant discrimination be enforced, Congress enacted the Civil Rights Act. However, the legislation was specifically limited to unenforced rights already present in our founding documents. Senator Hubert Humphrey elaborated: "If [anyone] can find in Title VII . . . any language which provide[s] that an employer will have to

HHH
HORATIO HIMSELF

hire on the basis of percentage or quota related to color, race, religion or national origin, I will start eating the pages one after another, because it is not in there." During the debate, Senator Harrison Williams assured the naysayers: "How can the language of equality favor one race or one religion or another? Equality can have only one meaning, and that meaning is self-evident to reasonable men. Those who say that equality means favoritism do violence to common sense."

Now entitlements are the norm. The civil rights movement is unfairly cited as precedent for the creative new obligations that overwhelm our resources and threaten our sanity. Ironically, Julian Bond, a civil rights pioneer, summed it up nicely: "Today the protected classes extend to a majority of all Americans, including white men over forty, short people, the chemically addicted, the left-handed, the obese, members of all religions. Surely there is a scholar somewhere who can tell us how we came to this state of affairs and how the road to civil rights became so crowded."

How crowded, you ask? Despite all the rules, regulations, and social restraints on prejudiced behavior, civil rights complaints in U.S. District Courts more than doubled between 1990 and 1998. Racial harassment charges filed with the Equal Employment Opportunity commission (EEOC) are five times what they were in the 1980s. By 1998 businesses settled 101,470 discrimination cases for $169.2 million dollars, up 44 percent from 1992. Either we are becoming more biased than ever, or the laws are having a perverse effect on our perception of human behavior.

Before anyone calls me a racist or other pejorative, let me categorically state that I support equal opportunity for all our citizens. No one should be discriminated against based on arbitrary measures including color, race, sex, and so on. I believe in voluntary recruiting, diversity training, and other measures to broaden minority participation in all areas of American life. Workplace diversity is a tremendous strength. Furthermore, its achievement is inevitable. By 2010, it is predicted that only one in six jobs will go to a white male. Women and minorities will take the rest. What I object to is the manner in which we have pursued this goal.

2010

Affirmative action, for example, began as a worthy policy. It was designed to insure a nondiscriminatory search for the best, regardless of race, gender, and then disability. If outreach, education, or job training were needed to increase qualifications among the underrepresented, then such help would be forthcoming. There was never an intention to lower standards. We would lift the performance of all citizens instead.

Yet look at the results: quotas, preferences, and consent decrees that admit and hire by every factor ostensibly prohibited under the civil rights statute. We now justify a disintegration of merit standards in the workplace as an effort to "right past wrongs." If people do not qualify, lower the bar.

In 1994 I was reporting for ABC's *20/20*. In a segment on reverse discrimination, I discussed a Defense Department memo that stated, "In the future, special permission will be required for the promotion of all white men without disabilities." In that same story, I met with U.S. Forest Service employees who showed me an ad for firefighter openings in their department. It read, "only unqualified applicants will be considered." The preferred group here was women, who filled 179 of the 184 openings during the hiring period. In that same year the Los Angeles Fire Department was faced with a court order requiring that 50 percent of the applicants passing its entrance exam must be minorities. Fearing too many whites would pass, the department simply denied many whites the right to take the examination. Few exams, whether for work or school, can pass today's test against discrimination.

How's this for discrimination? Recently a young man was denied a position as a police officer. Although he'd passed his training with flying colors, the department heads decided his IQ was too high and that he would likely get bored with the job. Of course he sued. The court sustained the department standards, ruling that since everyone with an IQ over 120 was rejected, this must not be discrimination. The plaintiff should have asserted that his brains were a disability; then he might have won.

Speaking of brains, apparently mind reading has become a requirement for employers, attorneys, and judges. We are to divine the intent behind every behavior and decision. A management piece in the November 1997 issue of *The Academy of Management Executive* entitled "Beyond Good Intentions: The Next Step toward Racial Equality in the American Workplace" certainly suggests this. While announcing that blatant racism is dead or dying, the article identified the new "more subtle form of racism" that involved "the unintentional promotion of segregation and discrimination. . . . [The] new racists will not act on their anti-black feelings unless given a non-racist justification for doing so. Executives must eliminate even seemingly reasonable business rationales that can be used as justification to exclude blacks. Vague talk of matching people to jobs in terms of such things as social background, lifestyle, or even attitudes, beliefs and values in order to achieve harmony, comfort or ease of adjustment is to be avoided." The article continues: "Discourse about doing business is too difficult to regulate completely . . . [so] organizational leaders must move beyond attempts merely to comply with such regulations. In regards to hiring, for instance, the following sort of affirmative action rule may be required: When choosing between black and white candidates with comparable credentials, the black is to be selected." According to these academics, everything is suspect. No "reasonable business rationale" can be advanced to explain employment decisions. Outright preferences are finally deemed the only appropriate response—a complete reversal of the Civil Rights Act.

In 1989 a white schoolteacher in New Jersey was laid off in lieu of a black teacher hired on the same day and possessing the same qualifications. The school board candidly stated its decision was based on race and a desire to promote diversity. By 1997, after the white teacher won her reverse discrimination case at several levels, the matter was headed for the Supreme Court. Attorney General Janet Reno initially supported the school board, then became hopelessly confused. She was let off the hook when several civil rights groups raised money to settle with the plaintiff, fearing the precedent would overturn their good works.

Our legislative and legal maneuverings in this area have been disastrous for all concerned. In his book *The Disuniting of America,* liberal historian Arthur Schlesinger, Jr., recognized this outcome: "Militants of ethnicity now contend that the main objective . . . should be the protection, strengthening, celebration and perpetuation of ethnic origins and identities. [This] nourishes prejudices, magnifies differences and stirs antagonisms."

Our regulations demand that we all come together but in a way that exacerbates our differences, mandates further legislation, and sets up inevitable conflict at every turn. We don't want equality for all Americans but instead, for every unique group, characteristic, thought, or trait.

The government encourages this by institutionally segregating countless categories. A few years ago golfer Tiger Woods protested the Census Bureau requirement that he check a box denoting his heritage. Which group should he deny? Which should he acknowledge? He created his own category, with tongue firmly in cheek. He is a "Cablinasian," a mix of Caucasian, black, American Indian, and Asian. In the early 1960s the American Civil Liberties Union (ACLU) recommended that our government simply eliminate the racial designations all together. Unfortunately, the business of categorizing provides too much political hay for politicians and bureaucrats to abandon. In fact, they eliminated the "other" category, so that you have to choose.

However, some groups are still not satisfied. In June 2000 the Dominicans in New York called for a redo of the entire national census. They claimed discrimination since the Puerto Ricans, Mexicans, and Cubans all had special categories. The Dominicans had only the generic "Hispanic" box to check. The government had provided a place for respondents to write in any unlisted group, but that was not good enough.

Entitlements also are emerging for every divergence from some imaginary norm and, with them, an increasing number of disability lawsuits are being filed in our courtrooms. The original Americans with Disabilities Act (ADA) protected an estimated 43 million Americans under the first part of the act, which defined as a disability "a physical or mental impairment that substantially limits one or more major life activities," although the number of traditionally handicapped individuals is only about 3 to 4 million. The ADA category regarding the obvious disabilities—blindness, hearing, and mobility—came later (as did a section for those "individuals *perceived* as having such impairments").

Our founding fathers bravely declared that all men are created equal. In the eyes of God, if you will, we are indeed equal. That one person is smarter, faster, or more attractive does not elevate an individual to a higher state of grace. It may, however, assist the person in everyday life, where the standards of judgment were never meant to be so celestial. We seem to have rejected this natural law in favor of a fanciful quest to equalize *results,* no matter the individual differences. The expense is outrageous, the outcome wildly disparate, and the resulting case law, a nightmare.

The growing number of disability laws is a source of confusion and absurdity. In a vain attempt to ignore both physical and economic realities, we have created an impossible dilemma for our schools, businesses, and institutions. The original legislation may have been undertaken with the best of intentions, yet I suspect that political correctness backed by a litigation machine now dictates the legal outcomes. Let's take a look at just a few examples.

On the face of it, the Rehabilitation Act of 1973 seemed reasonable. All new or rehabilitated public buildings would be made wheelchair accessible. But attorneys from the Office of Civil Rights of the Department of Health, Education and Welfare (HEW) slipped in a little something extra just before passage: "No otherwise qualified handicapped individual in the U.S. . . . shall solely by reason of his handicap, be excluded from participation in, be denied the benefits of, or be subjected to discrimination under any program or activities receiving federal financial assistance." Applied literally, this meant that every school, hospital, nursing home, library, and transit system receiving federal aid had to be rebuilt to handicap codes. Furthermore, when such codes start stating that the arc of water from a fountain shall be four inches high, or carpet shall be three-quarters of an inch thick, surely something has gone awry. Three decades ago, the cost was expected to exceed $100 billion. Today, who knows?

The Americans with Disabilities Act of 1990 expanded these "rights" to most aspects of public life. To prevent discrimination against those with disabilities, physical access to many private buildings would be required and businesses could not forgo an interview or reject an applicant simply because the person was disabled. This allowed virtually every establishment, public or private, to be sued for discrimination. According to author Philip K. Howard, "Not 2% of the [nation's] disabled are in wheelchairs, and many of those are confined to nursing homes [yet] billions are being spent to make every nook and cranny of every facility in America wheelchair accessible." I can just imagine what Howard would say about the new rules passed in 2002 in three communities in three different states that legislate a "right to visit." In Pima, Arizona, for example, builders must now make the first floor of every new home wheelchair accessible with at least one accommodating bathroom. The owner, architect, or buyer has no say in the matter.

This unyielding position has infected every debate. ADA supporters argue that equal treatment means just that: The disabled should be able to board any bus, attend any event, and enter any bathroom without help.

Warming huts perched along ski slopes and hiking shelters miles off the nearest road must now accommodate wheelchairs or be closed down. Disabled activists in Connecticut lodged a complaint against the schooner *Amistad,* a traveling historical exhibit, saying it was not wheelchair accessible. The ship re-created the overcrowding and inhumane conditions of the original slave ship, but historical accuracy was no excuse.

When it comes to public facilities, we are now having a debate that goes well beyond actual access. Movie theaters may provide areas for wheelchairs, but what if the disabled patron doesn't like that location? Given traditional "tiered" seating, how do you let wheelchair-bound patrons move around? The same holds true for stadium seats at sporting events or concerts. The disabled require special accommodations, but they also want complete freedom of choice. Developers are now scattering handicapped seating throughout arenas, but without special areas, how can they insure that some rowdy fan won't stand up during the game and block the wheelchair occupant? Country singer Garth Brooks was sued because he allegedly reserved the first two rows at his concerts for "pretty women" (although his spokesman said it was for friends). This was seen as a limitation on wheelchair seating. Perhaps the "homely" should sue. This summer a Florida man, wanting wheelchair access to a lap-dancing room, sued the strip club for noncompliance with the ADA. And East Sussex, England, is considering permitting vision-impaired patrons to touch lap dancers.

Traditional sporting rules are falling as well. When golfer Casey Martin went to court to win the right to ride rather than walk in Professional Golf Association (PGA) competition, I knew there would be trouble. He is a lovely young man and a very talented player. However, he suffers from a truly debilitating circulatory disorder that prevents him from playing without a golf cart. The Supreme Court in all its wisdom decided that "shot-making" was the essence of golf, and that walking the course was not integral to the sport despite arguments from players like Jack Nicholas and Arnold Palmer. Interestingly, another federal case was proceeding at the same time that Martin's was moving up the ladder. That case reached the opposite conclusion. The attorneys wisely noted that those judges were golfers, and Martin's were not. (I must note one exception. Justice Sandra Day O'Connor has a hole-in-one to her credit.)

So now the ADA applies to more than public accommodation. Other sports might as well be redesigned with "fairness" in mind.

Commentators have suggested baseball could assist the poorly sighted with extra strikes, or maybe we should change the length of the football field for players with asthma. Why not? After all, every one of these rules is ultimately arbitrary. Why shouldn't they be drafted to accommodate everyone who would like to play? This rationale is not far-fetched. It is already in effect. Remember the child with cerebral palsy who can now stand on the soccer field? High schools cannot reject athletes with "alcohol disabilities" or special ed players who cannot keep up their grades. The courts are making rules for our most time-honored activities.

The mere suggestion that someone might not be able to participate, or should use a special entrance or find a different job, will invite a race to the courthouse. Cost is no concern; inconvenience is insufficient, even rational need is ignored. The resulting expense is exorbitant. Inevitably, reality will rear its ugly head as we realize society cannot bear the burden of accommodating every unique human condition everywhere. Even with all our money, personnel, and national will, the goal is simply impossible.

In the meantime, the nation's attorneys are smiling. As with the civil rights bill in 1991, Congress built in an incentive to litigate ADA claims by providing for attorney's fees. A lawsuit may give the plaintiff statutory compliance, but the lawyer gets $275 an hour. From its inception to 1996, the number of annual lawsuits tripled, according to Trevor Armbrister in *Reader's Digest*. He also lets us know that the majority of cases were filed by those alleging bad backs or physiological and neurological problems, rather than categories like mobility or sight. A rash of cases in California and Florida have demonstrated how the "victimized" can become the "abusers" in an instant.

Two lawyers on the West Coast are notable for filing 230 such suits on behalf of a single client. In South Florida, John D. Mallah and his partner have sued over 500 businesses since 1998. Many of the suits were brought in the name of Mallah's uncle. Often the businesses that were sued had been certified by their local building inspectors and never realized they were in violation of the accessibility statute. But ignorance of the law is no excuse!

One case I found in Florida was particularly galling. Mobility Access is a mom-and-pop store. Both owners are in wheelchairs. Their company serves the handicapped community. Suddenly it was hit with a lawsuit for noncompliance with the ADA. The owners had failed to designate handicapped spaces in their parking lot, although no customer had ever complained. When served with the lawsuit, they posted the requested signs at a cost of about forty dollars. Unfortunately, the plaintiff's attorney fees ran another $1,600. Sadly, the willingness to conform to the law makes no difference. If attorneys scout violations, they can collect.

Two Florida representatives proposed a bill that would require ninety days' notice to a violator before a suit could proceed. Businesses then could spend their money fixing the problem rather than going to court. Not surprisingly, this elicited objections from Florida attorney Robert Bogdan. He wrote an editorial in *USA Today* saying "I believe it is unfair to place the burden of policing the law on the disabled, as notification would do. The disabled would be put in the position of asking these violating businesses to please stop." In fact, a website called the Washington Protection and Advocacy Service rallied its members by saying this was a "direct attack on the civil rights of 56 million Americans with Disabilities." (The numbers keep going up.) Now, that sounds like a heinous burden doesn't it? It must be easier to hire a lawyer and go to court than send a letter. Maybe so, if there is no cost to the plaintiff and the attorneys make out like bandits.

Not only must businesses accommodate the disabled, they also must keep up with the shifting standards for who actually qualifies. I held my breath back in 1999 as the Supreme Court reviewed three disability lawsuits. Two plaintiffs, sisters in fact, were both nearsighted. With corrective lenses they were able to work as pilots for a regional airline. However, that wasn't good enough. They wanted to work for United Airlines, which required its pilots to have natural 20/20 vision. Plaintiffs argued that their contacts gave them 20/20 eyesight but nevertheless asserted their uncorrected vision made them disabled. They wanted it both ways. We're disabled, so you cannot discriminate against us, but with corrective lenses we also qualify. If the Court had sustained their action, about 160 million people with correctable eyesight would have immediately become "disabled" under the ADA, including several of the eyeglass-wearing justices. Thankfully, the Court ruled that a correctable problem was not a disability and, furthermore, that United's standards were permissible.

In a similar case, the third plaintiff was hypertensive. This condition was controlled through medication, but the trucking company he wanted to work for had tough blood pressure requirements for its drivers. In all three cases, the Court did not find that discrimination had occurred, saying instead that a physical criterion for a job ordinarily will not violate the act. "The statute protects you from discrimination in a class of jobs, but it does not guarantee you a particular job."

These rulings do not give me much comfort. Self-inflicted diseases like alcohol or drug addiction, which certainly can impair performance, are regularly judged to be disabilities. The EEOC attacked Exxon's policy enacted after the *Valdez* disaster, which now prohibits anyone with substance addiction problems from holding a safety job. The oil company had incurred millions of dollars in liability costs after its tanker ran aground with an intoxicated pilot at the helm. It would be gross negligence to allow a recurrence. Yet, in its wisdom, the EEOC said that this so-called disability should *not* be the basis for discrimination against an employee, even one holding a job that demands sobriety at all times. Should a company and the public be put at risk so that someone with such problems can pursue any job he or she desires? I think not. Isn't it fair to say that some jobs are simply off limits? Aren't there times that discrimination merely demonstrates responsible hiring practices?

I guess not. The EEOC argued to a federal appeals court in Philadelphia that a train dispatcher should not be relieved of his duties with Conrail despite a heart condition that could cause him to lose consciousness. The EEOC actually asserted that consciousness is "not itself a job function" (that explains a lot these days). It says that "while consciousness is obviously necessary to perform" train-dispatcher tasks . . . "the [job] involves directing trains and taking emergency action to prevent crashes." The commission said that this employee's condition was not a "direct threat to others." There's logic for you. Similar arguments have been made for truck drivers who are epileptic or blind in one eye. While these problems may rarely result in injury on the job, who should bear the risk? Where is the greater duty: to the individual employee or to the public safety? In my book, there is no debate.

Various rulings have established a definition of disability as something that prevents us from undertaking a major life activity. This seems logical. Most of us would agree that seeing, walking, and hearing all are major life activities. But now having children has been ruled a major life activity, and infertility has become a disability. A company was successfully sued for firing a woman after too many absences while she sought infertility treatments. She wasn't fired for her so-called disability but for her repeated failure to show up for work. The fertility treatments were entirely voluntary on her part. She was not ill. There was nothing life-threatening about her condition. If she used up her allotted sick and personal days, then I believe the company owed no further accommodation. Maybe an unpaid leave would have helped, but that shouldn't be required. The burden for lifestyle choices should fall on the individual, not the employer.

Dr. Carol Gill, former president of the Chicago Institute of Disability Research, unintentionally summed up my feelings about many of these trends when she said, "Disability is a sociopolitical phenomenon as much as it is medical. Our issues are not caused by biology, any more than the issues of women's oppression are caused by sex. We have that kindred source of oppression, in a society that is all too quick to blame our second-class citizenship on our biology." Those feelings may have been apt for those in wheelchairs or without sight, but it doesn't apply to the millions of people who are now lumped into this category.

A dyslexic woman, who prior to tackling the law exam had acquired a Ph.D. in education administration from New York University and a law degree from Vermont Law School, managed to fail the New York Bar exam five times. Although her various disability lawsuits had awarded her extra time to take the test, a private room, and a scribe to read the questions aloud and take down her answers, she still did not pass. The U.S. Court of Appeals for the Second Circuit ruled that the Law Board had violated her rights by refusing even more accommodation and that she could try again with twice the allotted time and a computer at her disposal. The court originally ruled her dyslexia to be a disability because it substantially impaired the major life activity of reading, but thankfully there was dissent about whether this affected her ability to find work. Our laws do not and should not guarantee a particular kind of work as a remedy.

Here's a scary thought. These education disability cases are now affecting all areas of study, including medicine. Future doctors are claiming learning disabilities and getting those extreme accommodations as well. Remember, an employer can't ask if someone has a disability, so no information about the special dispensation is carried forward. Comforting, huh?

There is a job I have wanted all my life. I have the qualifications, the training, the strength and experience to do it, but I'm too big. I am bodily challenged. No matter how hard I try I will never be a jockey.

Is it discrimination if I'm turned away from the track? Of course not. Thankfully, the Supreme Court is slowly taking that position. It has asked the appellate court to take another look at the dyslexic's case, asking essentially "How far do we go?" Is a difference in test-taking ability a disability that should invoke the ADA and the courts? How much accommodation is too much? Should this assistance extend to other professions, say to our future surgeons and pilots?

Then there is attention deficit disorder (ADD). I will talk more about this exploding phenomenon when we look at education, but for now, consider the poor employer. Let's say some enterprising soul has received a diagnosis from his doctor that he just can't concentrate with all the distraction in his workplace. Maybe the pressure of deadlines is too great. Something has to give. Well, it won't be the job, I assure you!

Despite the fact that ADD is a questionable diagnosis in many patients, its use has become a social epidemic, and the courts have responded. Most of the cases deal with children, but there are broader implications. I interviewed a young law student a few years ago. Like most first-year students, she was having difficulty, but then she was diagnosed with ADD. Now she had a reason for her troubles—an actionable one. Please note that up to this point her grades had been good enough to gain her entrance to law school. Nevertheless, following this "diagnosis," she sued for additional assistance to compensate for her "disability." She was given note takers and tutors at the university's expense, along with additional time in which to take her exams. At one point I asked her about the future. She wanted to be a trial lawyer. "What if," I proposed, "your senior partner rushes in one afternoon and assigns you an emergency motion that must be filed before the courthouse closes." This sort of pressure and time crunch happens all too often in real life. She responded that she wouldn't do it. If he insisted, she'd sue. What happens when a medical emergency requires a doctor diagnosed with ADD to take quick action?

People with this "condition" can enter buildings, use the facilities, read, and write, you name it. They do not need lowered door handles, ramps, or Braille elevator keys. Being "distracted" does not affect some major life function. If it does, then we're all in trouble. It simply cannot be discrimination to recognize that some jobs are highly stressful and require an employee who adapts well. Ask Red Adair.

Now it seems that the law requires employers to design a job for every applicant. You have a lateness disorder? No problem. The job should start when you decide to arrive. You panic at deadlines? Don't worry. Take all the time in the world. In December 2000 a federal court ruled that although a woman employee had been "belligerent and displayed an unprofessional attitude" at work, had "difficulty controlling her emotions," and was "incredibly sensitive to criticism," she was entitled to sue for discrimination. The woman argued that these personality traits were caused by severe depression and should have been accommodated under the ADA by her employer, UNISYS.

What if an employer refuses to hire someone for a job that might injure that particular employee? In 1991 the Supreme Court ruled that battery maker Johnson Control could not restrict women from certain jobs on the basis that lead exposure could harm a fetus. This practice was ruled sex discrimination. But there's a catch. Any child born with a defect can later sue, arguing that it had no choice about the exposure to potential toxins.

Finally, on June 10, 2002, the Supreme Court unanimously decided that employers can protect applicants or workers from dangerous conditions even if such action would limit job opportunities. In *Chevron U.S.A. v. Echazabal, No. 60-1406,* the company turned down an applicant with chronic liver disease because the inevitable exposure to chemicals and solvents at the refinery could be harmful if not fatal to him. The federal appeals court in San Francisco said this was paternalistic and that "disabled persons should be afforded the opportunity to decide for themselves what risks to undertake." Yet while the man is qualified for the work, giving him the job is clearly a safety violation on the party of the company. The Supreme Court did not take some principled stand however since its decision simply followed EEOC policy, thus affirming the EEOC's right to interpret the ADA.

Yet the nine justices have helped to slow the expansion of the ADA in recent rulings, but they can act only when a specific case is presented. As of now, there is little to stop this march toward a nation dominated by disability labels. When you read about the effect of these policies on our education system, you may agree with the activist who recently proclaimed that the ADA protects *everyone,* because we are all "potentially disabled."

THREE | The Legal Perversion of Education

In an effort to halt the downward slide of our public school system, the government has, predictably, thrown a lot of cash and even more rules at the problems. Our institutions of education are a mass of laws and regulations that both burden and shelter educators and their pupils. While children are always the subjects of political grandstanding, lawyers have discovered an entirely new field of litigation under the umbrella of students' rights. Teachers now are constrained by ludicrous regulations that inhibit the education and discipline process. They have their vengeance, however, with the morass of laws that protect their jobs. The powerful teachers' unions still wield a strong lobbying and election sword that prevents serious reform within their ranks.

As in the workplace, rules and regulations have not improved the educational system. Administrators won't rock the boat for fear they might tumble out with everyone else. They hire teachers who cannot teach rather than face discrimination lawsuits. They cannot fire for the same reasons. They stress special education programs that bring in extra funding. They take money from Channel One so that commercials can barrage our kids during school as well as at home. They've sold out our children's health to the soft drink companies; virtually every district in the country now gets a percentage of the sugary substances sold in vending machines throughout school buildings. Politicians have become so beholden to the teachers' unions and contributing organizations that they are unwilling to offend obvious culprits. Equality of outcome in the classroom has replaced equality of access to a good education as our primary goal. To accomplish this, we must use the least capable students as our models. The weakest teaching and testing standards become the norm so that "everyone succeeds."

As our kids move through elementary school, they rank near the top of the world's students. According to the Department of Education, that ranking begins to slip around grade five. U.S. performance then drops for every year a student remains in school. By high school graduation, math and science scores of U.S. kids have plummeted to about eighteenth among developed nations, ranking alongside Bulgaria and Latvia. Similarly, most immigrant children exhibit self-discipline and respect for school in their first years. These youngsters often outperform American kids, spending more time on homework and less in front of the television set. However, as they assimilate, their performance and aspiration deteriorates. How do we explain these perverse outcomes when we are spending more per capita on our students than any other country on the planet?

Education is a "right" for children in America. As such, we must distribute it equally. What does that mean? Should everyone have equal access to the very same education? Should we spend the same money and attention on each child or chip in whatever it takes for that student to match up to his or her classmates? Must we put all kids in equivalent classrooms with no distinctions? Let's see where this equality debate leads us.

Children with no recognized disabilities often learn at different speeds or in a different ways from one another. The more difficult the lessons, the more differences we will see in their performance. Some children grasp math quickly while others excel at language or literature. Some grasp spatial concepts while others cannot see beyond two dimensions. It used to be acceptable to recognize and accommodate these differences with accelerated or remedial classes bracketing the standard setting. Teachers could better target their audience when these distinctions were made.

Today mainstreaming every child, no matter the disability, is deemed a critical goal. To avoid the appearance of discrimination or (God forbid) the loss of self-esteem, we lump kids of various abilities together and teach to the lowest common denominator. We expect one instructor to handle children with learning disabilities, severe emotional problems, physical handicaps, and accelerated abilities in the same setting at the same time.

Back in the 1960s we wanted to "meet the special educational and related needs of handicapped children." Laws were passed to address those who had been excluded from schools, institutionalized, or placed in programs with little or no learning. The primary goal was to mainstream those children who would have been in traditional class-rooms but for physical disabilities like mobility or sight. In the 1970s, however, courts made education for mentally, physically, and emo-tionally disabled children an entitlement that "must be made available to all on equal terms." By 1975 disabled children were awarded the right to "specially designed instruction, at no cost to the parents or guardians, to meet [their] unique needs."

How have the courts interpreted this? Philip K. Howard points to two amazing cases in his book, *The Death of Common Sense*. "Timothy W. was a profoundly disabled child. He was born with virtually no cerebral cortex and suffered severe brain damage. . . . His other hand-icaps included cerebral palsy and cortical blindness, and he was quad-riplegic. He could react to strong sensations like pain [but] he could do virtually nothing for himself except part his lips when being spoon-fed." School experts in Rochester, New Hampshire, concluded that Timothy was "not capable of benefiting from educational ser-vices," but his mother wouldn't listen. Finally a federal appeals court ruled that "under the Individuals with Disabilities Education Act, it didn't matter whether Timothy could benefit from education. The Rochester school district was obligated to provide an educational pro-gram."

It is one thing to provide an education, but should the school bear even more costs? Howard had another example, even more outra-geous. "Drew P., a multihandicapped child from rural Georgia, suffers from infantile autism and severe mental retardation. Although the state provided an extensive educational program, including an expert in autism, Drew's parents were dissatisfied. They heard about a spe-cial school [in] Tokyo. A court ruled that the school had to foot the bill."

Here are two other cases from a piece in *The Washington Monthly*. In an Iowa Supreme Court ruling, "the school district had to pay for full-time nursing care for a then high school sophomore named Gregory Frey who is paralyzed from the neck down," while in California, a "school district [paid] for a severely brain-damaged boy to attend a specialized school in Massachusetts, at an annual cost of roughly $254,000. The superintendent only balked when the family demanded extra visits for the boy's sister." Most schools react this way, provid-ing expanded, often unreasonable accommodations rather than fight

ARE THESE

about it in court. Is this the meaning of "an equal education"? Children with extraordinary needs get a disproportionate share of scarce education dollars. Some of them may get no benefit from such regular schooling yet they are now integrated into the system at tremendous cost.

I read once that "the only thing special about special education is its cost." On average, about three times more funding is required to teach these children than so-called regular kids. In New York City the special education program costs, on average, $20,000 per child, compared to $7,000 for the rest. This program saps about one-quarter of the school budget for only 10 percent of the students. Frighteningly, this category has increased about 370 percent in the city since 1976, although referrals have finally begun to slow. As of 1999, one-third of the Washington, D.C., school budget went to the 10 percent of students designated for special education. Nationwide, the diagnosis of "learning disabled" increased about 38 percent between 1988 and 1998. The diagnosis for one category alone, attention deficit hyperactivity disorder (ADHD), increased about 270 percent during this period. Some 6 million kids receive special education instruction and services at a cost of almost $40 billion. Some experts put the figure closer to $60 billion. Yet the U.S. National Council on Disability still asserts that, to date, the "federal efforts to enforce the law have been inconsistent, ineffective and are lacking any real teeth." You decide.

As with other disability designations, the definition of an education disability is growing ever larger. Learning disabilities (LDs) now encompass everything from dyslexia to emotional disorders. Emotionally disturbed or disruptive children now dominate the category of learning disabled. If these students do not receive special instruction in their regular classroom, parents can sue, and plenty of them do. This emotional disability triggers a mind-boggling set of procedures for testing and review. The result is a catch-22. A child who regularly disrupts a class may be able to avoid removal or relocation, because any action based on this emotional disability is legally tagged as discrimination. Not surprisingly, discipline problems are exploding. In February 2002 the Los Angeles school district bragged that it was assimilating thousands of its emotionally disabled students into regular classes. That these actions often are detrimental to the rest of the class is not considered.

To avoid costly litigation, many times schools must assign several teachers to cover the varying needs within any particular class. Given the tremendous shortage of qualified teachers, this is a very inefficient, ineffective use of resources, all in the name of "normalizing" kids. The ensuing disruption and confusion often prevent any meaningful teaching. The interests of one child can now dictate the outcome for every other kid in the room. Just as in the workplace, where each character trait, unique problem, or personality quirk must be accommodated, the normal classroom now revolves around our differences. This is not the elimination of discrimination. Instead, it is the practice at its peak.

The special ed category ADHD needs a bit of special attention, given the extraordinary abuse of this designation. First the "H" stands for hyperactive and is the usual characterization for children rather than ADD for adults. The number of children being diagnosed with ADHD is exploding. A study notably commissioned by the manufacturer of the ADHD drug Adderall asserted that many kids go undiagnosed and untreated. Dr. Peter Jensen, a professor of child psychiatry who, notably, is affiliated with the company's survey, said that half of the afflicted children are not diagnosed due to poverty, poor healthcare, or teacher/parent disinterest. Interestingly, Jensen noted that even children without ADHD, but who experience "temporary difficulties," will benefit from drugs, but he added, "That would be inappropriate treatment." Any college student who scored a little Ritalin during exam time knows what Jensen's talking about.

So do some parents. On a more mercenary note, this LD designation has become a source of extra help for relatively normal children, courtesy of the taxpayer. One-third of the students in the wealthy community of Greenwich, Connecticut, are "special ed" students. If you can get a doctor to write a note about little Johnny's distraction or inattention and get a bit of free tutoring, why not? It just might insure higher grades that will pave the way to Harvard. Walter Olson interviewed experts for a 1999 piece on disability accommodation in *Reason*. One professional, Mariann Rossi-Odusky, said, "Anyone can be 'special education.' I've just got to give you the right tests." Norwalk Superintendent Ralph Sloan told him, "Nobody is slow anymore. If you are not in the fast track, you have a disability."

Lawsuits are now preventing schools from making any notation on a student's records about special dispensation in schooling or testing, so colleges can't consider those factors. Almost nine of ten disabled students asking for accommodations are those with ADHD or learning disabilities like dyslexia. Testing experts don't know what appropriate help is and what gives unfair advantage to these students. Some frustrated experts have suggested removing time limits for everyone on all tests. Professor Diane Pullen, an education law instructor at Boston College, says, "If you make a decision that a test doesn't have to be timed, you can eliminate most of the requests for accommodations, and the problem goes away." Why not just eliminate grades (which some schools are doing), then testing, and finally any competition altogether? If successful, the new push to make college a "right" will effectively accomplish this goal.

For those parents who resist the medicinal path, watch out. In 1995 the Wisconsin Supreme Court upheld a $170,000 jury verdict against parents whose fourth-grade special ed student attacked his teacher after they took him off medication that had reduced his aggressive behavior. The court did say that it was not imposing on parents a duty to keep the child on medication but rather a lesser duty to warn the school if they decided to discontinue the drug.

The obvious next step came a few years later. This newspaper headline in 2000 caught my attention: "Parents Pressured to Put Kids on Drugs." I couldn't believe my eyes as I scanned further to learn that "some public schools are accusing parents of child abuse when they balk at giving their kids Ritalin." Even more frightening was the next bit of information.

According to the article, a precedent-setting case occurred in a family court in Albany, New York, when upon complaint by the school, a couple was ordered to continue medicating their child for Attention Deficit Hyperactive Disorder. Around the same time, another New York family had been visited by child protective services to check out anonymous charges of "medical neglect" after they took their son off Ritalin due to side effects. Fearing refusal might lead to abuse allegations, even custody issues, these parents succumbed to pressure from schools and courts to drug their children.

Some states, such as Minnesota, in response to what advocates call the overprescription of drugs, have reacted with legislation that prohibits schools and child protection agencies from telling parents that they must put their children on drugs to treat disorders. In 2000 doctors wrote about 20 million monthly prescriptions for Ritalin, a Schedule II controlled substance, thanks in part to the dynamic marketing campaign by drug makers directed at parents.

Advocates of drug treatment actually compare the treatment to the government requirement that children be immunized against certain diseases before they begin school. However, the issues regarding ADHD are very different. The diagnosis is still uncertain, and the long-term effects of drug treatment are unknown. Many children have dramatic reactions to the drugs used, including sleeplessness and appetite loss. And finally, one person's hyperactivity may be another person's boredom.

I do not believe that all children currently diagnosed with ADHD are candidates for medication such as Ritalin. A large percentage of them would be better served with less sugar in their diets, more exercise in their systems, and some serious stimulation for their brains beyond the one-way input from a television set or the often mediocre teaching that simply drills facts and figures with no real intellectual challenge.

The debate over bilingual education is a variation on the discrimination theme and further demonstrates what perverse outcomes can arise from the creation of new "rights." In 1998 Californians were faced with an ethnically balkanized education system. Some sixty-eight languages were spoken in the state's schools. The cost of following the law by accommodating each immigrant student with bilingual assistance was overwhelming the districts. Amid tremendous rancor, voters overwhelmingly supported a state referendum to require an English-immersion program. Almost overnight, second-grade students with limited proficiency in English were improving in math and reading.

In Oceanside, where they took the law seriously and refused to issue waivers to the change, reading scores were up 19 percent. Next door in Vista, they weakened and change was negligible. The Vista principal, Ken Noonan, quickly abandoned his reservations. "I thought this would hurt kids. The exact reverse occurred, totally unexpected by me. The kids began to learn—not pick up, but learn—formal English, oral and written."

At the same time that the West Coast was experimenting with the obvious, New York City was clinging to failure. In 1974 a Puerto Rican youth agency sued the city. Puerto Rican children were not receiving the education promised by the public schools. A consent decree was issued, calling for bilingual education for these students. It became financially lucrative for school districts to sustain this program, as hefty subsidies flowed in to implement the policy. Anything that involves extra money will be protected at all costs (as with special education). In fact, by 1988, any kid with a Spanish surname who was also in the lower 40 percent of a class was placed in bilingual education, even if he or she was fluent in English. As the monies increased, schools began to inflate the number of kids needing such instruction; the numbers jumped from 94,000 in 1988 to 187,000 just one year later.

Then suddenly Latino parents caught on. Wait a minute, they said, our kids aren't learning! Furthermore, they recognized that assimilation is critical to success in this country. Since that time the number of children in bilingual education has dropped, but about 25 percent of the Hispanic students in New York City still reside in special classes. This city should take a page from California and move those students quickly into the environment they will have to compete in throughout their lives.

Unfortunately, national officials ignore success stories in favor of political expediency. During his administration, Clinton education secretary Richard Riley took the politically correct stance on the "dual language" approach to education. Recognizing the growth of our Hispanic population, he supported the two-language method of instruction in schools. At the time, a letter to the editor in *USA Today* supported Riley by saying "Spanish is the most important reality in self-identification of most Hispanics." What happened to the notion that we were all Americans first?

Another letter in that same day's edition said "Go to Europe or South America. No one is confused, despite the mixed population, as to what the national language is. There are no concessions in the classroom for those speaking another language." Peruvian by birth, this writer commended her father for insisting his children learn "proper English," not Spanglish or poor English. He knew, as did she, that assimilation is the pathway to success when you enter another culture. To suggest otherwise is denying reality. We are doing a long-term disservice to children when we refuse to tackle the short-term language deficiency. Yet in large part because educational bureaucrats use outdated ideology to justify massive funding, we hobble these children with a bilingual education.

Simply managing students is the most time-consuming thing teachers do these days. You can see why. After paperwork, mandated discrimination, and disciplinary activities, there is little time left for instruction. Maybe that is just as well. Sometimes I wonder if we really want our kids to learn.

In July 1999 *Reason* magazine published a teacher's lament, "Why Johnny Can't Fail." The author, Jerry Jesness, wrote of his ultimate submission to what he termed the "floating standard." It begins: "I confess. I am a grade-inflating teacher guilty of 'social promotion.' I have given passing grades to students who failed all of their tests, to students who refused to read their assignments, to students who were absent as often as not, to students who were not even functionally literate. I have turned a blind eye to cheating and outright plagiarism and have given A's and B's to students whose performance was at best mediocre. Like others of my ilk, I have sent students to higher grades, to higher education, and to the workplace unprepared for the demands that would be made of them." This was the encouraging part!

Jesness asserted that all our talk of reform is meaningless because we are no longer willing to honestly evaluate our students. Schools can create tough curriculums, list outstanding courses, and hire credentialed teachers, but if the measure of the student is artificial, the outcome hasn't changed. He blamed not only the teachers and administrators but also the government and parents for this situation: "Americans want quality education, but when lower grades and higher failure rates reach their own children's classes, they rebel and schools relent. Americans hate public education because standards are so low but love their local schools because their children perform so well there." Jesness says that parents are happier, students better behaved, and teachers less burdened when everyone goes along to get along: "Students build self-esteem, parents gain peace of mind, and schools save money. When the payback comes, time and distance keep the student and the school well separated."

He described his own heartbreaking experiences as he tried to teach. If he graded honestly, the parents complained and the principal found fault with his teaching. If he disciplined a child or sent someone to the office, the event was noted in his record as an inability to handle students. He was fired several times before he began to toe the line.

I didn't know whether to laugh or cry when Jesness talked of teaching *Hamlet* to an unwilling or incapable audience. "If you demand that your charges read and understand the play, most will fail and you will be blamed. If you drop *Hamlet* and convert the class into a remedial reading course, you will be out of compliance with the curriculum. If you complain that your students are not up to the mandated task, you will be labeled insensitive and uncaring." He suggested several alternatives: Read it to them. If they can't sit still, get it in comic book form or rent the movie. Test with true or false, fill-in-the-blank or maybe let them do an art project (draw a picture). "Keep dropping the standard and sooner or later everyone will hit it. If anyone asks, you taught *Hamlet* in a nonconventional way, one that took into account your students' individual differences and needs."

As he inflated his students' performances, his own evaluations soared. About the time he abandoned all honesty, he was regularly classified as "clearly outstanding." "Grades are educational quality control, and passing grades 'prove' that teacher, student and school are successful; therefore the best teachers are those who give the highest grades, and the 'best' administrators are those who can convince their teachers to do so," he said.

Jesness debunked all our excuses. What about our impoverished kids with single parents or diversity problems? Surely concessions must be made. Jesse suggested we look at Korea, Sweden, or Singapore. Those countries face similar challenges with a fair degree of diversity but are doing quite nicely thanks to discipline, testing, and fixed standards.

The lawyers have insured we cannot discipline, and fixed standards may be discriminatory. After all, just whose standards are going to be fixed? As for testing, opposition to standardized exams is the new line being drawn in the sand by teachers and some concerned parents. Teachers don't want the obvious and immediate evaluation of their teaching skills that would accompany a classroom full of grades. Some parents imagine that their kids might get through school without ever confronting an objective evaluation of their abilities. I realize there have been many innovations since my time in school. Nevertheless, I can't quite figure out how all the testing I endured actually hurt me. As students we expected to receive grades and knew that those numbers were accepted as a measure of our acquired knowledge. Education, not self-esteem, was the goal.

Today, however, we pretend to discourage distinctions or, to be perfectly candid, any discrimination. Discrimination is not a dirty word. It is that distinctly human ability to sort and select. But now our politically correct concepts of equality and self-esteem tell us to refrain from labeling or categorizing a child in any way. We encourage a value-neutral approach to everything such that getting all the questions right on an exam is no better than just showing up for the test. Testing companies long ago made racial norming of exam questions standard procedure; any question regularly missed by a particular minority was tossed out the next year. Today we complain about any distinction, period.

While I do not believe that every student or school must conform to a certain curriculum, there should be a required level of knowledge to gain promotion through our schools. It doesn't matter which test is used to measure that knowledge as long as levels of proficiency can be determined. We are on the verge of undermining or outlawing any such qualitative comparisons not only in school but in the workplace and beyond. How such a competitive society could arrive at this point, where such assessments are regarded as discriminatory, psychologically harmful, or entirely meaningless, is beyond me.

This brings me to the rest of the equation. The appropriate rallying cry in the education battle should be that of equal access to a good education. Educators, not legislators, should determine which classroom a child is placed in or what sort of accommodation a school can reasonably make for various problems. What the legislature should worry about is mandating that all those schoolrooms, no matter the category of pupils, be staffed with qualified teachers. Unfortunately, now you are talking about political warfare.

I have tremendous respect for the teaching profession. Education is the most important contribution we can make to better society. Because of that, I am thoroughly dismayed at the deterioration in the quality of our teachers and their inability actually to educate our children. The president of the United Federation of Teachers, Randi Weingarten, put it more diplomatically when she said, "To succeed in improving our schools, we must, above all, look to the educators who work with the children." Unfortunately, these words were the opening salvo in a union fight where the goal was not improved instruction but better salaries, less class time, and more benefits for teachers who could not or would not do their job. Through contributions and other political pressures, the unions have succeeded in preventing major reforms that include raising teacher standards, removing unqualified instructors, and recognizing quality through merit pay.

The 2000 contract struggle in New York City is a good example of the intractable stance the unions keep taking. The city's 180-day school year is the shortest in any major city, yet union rules give teachers one-third of every workday for administrative and preparation activities. Salaries currently range from about $32,000 to $70,000 a year. With school holidays, summer vacations, in-service days, and other time away, these workers spend about 120 days a year actually working in the classroom. I realize plenty of work occurs after hours, but such is the case with most jobs we label as a profession rather than a trade.

Despite this, New York City's teachers were arguing for even less classroom time for new teachers. They wanted more mentoring experience while still being paid to teach. I know of few professions where mentoring is a salaried activity. It is something that occurs naturally in the course of job growth and development. Nevertheless, that argument has taken hold around the country as school districts are hiring full-time teaching coaches to mentor employees.

Unions argue that other professionals, such as lawyers and business executives, extensively tutor their new employees. I have to laugh. My first job out of law school was as an assistant district attorney. My initiation occurred less than twenty-four hours after acquiring a desk. I was given a file to take home that first evening and told I would try that case before a jury the next day. I had yet to find the ladies' room. It was, in fact, trial by fire, but everyone walked those coals. If you couldn't cut it, you were out of a job. Doctors have their internships, but we all know the horrifying stories of days without sleep and endless on-call status for these young medics. They too will lose their jobs if they can't keep up. No unions protect them. No long Christmas or summer vacations break up the days. Emerging business executives are in the same boat. The dog-eat-dog competitive environment insures all of these professionals hit the ground running, work overtime, and prove themselves before someone else takes their place.

Interestingly, the teachers' unions have insured that such coaching and observation cannot be used to negative effect. The mentors are union members who will not recommend discipline or further training for poor teachers. Their evaluations are not to be shared with principals under the theory that teachers would not cooperate if their performance might be reported. In San Diego, these specialists can observe only on invitation of the teacher.

We desperately need better teachers. Maybe such mentoring will increase the quality of instruction. (It certainly provides more jobs.) Nevertheless, the laws that literally prohibit repercussions for bad teachers are ludicrous. The New York State Board of Education finally allocated $450,000 in 2000 to give a test preparation course to some 441 teachers who had failed to pass their certification exams over four, five, even six years. One teacher had flunked the exam twenty-four times. All of these people continued teaching despite repeated failures to pass their own competency requirements.

Education boards complain they have to prop up these teachers because many are handling hard-to-staff subjects like math and science. One New York Board member said, "If we didn't help these people, there might be no one in these classrooms." Now there's a comforting thought. Our kids are illiterate and failing math and science by the thousands, but as long as there is a warm body, *any* body supervising the room, we're satisfied. According to the Education Trust, 25 percent of teachers in high-poverty secondary schools lack either a major or minor in the subject they teach. Thanks to the rules and ridiculous due process measures pushed through by the United Federation of Teachers, these unqualified teachers stay in the classroom while we spend millions to provide them the same sort of remedial help their students will certainly need in the future.

The unions don't stop there. Incompetent teachers have an almost unlimited ability to thwart dismissal. The notion of due process has become so absurdly bloated that it can take up to three years to terminate a bad or dangerous instructor. Throughout this process, the teacher remains on full salary. In New York a principal must document some ten to fifteen grievances before issuing an unsatisfactory review to a teacher. Complainants can appeal through four hearings, always accompanied by a paid union representative. Theoretically, this could mean that up to sixty hearings are necessary simply to validate the unsatisfactory ruling. This rating does not mean dismissal. In fact, the teacher can't even be transferred to another school for three years. Administrators have given up attempting to challenge incompetent instructors. It is therefore not surprising that of 72,000 teachers in New York, only 600 received an unsatisfactory rating in 1999. That is less than 1 percent in a system where about half the students are functionally illiterate.

What about a situation like this? In a Connecticut newspaper, the *Norwalk Hour,* Ashley Varese reported, "After an in-house investigation that lasted more than a month, Carleton Bauer, the Ponus Ridge Middle School teacher who gave an 11-year-old girl money to purchase marijuana, has been reprimanded with a letter in his file." The teacher's union had, of course, negotiated this resolution for the thirty-one-year teaching veteran. The interim superintendent of schools, William Papallo, called the penalty "fair and equitable," saying "For someone who has worked so long, a reprimand is very serious."

Remember the reason for unions? These organizations were designed to prohibit the abuse of the American worker. A fair wage, protection from unreasonable or discriminatory hiring and firing, safe working conditions; these were the appropriate goals of such groups. They were not supposed to insure work for lazy or incompetent employees. They certainly were not intended to pervert the quality of work or competence of employees such that no reasonable results could be achieved within a business or institution.

How do we get those unqualified teachers in our classrooms in the first place? Look no further than the schools that produce them. Teacher colleges are a strange world unto themselves. These institutions were supposed to begin issuing so-called report cards three years ago to tell the public exactly what they were teaching and who was graduating. Nothing has been forthcoming, and no one is pressuring for compliance. Instead, the colleges' bureaucrats are still whining about the need for millions of dollars and man-hours to comply with this demand. They protest any upgrading of the certification process or any testing of teacher proficiency. Heaven help the states that are trying to increase the use of competency exams for new or long-term teachers.

Right now these teacher colleges have a stranglehold on teaching jobs. Thanks to the rule makers, many professionals with extraordinary credentials in their select fields cannot teach because they have not taken a litany of "education courses." Some instruction in teaching may be necessary, but the heavy burden to learn rote exercises in methodology should be rejected in favor of attracting intelligent, qualified instructors.

So as not to discriminate, let's look at the administrators next. I am afraid this review will be no more comforting than the last. The principals and superintendents who set the curriculum, guide our teachers, and mentor our students should display the educational excellence we desire from our children when they graduate. This is not the norm.

Paul A. Zoch, a Latin professor in Houston, wrote a scathing article about these leaders. From the late 1980s on, he found that "one-third held degrees in business, education or physical education" before taking the reins of a school. Their academic career as a whole was relatively abysmal. Both in SAT and GRE scores, the education and business majors were at the bottom of the entrance list, rating even lower than the "supposedly verbally challenged engineers." In the 1992 National Adult Literacy Survey, the school administrators' scores in prose literacy surpassed only sales supervisors and business proprietors in the race to the bottom.

It is now politically incorrect to use test scores as a measure of talent, even with school supervisors, but you can draw your own conclusions. In his article, Zoch included several letters from new principals to incoming teachers. One such missive went like this: "In recent weeks, I have previously had the pleasure of meeting many of you, however there are many that I have yet to make your acquaintance. It will be my personal vendetta to meet each of you and remember your name as well as what you do before the year's end." There's a comforting introduction!

Education administrators have no obligation to excel in any particular core subject. That great black hole known as the education degree will suffice, with stimulating requirements like curriculum management, education law and finance, and educational leadership. The National Board for Educational Administrators actually wanted to require at least a master's degree in education, saying administrator certificates were worthless.

Zoch described an exercise he was required to do with a group of incoming teachers. The administrator asked them to break into groups and list the accomplishments their high school graduates should achieve. At the top of the overall list were things like "high self-esteem, good grooming, and good ethical character, even happiness." Only one group added to its list "the ability to read and write and do math at the 12th grade level." The administrator never challenged these goals or suggested what was truly important. I am not surprised. The higher the goals, the harder it is to accomplish them. Student failure means loss of money, loss of eligible athletes, an increased dropout rate, and maybe loss of the administrator's own job. Then again, maybe these personality traits are the new qualifications for an educated American.

One of my very favorite writers, Lewis Lapham, edits *Harper's* magazine. In a piece entitled "Why Our Schools Will Never Improve," he ravaged politicians, corporations, and the media for making deceptive promises of reform. He said the so-called revolution will fail regardless of more money or teacher accountability. Lapham asserted, and I agree, that education is now handled as another "commodity . . . the graduating classes an assembly-line product [where] contented computer operators" are manufactured for the needs of the business community. Better yet, kids are instructed in the art of consumerism thanks to ad-driven Internet servers, corporate education programs that tout their products, and commercial-packed TV channels that deliver a bit of news to soften the blow.

He said that "much of what passes for education in the U.S. deadens the desire for learning" and, even worse, such a result is "deliberate." Many high schools today look like lenient prisons that warehouse kids until most are released to find jobs they're not qualified for with an "unbridled appetite for goods and services they can't afford." "The consumer society," Lapham says, "rests on P. T. Barnum's great economic truth that a sucker is born every minute" and our nation's "reserves of ignorance" are indeed a "precious resource." He concluded with faultless logic that an educated mind is an independent one. "To learn to read is to learn to think, possibly to discover the strength and freedom of one's own mind. This is not a discovery that the consumer society wishes too many of its customers to make."

A bright, independent mind can ask too many intrusive questions, refuse to accept what is force-fed over the airways, and even challenge dogma delivered by leaders of industry, politics, and the church. As Lapham states so succinctly, "a too well educated public might prove more trouble than it's worth." As a final note, the accompanying *Harper's* Index included these stats: The average number of words in the written vocabulary of a six- to fourteen-year-old American child in 1945 was 25,000. Today the average number is 10,000.

Have we become so blinded by lobbyists, lawyers, and unions that we can no longer see the relatively simple steps to success? All we have to do is read about real classroom achievement to understand what works and what doesn't. In countless small programs implemented at the local level, parents, teachers, clergy, and business leaders give their most precious asset, their time and commitment, to create safe, healthy, and dynamic learning environments in our schools. Most important, they have high expectations for the children, and no matter the locale, the kids rarely disappoint. These ideas can be replicated across the country, not through more money, regulations, or bureaucracies but by replicating personal involvement in our children's futures.

FOUR | Regulatory Agencies: Laws Without Legislation

Years ago a vacationing group gathered on the banks of the Colorado River for a pre-rafting barbecue. I decided to hike up a nearby hillside for a look around. When almost at the top, I ran into an old barbed wire fence blocking the path. One glance showed that the wire sagged from many travelers snaking their way through the barrier to take advantage of the view. Following suit, I was cut short by a stern voice. "You can't go up there!" Turning back, I queried my friend, who worked for NASA, "And why not?"

"Obviously, that fence is there to keep you out," he said.

"Or it might be here to keep something in," I replied.

And thus began a nightlong debate about law. The discussion degenerated into his shouts of "libertine" and mine of "bureaucrat." The lines were clearly drawn. Despite my professional devotion to the subject, I have always asked about the purpose of rules. What goal was intended? What limitations are required? Who benefits and who is harmed by the enactment? Finally, should those rules exist at all?

Over the past several decades I have watched as the art of rule making has swept Capitol Hill. You would think this nation would explode if the government mandated what we plant in our yards, how we safeguard our homes, or where our children sit in a car. Instead, we simply comply with no questions asked. If you think civil laws are absurd and overwhelming, just wait. Regulations have the effect of laws but don't even need a majority vote to implement. So, like rabbits, they breed exponentially until the landscape is overrun. Entire institutions are devoted to the contemplation, passage, and enforcement of statutes so complex and minute that no single person could ever know, much less obey, them all.

An enormous bureaucracy supplements and often supersedes the rule making by our representatives. This segment of government has become an independent source of power as well as a foil for legislators and lobbyists. Most agency work is done in relative obscurity, yet on inspection, the favors and influence peddling are as apparent as in the more public realms of politics. Agencies are often scapegoats for actions actually taken by lobbyists and members of Congress. Since decisions by bureaucrats are easily disguised amid the thousands of regulations churned out daily, it is harder to find the fingerprints, but they are there.

The following agencies govern almost everything we do. The Food and Drug Administration (FDA) and U.S. Department of Agriculture (USDA) control the foods we eat, the Internal Revenue Service (IRS) determines the taxes we pay, the Department of Health and Human Services (HHS) governs Medicare and Medicaid, and the Social Security Administration (SSA) handles our retirement. The Consumer Products Safety Commission (CPSC), Department of Housing and Urban Development (HUD), Education Department (ED), Environmental Protection Agency (EPA), Department of Labor (DOL), the Department of Defense (DOD)—well, you get the idea. Fifty-four federal departments and agencies employ more than 130,000 federal workers who do nothing but specifically regulate. On Bill Clinton's watch, the number of full-time positions in regulatory agencies reached an all-time high. (This despite Al Gore's pledge to "reinvent government.") These people spent over $18.7 billion simply writing and enforcing pronouncements. As the twentieth century ended, economist Thomas Hopkins estimated that the cost of complying with these regulations cost U.S. taxpayers $721 billion a year, about 40 percent of all federal spending. President Bush's newly proposed Department of Homeland Defense would have a $37 billion budget and would attempt to meld about 169,000 federal workers from the component agencies (before hiring new personnel). A large percentage of these workers will join the ranks of the rule makers to confront the Herculean task of uniting the factions from twenty-two new and existing agencies. The prognosis for success is dire.

Worse yet, these agencies have built-in survival mechanisms that guarantee the bureaucratic nightmares we now encounter. Whether local, state, or federal, most agencies have common characteristics. First, they are self-sustaining bodies. Their mission is to become indispensable. Employees will create problems and make work to elevate their importance. Civil servants know they are not judged on quality but on quantity. The more rules and citations an agency produces, the more files that are opened then closed, the more productive it is perceived to be. Second, every dime in the budget must always be spent. No money can be left on the table. That might (horror!) suggest the need for a cut in subsequent allocations. Overruns suggest the opposite and are always appreciated. Since legislators build in the effects of inflation, annual allocations usually result in a funding increase. If an agency's budget remains the same from one year to the next, sponsoring politicians will ring the alarm, that "They're cutting our program." Third, every talented bureaucrat is constantly scanning for future opportunity. As with congressional staff positions and even elective office, agency work is a great stepping-stone to the big bucks. The more important your contacts, the more influential your agency, the more value you will have to private industry seeking favors from the government. Display the appropriate "flexibility" and you will be richly rewarded when you seek employment in the private sector.

Equally, politicians know how to manipulate these agencies. Civil servants learn they must "go with the flow" to keep their jobs. Those who stay on through different administrations learn to adapt so that they pacify a liberal administration by strict enforcement of the rules and slack off during a conservative term. They simply pretend to get tough during a moderate administration like Clinton's, when both sides of the fence need mollifying. The rules and problems don't change, but the agenda does. If someone rocks the boat at the wrong time, the punishment is swift. During the Reagan administration, the EPA got a little too cocky. What happened next? The agency's office of enforcement was simply abolished in a "reorganization" ploy. Those employees completely mistimed their mandate.

On the other hand, the EPA showed it had wised up by 1990. In the Clean Air Act revisions that year, Congress called for the development of alternative fuels, certainly a worthwhile goal. The EPA used this legislation to specifically mandate ethanol support. Methanol, a corn by-product, actually delivers less energy than it takes to generate the product. It produces an abundance of nitrogen-oxide emissions, only slightly lowers other organic compounds, and doesn't even affect the worst polluting culprit—the airborne particulate matter. However, Archer Daniels Midland, a huge political contributor that coincidentally manufactures about 41 percent of the nation's ethanol, makes a bundle on the alternative fuel. Congress touts the benefits, particularly to the small farmer, while using the EPA to pay back ADM for its largesse, which according to the Center for Responsive Politics, totaled almost $1 million to the Republicans and Democrats between 1999 and 2002. The 2002 Farm Bill again increased the government's commitment to this giveaway.

As with most government activity, procedure trumps substance. The process is all-important, even if the outcome is ridiculous. When a problem is identified, it must first be defined—what damage is occurring, who is affected, and how much does it cost to reduce or eliminate the problem? Agencies then compile massive statistics, obtain testimony from affected parties, prepare scientific reports, and provide countless hearings for additional input. If the process is faulty, even a correct result might be challenged in court. A single enactment can take decades to achieve. Airbags took over twenty years to approve and implement. Removing the carcinogenic red dye from foods took twenty-five years. This delay is not due to the democratic process in action but to the ability of lawyers and lobbyists to obfuscate and delay for more mercenary reasons. These delays have become possible because of the ridiculous extent to which the notion of due process has been expanded. It's no longer one notice and public hearing but repeated engagements with procedural (not substantive) objections every step of the way. Remember, if you can delay an action, that is money in the bank until the new rule is enforced. Litigation is usually preferable to any finalized rule on the books. Once regulations are enacted and enforcement is attempted, the real games begin.

Rule making by agencies often produces results that were not intended by Congress. Since our courts give deference to agency interpretations, the original mandate sometimes disappears entirely. The bureaucracy takes on a life of its own, controlled by the whim of the regulators. Some of the real messes we now encounter were created almost entirely in this manner. The Civil Rights Act of 1964 established an enforcement agency, the Equal Employment Opportunities Commission (EEOC). Remember Senator Humphrey's line, "If [anyone] can find in Title VII . . . any language which provide[s] that an employer will have to hire [minorities] on the basis of percentage or quota, I will start eating the pages one after another, because it is not in there"? The EEOC's first compliance officer, Rutgers law professor Alfred W. Blumrosen, decided otherwise. He literally bragged of what he called his "free and easy way with statutory construction" and praised his agency for working "in defiance of the laws governing its operation."

As amazing as it now seems, this bureaucrat practically rewrote the legislation single-handedly. In his 1971 book *Black Employment and the Law,* Blumrosen stated, "If discrimination is narrowly defined . . . by requiring an evil intent to injure minorities then it will be difficult to find that it exists. If it does not exist, then the plight of racial and ethnic minorities must be attributable to some more generalized failures in society, in the fields of basic education, housing, family relations and the like. [The] answer can only come gradually as basic institutions, attitudes, customs and practices are changed."

Since this might take generations to remedy, Blumrosen continued: "But if discrimination is broadly defined . . . by including all conduct which adversely affects minority group employment opportunities . . . then the prospects for rapid improvement in [those] opportunities are greatly increased." His mission was clear. Discrimination would simply *be assumed* if minorities were "underrepresented" in some job. He suggested that the EEOC should prosecute employers, even in the absence of complaints, if their racial composition gave *the appearance* of discrimination.

As head of the enforcing agency, Blumrosen knew that the courts give great deference to an agency's interpretation of its own activities. He bet on that construction, and his gamble paid off. Despite the explicit prohibition against quotas, Blumrosen instituted exactly that, and no one objected. Minority preferences and affirmative action became the accepted interpretations.

In a history of the EEOC prepared for the Johnson Library, this transformation was noted. The record reflects that the EEOC rejected the "traditional meaning" of discrimination as "one of intent in the state of mind of the actor" in favor of a "constructive proof of discrimination" that would "disregard intent as critical to the finding of an unlawful employment practice." For example, if a company gave an objective employment test but too many minorities failed, then that was discrimination, period. Chief Justice Warren Burger, writing in *Griggs v. Duke Power Company* (1971), affirmed this approach. The company could not require a high school diploma or passage of an equivalent exam even if the requirement was not intended to discriminate. He noted that blacks were less likely than whites to have completed high school or do well on aptitude tests, so he ruled that "the Act proscribes not only overt discrimination but also practices that are fair in form, but discriminatory in operation." Essentially, minorities could sue without showing any personal discrimination, thus violating the democratic notion of equality before the law.

By 1976 the die was cast. In *International Brotherhood of Teamsters v. U.S.,* the Court clarified that any requirement that had a disparate impact on the races, regardless of intent or reasonableness, constituted discrimination. Subsequently, liberal Justice Harry Blackmun warned this would lead to hiring based on race rather than merit. Sure enough, it did. Another avowed liberal, Justice William O. Douglas, tried repeatedly to scrutinize the new crop of reverse discrimination cases emerging in the area of college acceptances. In his autobiography he quoted Justice Thurgood Marshall as saying "You guys have been practicing discrimination for years. Now it is our turn."

By the time *United Steelworkers of America v. Weber* (1979) was decided, Justice Burger was aghast at what he'd set loose and dissented, saying that the Court "introduces into Title VII a tolerance for the very evil that the law was intended to eradicate." Yet in 1987 *Johnson v. Santa Clara County* expanded preferences to women. The Court ruled that discrimination against a white male in favor of a less qualified female was perfectly legal even though the defendant had no record of prior discrimination. The dissent was succinct: "We effectively replace the goal of a discrimination-free society with the quite incompatible goal of proportionate representation by race and by sex in the workplace."

All of this started with one renegade bureaucrat who clearly knew better. In 1972 Blumrosen bragged that the EEOC's power to issue guidelines "does not flow from any congressional grant of authority." For forty years we have been directed by his misguided intentions and by blind cooperation from the courts.

The ability to control and thus expand statutory interpretation has given the EEOC influence beyond any rational comprehension. In *Jacques v. DiMarzio, Inc., No. 97-CV-2884,* the plaintiff was fired from her job after seven years due to a "series of conflicts with fellow employees" and "her confrontational and irrational behavior with her supervisor." She said her behavior was as a result of a mental disability. Both her 1996 complaint to the National Labor Relations (NLRB) and one to the New York State Division of Human Rights were unsuccessful. Then the EEOC gave her a right-to-sue letter.

POWERFUL

In determining she could go to the jury with her case, Judge Fredrick Block wrote, "the ability to interact or get along with others is a *major life activity* within the meaning of the ADA." The defendant responded by filing a counterclaim seeking damages for harassment, interference with business operations and employee morale, and damage to the company's reputation. Not for long! The judge threatened the company with sanctions, saying that this counterclaim was "in apparent retaliation against a vulnerable plaintiff who suffers from a significant mental impairment for filing her lawsuit. She should not be subject to 'terrorism tactics.' "

There are now about 160 different federal programs that deal with affirmative action and setasides that accompany government contracts, grants, and other financial dealings. Even if you don't discriminate, there are "goals and timetables" for hiring and promotion that businesses must recognize if they want to deal with the government. As with other conflicting and confusing federal regulations, no one can ever know if they are in full compliance. The best intentions will not save you from the rules!

Pretend for a moment, though, that you know all the rules. Then you're faced with the question of which ones to obey. Throughout the regulatory world, there are major conflicts to sort out. The trucking company that rejects a driver with sight in only one eye is complying with the standard required by the U.S. Department of Transportation, but the EEOC may sue it for discrimination. Watch out if you screen for alcoholism, drug abuse, even criminal records. You may come under fire regardless of the safety considerations that should be paramount. The U.S. Department of Agriculture (USDA) and the Food and Drug Administration (FDA) often butt heads, requiring different standards for the same products. Environmentally conscious businesses can get really confused. Follow the Resource Conservation and Recovery Act to properly dispose of waste and you may violate the Toxic Control Substance Act. The list goes on and on.

In 1936 there were 2,411 pages in the *Federal Register,* the assemblage of all new federal pronouncements. Today there are about 75,000. Why so many? The answer is political, not rational. In his last two months in office, between November 2000 and January 2001, Bill Clinton added about 29,000 pages to the *Federal Register,* beating Jimmy Carter's last-minute push by 5,000 pages. Why would Clinton wait eight years to drop in these new rules? Did we desperately need them right before he left office? No. Clinton clearly was manipulating federal agencies to accomplish what couldn't be achieved through the democratic process. In fact, our last fourteen presidents all increased rule making by an average of 17 percent as their administration ended. Most of these new regulations were either gifts to contributors or an attempt to preempt political decisions that properly belonged to the next administration. The procedural task of overturning rules is so difficult that presidents can count on a large number of these final regulations surviving or at least frustrating a successor for years to come.

The ability to promulgate rules offers extraordinary power. Legislators have learned that the ability to authorize and manipulate law is their meal ticket. They now sell access to the legislative process like tickets to the races. I once saw a Dennis the Menace cartoon that showed Dennis whipping a confused little Joey at Monopoly. Smiling, Dennis explains, "Don't you know? Whoever makes the rules, wins." Yes, indeed. Even more than the debilitating effect of money on politics, the ability to manipulate the law is corrupting our system. Once our elected officials understood how much could be gained through the exercise of this authority, they were off and running. It has been hell to pay every since.

Writing laws is an amazing way to deliver favors to influential groups. Lobbyists have been known literally to set up shop in the White House or a congressional office, penning submissions to an agency or government committee. The former EPA administrator in the Carter administration, Douglas Costle, has said "probably three out of every four [White House] comments on our rule-making were cribbed from industry briefs."

President Bush made an obvious about-face when he reversed his campaign position on regulating carbon dioxide emissions, but had Vice President Dick Cheney not been so blatant about his exclusive meetings with energy giants, we might not have realized how much our energy policies conformed to that industry's requests. In April 2001 Enron's CEO, Kenneth Lay, delivered the company's wish list to Cheney. When the administration's ultimate plan was announced, the parallels were remarkable. *Washington Post* reporter Eric Pianin wrote at the time, "A senior EPA official resigned this week protesting what he described as the Bush Administration's effort to undermine tough legal action against dozens of aging coal-fired power plants and refineries that have violated federal emission standards. Eric V.

Schaeffer, who headed the EPA's Office of Regulatory Enforcement, said that 'energy department officials treat the power industry as their 'client.' " The practice continues unabated.

The conservatives cloak themselves in the mantle of regulatory reform, but you can see that the GOP is just as adept at writing rules as the Democrats. One party pushes for labor or environmental rules while the other hands out tax breaks and subsidies. If the Republicans deny they are adding to the *Federal Register,* just examine their contributions to the Internal Revenue Code. Ultimately, the ideological facade each side displays just disguises the fact that more often than not they both manipulate rules to cater to the same big contributors. The shadowy world of regulatory law allows them ample opportunity.

There is one area of federal regulation that I support, at least in theory, and that is the Environmental Protection Agency. I do not condone its every rule, its haphazard operations, or its extremely selective enforcement, but the subject of environmental protection is appropriate for federal supervision. We now understand that everyone shares the nation's air and water. Widespread damage can occur from one action or a single industry. We are learning that the mutation and extinction of flora and fauna is reflective of our own well-being. This understanding has focused needed attention on the environmental causes.

Even former opponents of the EPA and its work now recognize the need for limits on harmful activities. Unfortunately, as we move from identifying problems, through regulations, to enforcement, something goes terribly wrong. Our wetland laws are a perfect example. While the big corporations, developers, and industrial farms pollute at will, delay prosecution for decades, and negotiate minimal fines if finally nabbed, a homeowner cannot fill in a damp patch of skunk cabbage without a permit. Rules that were never intended to apply to a few square yards of turf are being enforced against the little guy, while those who seriously damage our wetlands and waterways proceed with abandon.

The raging controversy over the New Jersey Meadowlands is a perfect example. This large, pristine swampland, once an environmentally ravaged ecosystem, now on its way to a fragile recovery, is located in a prime building area. Many federal waivers occur where a building site affects only a small reclamation, but the Mills Corporation wanted to build a megamall complete with office, retail, and entertainment space right in the heart of the protected acreage. All pertinent federal and state agencies, including the EPA, had opposed this, so how would the corporation accomplish its mission?

First, Mills hired a lobbying firm headed by Judy Shaw, former chief of staff for New Jersey governor Christie Whitman, and another that employed Jerome Benny, former chief of staff for Bergen County executive Pat Schuber. Mills then forked over hundreds of thousands of dollars in lobbying costs and campaign contributions to local, state, and federal officials. That, and the promise of huge sales tax revenues, got a bill floated to use government bonds for road and infrastructure improvements around the site. A $43,000 contribution to Gore 2000 was made in April 1999, the same month the vice president's own creation, the Council on Environmental Quality, was discussing ways of obtaining EPA approval for the development. When asked about this apparent conflict, Gore's office responded, "He hasn't been involved on a daily basis in the Meadowlands dispute."

Mills Corporation is no stranger to the intricacies of the political process. In Texas it managed to skirt environmental objections to a mall project in only three years. When faced with objections from the Sierra Club, it simply donated $200,000 to the conservancy for land acquisition and the opposition disappeared. "In the end, we decided not to litigate," the Houston Sierra Club president said. "That way, we were directing some money to preserving wetlands areas. We didn't have much hope of being successful. In retrospect, Mills really didn't cough up much money."

Thus far, opponents have been able to thwart the Meadowlands project by making a statewide stink, but as I write, the final outcome is still unknown. Gore was defeated, but Governor Whitman now heads the EPA and will be negotiating with her former employees. New Jersey State officials have proposed locating an alternative site, but Mills has not withdrawn its permit applications to build in the wetlands. Mills Corporation also has a fallback position. If the environmental agencies reject the plans, and the state doesn't hand over another satisfactory site, the company will pursue a constitutional private property rights challenge in court. Failing that, corporate attorney Michael Luchkiw said that denial of the project is the equivalent of land condemnation and "would require the federal government to purchase the property" at fair market value, with no discount for the wetlands. Either way, he plans to win.

Hackensack riverkeeper Bill Sheehan said about the Meadowlands project: "We have to get the polluters and the developers and the chemists and the agribusiness out of the pockets of our elected officials if we're ever going to be able to take back our rivers and our bays." According to environmental activist Robert F. Kennedy, Jr., "Nobody has the right to liquidate [wetlands] for cash," but this is exactly what occurs thanks to waivers, exceptions, and trade-offs. A few powerful contributions can clear the way where rules seem to dictate otherwise.

My own experience with a wetlands commission has unquestionably prejudiced these pages. Having grown up in the country, I have tremendous respect for the land. A bit of a tree-hugger, I would never knowingly injure or pollute anything. However, when I moved to Westchester, New York, I was amazed at the extent to which local government had intruded on personal behavior. You cannot burn leaves. You cannot cut down a tree over twelve inches in diameter without a permit, nor can you dig a pond without permission for fear it may disturb a wetland . . . or create one. The building lots are a minimum of four acres, so it is rare that my activities would impinge on the neighbors. Nevertheless, rules are rules, and my town's committees need something to do.

I had the audacity to dig a small pond in a flat open field previously inhabited by nothing but lawn grass. I then cleaned out an existing channel that ran from that location to a lower pond to insure against flooding. A neighbor two doors down called the wetlands board. Suddenly a man was in my driveway wanting to see my permit.

I had reviewed the wetland rules before beginning the project. The laws were drafted to protect nature's intricate filtration system for our water supply. The primary targets were developers who reclaimed large wetlands for building sites or industries that cast off pollutants into such areas—the Mills Corporation and the Meadowlands, for example. Noting that dry areas were not regulated, I concluded that adding a pond was not a problem. I also noted that regulations permitted the maintenance of any "watercourse" (ditch) to prevent flooding. It seemed logical that I could also clean the old drainage ditch that linked the new pond to my existing one to protect against overflow.

I explained this to the town official, adding that I'd done nothing that required a permit. He shrugged and left. I never got an answer, but I did get a summons. I had been cited for violations and was to appear in court.

As an idealist, I believe the courts are designed to seek justice. There should be reasons for issuing tickets and, of course, some relationship between the punishment and crime. So, on the appointed day, I awaited my hearing by eavesdropping on other cases, primarily traffic offenses, where I received a side lesson in the art of selective enforcement. What I witnessed during my wait was nothing less than a legal bazaar or the equivalent of *Let's Make a Deal,* where the only purpose was to make money for the town, not to punish offenders for their particular transgression. Plea-bargaining occurred at a frantic pace. Cases were reduced to completely unrelated crimes to lessen the impact on insurance rates or eliminate any "points" on the offender's driver's license. If anyone balked, the offense was morphed again until some agreement was reached. Fines averaged about $100 a pop, and each carried a nice $30 state tax.

What effect did the punishment have on the offender? Was the community's safety protected? The only real winner was the town revenue department as the cash register rang nonstop. As for the violators, they realized their only crime was getting caught. If it happened again, at least they'd know how to negotiate.

My turn at the desk finally came. Before I could sit down, the town prosecutor began explaining to me how to plead guilty. He had already assigned a $100 fine. I interrupted, asking "What if I don't think I committed any offense?" His eyes narrowed. I could hear the wheels clicking as he realized someone was disrupting his well-planned schedule. I explained that I was perfectly willing to take responsibility but simply wanted to know what I'd done wrong. With no information beyond the complaint form in his folder, he couldn't give me an answer.

Trying to be reasonable, I offered my explanation. The prosecutor couldn't have cared less. Finally he revealed that a guilty plea would not finalize this matter anyway. This was news to me. The wetlands board would require a consultant to walk the property and report back at a hearing. He suggested we postpone the whole thing until after the board acted. He sent me to the courtroom, saying he'd join me momentarily to schedule a new date.

I waited over two hours. When the courtroom had completely emptied, I was called up to the bench. The town prosecutor asked the judge to pass my case to a later date so I might discover the error of my ways, declare my guilt, and get this case off their docket. The court readily accepted this easy option, and the judge rescheduled my hearing. During that time, I listened to the judge sentence the traffic offenders with a joke or a smile. A lot of cops were hanging around collecting overtime in case someone actually wanted a trial. This intimidation was successful. Write a check, pass Go; refuse to deal, and the system will crush you. As you can imagine, it was a fire sale.

This exercise reminded me of the difficulty laymen have in confronting even minor problems in our court system. The magic show is amazing as attorneys and judges speak in code, ignore civilians, and subtly intimidate to compel a resolution. They know that most people will do or pay whatever it takes to get out of there as quickly as possible. That's what they count on.

Back to my environmental conundrum: The matter proceeded to the wetlands commission. I had to hire an engineer to do a survey of my property. He then had to testify before the board. My total cost for his services: several thousand dollars. Ultimately the board decided that the original complaint about my new pond was bogus. Not wanting me to escape so easily, the board declared victory by asserting that the two inches of soil I removed from the bottom of the drainage ditch was indeed a technical violation as my watercourse (ditch) may not have needed any maintenance.

I actually had some case law to challenge the ditch decision but decided discretion was the better part of valor. As I wasn't planning to move any time soon, I chose a pragmatic defeat over justice. Dutifully I called the court and arranged to mail in a guilty plea along with $250 (up from the original $100), thinking all this was now over.

Not so fast. Despite the board's findings that my new pond was no violation, it had its hooks in me now. The area around my lower pond included a patch of wetlands so the board decided to expand its authority. It was mission creep at its best. It wanted me to obtain a professionally prepared "wetlands planting scheme" for the area around the two ponds. Several weeks and expenditures later, I sent over the plan. There would be some blue irises, some yellow whatchamacallits, some green whatever. Surely the board would be happy now, but noooo. The plan was fine, but now the board wanted $2,500 to hold for two years as insurance that I would maintain the new plants. I still haven't sent over the deposit and expect another summons any day.

Wetlands are valuable wildlife habitats, coastal spawning grounds, and a natural means of flood control. My dry-land pond was none of these. In the meantime, judicial decisions and regulatory compromise allow tremendous damage to the areas originally targeted for protection. Rulings say you cannot "fill" but you can "drain." Others say you can "trade off" by creating comparable wetlands to replace those destroyed by development. (Just how do you "replicate" centuries of natural filtration?) Once companies agree to this deal, or pay a small fine, they rarely see inspectors again. Negotiation, not enforcement, is the rule and noncompliance the frequent result.

It's simply a game of power and money. This was never more evident than during the last presidential election. To the public, Al Gore was the ultimate environmentalist pitted against the big-oil team of Bush and Cheney. One assessment may be correct, but the other is suspect. Which is which? The Center for Public Integrity's 2000 report on campaign financing told an interesting tale. Most political junkies know about Al Gore's long-standing relationship with Occidental Petroleum. For the uninitiated, founder Armand Hammer used to say that he had Al's father "in my back pocket." When the senior Gore left the Senate in 1970, Hammer hired him for $500,000 a year. In addition to many campaign favors and contributions, the former vice president continues to draw $20,000 annually from a Tennessee lease deal with Occidental.

The company has not gone unrewarded. Since 1912 the U.S. Navy has owned two oil fields as emergency reserves, one in California, the other in Wyoming. Oil companies have been salivating over these properties for years. In October 1997, with Gore's recommendation, the Energy Department announced that 47,000 acres of California's Elk Hills would be sold to none other than Occidental. "It was the largest privatization of federal property in U.S. history, one that tripled Occidental's U.S. oil reserves overnight," according to a 2000 report by the Center for Public Integrity.

Interestingly, the Energy Department ignored its responsibility to assess the environmental consequences of the sale. Instead, it hired a private company, ICF Kaiser International, Inc., to do the deed. Coincidentally, of course, Gore's campaign chairman, Tony Coehlo, sat on that company's board. This sale also coincided with a Gore speech to the White House Conference on Climate Change. He talked about the " 'terrifying prospect' of global warming, instigated by the unchecked use of fossil fuels, such as oil." The press dutifully reported his official stance.

For twenty-five years, General Electric has stalled its cleanup of the upper Hudson River. GE has spent millions arguing against the dredging of PCBs (polychlorinated biphenyls) that deposited there despite three independent scientific panels that insist this action is necessary. Back in 1976, then GE chairman Reginald Jones told New York governor Hugh Carey to abandon the dispute or he'd move his 55,000 employees elsewhere. The problem was shelved. Each attempt to revive the issue was met with similar intimidation, and Democrats have been just as susceptible as Republicans.

Finally the current head of the EPA, Christie Whitman, has taken a stand. Estimated to take ten years at a cost of $500 million, this may be one of the largest industrial cleanups in U.S. history. I say "may" because the studies, polling, and planning are starting all over again with Whitman's pronouncement, the agency's (allegedly) final "record of decision." In a *New York Times* piece, Kirk Johnson recognizes that "Turning that legal order into a specific plan of action is an enormous task. Although dredging is not scheduled to begin until 2005, that leaves only three years, a crash course some environmental experts say—to build what will be an industrial complex for dredging, all under the scrutiny of a community still widely suspicious of whether it should be done at all, and doubtful it can be done right." In addition, this "record of decision" now triggers more negotiations with GE over its implementation. Ultimately a consent decree, subject first to public comment, must be approved by a court.

We're not done yet. Here's the clincher. The EPA will issue written performance standards on everything from "noise, to the impact on recreation and the spillage of PCB's back into the water, and the rules will then be reviewed by scientists and the public before they are issued." Opponents of the plan intend to use those rules to halt the project by suing over any violation. The EPA's regional Superfund director, Richard Caspe, acknowledged this tactic might work: "There are people who have said that if we truly develop objective performance standards, we will fail and the job will stop. We say 'make the standards fair and reasonable, then let the chips fall where they will.' "

Here is my prediction. As there is no such thing as "objective" criteria in the political arena, the "science" and standards developed for this project will fit whatever outcome the Bush administration desires.

If there is enough public pressure to push the project through, it will proceed. GE and its allies have at least another three-year window in which to alter that "final decision." I wager they will do just that.

There are many who firmly believe our country is headed for environmental devastation under Republican president George W. Bush. I'm not at all optimistic about his commitment to the environment, but we should recognize that he has plenty of company on the other side of the aisle. The recent battle over arsenic in our drinking water is a prime example. For at least seventeen years, experts have been arguing about acceptable arsenic levels with each side making a big show of what they term "sound science." Suddenly, in the very last days of his administration, Bill Clinton implemented a new regulation for the permissible levels in our drinking water by reducing the 50-parts-per-billion arsenic standard in effect since 1942 to 10 parts per billion. The environmentalists applauded, while industry, especially mining, began to scream.

Let's look at the process that led to Clinton's declaration. The Safe Drinking Water Act of 1974 mandated by amendment that the arsenic standard would be reviewed by 1996. After four "new" years of study (in addition to a decade's worth before), the National Research Council (NRC) said in 1999 that the EPA "should develop a stricter standard [for arsenic] as soon as possible." Note the sudden urgency. In addition, despite all the years of hard work, these NRC scientists, charged with advising the government on such issues, offered no appropriate levels. Instead, the EPA was to do its own calculations. (We're paying for this?) The agency threw out a range, anywhere between 3 and 20 parts per billion, for public discussion. ("Public" meaning the various interests groups on the Hill.) The EPA then "selected" 10 parts per billion. This was not the result of science but of political compromise, in the battle of cost versus benefits. It also happened to be the standard selected by the European Union (EU) and the World Health Organization (WHO). The environmentalists stayed with 3 parts, the water companies asserted 50, but the truth is reflected by Richard Wilson, a Harvard physics professor, who said: "I probably would have settled on 10 parts per billion, but I could argue why it could be anywhere in a massive range."

It turned out that EPA researchers had spent most of their time studying arsenic effects in other parts of the world rather than the problems here at home. Were there differences (due to diet, other pollutants, etc.)? What effect would they have? Does it matter? Who knows? Anyway, Bush told the EPA to prepare *another* study by August 2001. (This is always an effective way to stall.)

Opponents of the standards permitting more arsenic said that the new panel was weighted to support relaxed numbers. Of course it was. One former EPA official told the press that " 'sound science' often meant adjusting figures. . . . This should be the answer and you figure out how to get there." The process is not completely nefarious; some sort of compromise usually moves us a bit closer to "the truth." Nevertheless, the winning team proclaims that "evidence," "research," and "science" are on their side. They pretend, we all pretend, that there is something magical about this process and the numbers, rules, and standards that emerge. Don't kid yourself. It is the same game played by competing lawyers in the courtroom with their hired experts. Each side brings in its players. Usually the "best science" mirrors the current political climate.

Ultimately the Bush administration went with Clinton's 10 parts per billion. Why? Politics. The issue garnered a lot of press, and people actually paid attention because everyone cares about the water we drink. No matter the truth about those arsenic levels, if it sounds bad for us, we want action! The president decided it was better to take heat from industry in the press than upset the entire American population. The test, of course, will be enforcement of these new standards. If I were to go out to a major mine in a year or so and test the water, I'll bet the arsenic content won't have changed a bit.

Arsenic opponents are now fighting dirty: They're calling in the kids. In July 2001 *Time* magazine told us that the three-decade-old process of treating wood with CCA (a form of arsenic) might be dangerous to the children. The substance initially infused into lumber is apparently leaching out. "It's bad enough if decks, docks and maybe even a few picnic tables begin sweating arsenic, but the toxin was also widely used in children's playgrounds." By June 2002 the issue had made page one of the *New York Times*.

Here we go again. Doctors say they don't know what harmful levels are. Manufacturers reply that wherever they are, they haven't crossed that line. Charges are made that the $4 billion-a-year industry is stifling the truth. Its representatives respond that if the product is so dangerous, why aren't their workers sick? There have been no reports of a "measurable increase in disease among these groups."

Environmentalists then deliver the coup de grâce: "We've pretty much set up an arsenic delivery system for kids." You know which position made headlines. Please note that I don't want children soaking up harmful levels of arsenic. I am perfectly willing to see my tax dollars go to remedying any real problem for people or the environment. My point, however, is about the constant games we play with our rules and laws. We *don't know* the answers (and given the quality of science produced by the federal government, there is no guarantee we ever will), yet the EPA now responds to a thirty-year-old activity because consumer groups invoked "the children."

The EPA has known about this issue for years. Nine other countries have banned or restricted the use of CCA, but the EPA only requested that warning sheets accompany shipments of treated lumber to retailers. Nothing was targeted to the consumer. As the clamor grew, the agency issued warning labels for the wood products and some stickers and displays for the stores. Then the Consumer Product Safety Commission (CSPC) stepped up the action by gathering public comments and preparing petitions to call for a ban on the product. Playgrounds began shutting down. As Jeffrey Kluger said in his *Time* article, "While adults wrestle with the politics of the problem . . . it's kids who are paying the price." (*What* price? Kluger doesn't tell us, and I suggest he doesn't know.)

You can guess what will happen: The lawyers are going to legislate this for us. The use of CCA on consumer products is already the subject of a class action in four states. These defenders of our safety are "hoping to force [the industry] to pay for sealing existing structures built with CCA and cleaning up contaminated sites." I bet they're also eyeing the millions in attorneys' fees that would accompany a trial or settlement!

Then again, the EPA recently took serious action to protect us by revealing that many candlewicks still contain lead. Furthermore, the burning of *any* candles, especially scented ones, pollutes the air and can cause breathing problems. "Recent research found levels of soot and toxic chemicals from nine candles in a well-ventilated room were higher than would be considered safe outdoors," according to the *Daily Record*. Consider yourselves warned.

Our Safety Commission is also on constant vigil. Established in 1973, it was intended to "prevent *unreasonable* injury to consumers" from commonly used products. By August 1996 the *CPSC Monitor* found that over 50 percent of all recalls were on products that had caused no known injury. Today this agency acts as if its mandate is to prevent the possibility of *any* injury by creating a completely risk-free environment for us all.

Before its recent bankruptcy, Kmart was in the process of recalling 24,000 Martha Stewart teakettles because of fourteen reports of "boiling water improperly expelled from the spout" that could present a hazard. Three cases of minor burns were included in those incidents. The last time I poured boiling water from an open pan, it did the same thing. My teakettle produces hot steam that will burn me if I get in the way during pouring. Should I turn these items in?

In this effort to micromanage and safeguard our lives, ludicrous results are inevitable. We all know the history of airbags. After decades of fighting, they were installed only to produce countless lawsuits from the short, fat, small, and otherwise inappropriate body types for this exploding device. Now that we have this safety equipment, we must be able to disengage it.

Furthermore, no decent parents allow their children to ride in the front seat, airbag or not. We must have the appropriate child restraint seat in the back with the kids properly strapped in. You may get a ticket otherwise. In fact, there will soon be a "universal" adapter to make all child restraints fit any car, so there will be no excuse. Just in case these restraints and the 1,400 other auto-safety regulations aren't sufficient, there is a push under way to install mandatory speed controls on our cars. Forget the speedometer; you'll need it only for in-town driving.

I am amazed at the new rules governing baby bath seats. Apparently these dangerous instruments have "been linked" to the deaths of at least seventy-eight infants after babies either got out or tipped seats over and drowned in the tub. The CPSC chairwoman has responded, "Within a short period of time we will see some solutions or regulations that will ban baby bath seats or correct problems." But hold on. The problem in every case was the bather leaving the child unattended. There is nothing wrong with these devices. No matter. Counsel for the Consumer Federation of America said, "We believe this is a very significant acknowledgement of the hazardous nature of this product." I know this may sound cruel, heartless, and politically incorrect, but the cause of death in these cases was the negligence of the *attendant,* not the baby bath seat. Today, however, we are all victims, never the perpetrators of our own tragedies. Let the recall begin!

Let's take a close look at the United States Department of Agriculture. In charge of our meat and poultry safety, it received such high marks for its standards that a report by the Occupational Safety and Health Administration (OSHA) read, "If all meat-inspecting regulations were enforced to the letter, no meat-processor in America would be open for business." In July 2001 Reuters reported on a federal investigation into forty-four small meatpacking plants in New York City that found violations in forty-one of the facilities. Thirteen were in such flagrant violation that they required a follow-up investigation. So what did USDA inspectors do? Only four plants were closed even temporarily, and three of these were reopened almost immediately. However, something was accomplished. Several federal inspectors were investigated for failing to show up for work or drinking on the job. The USDA audaciously asserted, "We have no indication these conditions were existent to the extent they were in New York anywhere else in the country." Huh?

Let's not diagram that sentence. Instead, we'll examine the noted violations. Most of them were for the failure to follow the Hazard Analysis Critical Control Point system (HACCP). (Without government acronyms, this book would be much longer.) Translated, this is a "science-based" (ah!) program designed to identify the steps in food production where contamination is most likely to occur and then establish controls that prevent or reduce contamination. O.K., this sounds good. In practice, it is something else entirely.

Once again process trumps real safety. Every article I read about this HACCP system primarily discusses the need to verify compliance with this plan. Manufacturing methods that have been universally recognized as safe and appropriate were considered "in violation" if they didn't strictly follow government guidelines. "USDA recognizes the usefulness of quality control programs and good manufacturing practices. However, USDA maintains that to ensure the effective oversight of HACCP systems it must be able to verify plants' compliance with HACCP regulations, and inspectors cannot verify non-HACCP plans," says a report from the General Accounting Office (GAO). Got that?

Translated, the focus of these inspections is not plant safety but only whether the government system is being complied with. This is essentially a paperwork function. If the records are in order, then compliance is assumed. The GAO states this clearly: "The Department's inspector training emphasizes compliance rather than the development and implementation of HACCP plans." It is up to the industry to learn what the policies mean and then implement them. The USDA just comes in to check the file cabinet.

That same report indicated that federal inspectors don't even do that very well. Inspectors were tested in three primary areas of enforcement. The GAO found that, "In summary, the responses to these three questions indicate considerable confusion about these aspects of an inspector's HACCP duties. For example, only 13% of the inspectors selected the responses that the Center provided as the correct answers to all three questions, and one-third provided the correct responses to only one of the three questions." So, about two-thirds of these employees failed the test. This sounds like our secondary schools!

Remember that the issue is not food safety. We all agree on the concept. The question is: What is the goal of any particular regulation? Will application of the rules accomplish this? Can those rules be effectively enforced? My conclusion is this: In response to the estimated 76 million illnesses, 325,000 hospitalizations, and 5,000 deaths in the United States each year from food contamination, we send out a handful of basically incompetent inspectors to check paperwork in plant offices. If the plant is doing things right but isn't "in compliance with HACCP plans," it is cited. If it is doing things wrong but has the correct paperwork, two gold stars.

The 2000 GAO report gave us a good look at the FDA today. It concluded: "The FDA's efforts and federal laws provide limited assurances of the safety of functional foods and dietary supplements, . . . provide limited assistance to consumers in making informed choices and do little to protect them against inaccurate and misleading claims." Yet I still have a fondness for this agency. While the purity of our food is questionable, the labeling rules are in tiptop shape. In this area, the FDA really shines. With our superficial concern about health and fitness, calorie content is carefully noted on almost every product. But you'd better double check how many servings there are in a package. That calorie count can be deceptive. The food pyramid appears on many containers to guide our food choices, but after years of telling us one thing, it has now been completely changed.

In May 2000 the National Nutrition Summit, attended by about 1,800 researchers, policy makers, educators, and public health professionals, was held in Washington, D.C. Experts gathered to issue proclamations like "Fast food and junk food are not good for you" and "Eating too much will make you gain weight." One major event was the release of the government's new Dietary Guideline for Americans. The two biggest messages to consumers, according to one dietician, were "be physically active and manage your portion sizes." A participating New York University professor criticized the results by saying "Do the dietary guidelines help people lose weight? I would say flat-out no because they don't tell people what not to eat."

Certainly the flood of rules and regulations is not producing results. Over the past several decades, the number of gyms, diet materials, food products, and regulations to improve our fitness has skyrocketed, yet so have out waistlines. Obesity is now a health crisis in this country, affecting people earlier and more severely than ever. Of the ten leading causes of death in the United States, four are associated with bad diets. Coronary heart disease, cancer, and stroke are the top three. Add in diabetes and you account for over half of the annual deaths in the country. These alarming numbers are like a red flag to the bullish regulators. While improved diets would certainly help the nation, the FDA and USDA see these statistics as justification for more labeling rules. With impressive cost benefit calculations, they plot the next wave of social engineering for our eating habits.

One of President Clinton's regulations issued days before he left office required nutrition labels on raw meat and poultry products. The fat and nutrient content of the products is to be placed on packages or posted in the meat case. While many stores and processors provide these labels voluntarily, Clinton decided they should be mandatory, right down to the water content of raw chicken.

Here is an example of the information provided: "A cooked 3-ounce patty of 80% lean ground beef has 6 grams of saturated fat, 30% of the daily limit for an average person. By comparison, a 93% lean patty has half as much fat. A 4-ounce serving of chicken with skin has 3 grams of saturated fat. Without the skin, it has 1 gram." With a straight face, then secretary of agriculture Dan Glickman said that such "labeling will allow consumers to easily and accurately obtain helpful nutrition information such as fat, calorie and cholesterol content." No one is alleging this product is unsafe. No one says the current labeling is misleading. Why then should the government mandate further information? Show me where such elaborate knowledge has helped our choices or our girth?

All of this manipulation is for naught. Americans are gaining weight by the hour, and there is no mystery as to why. We have become a nation of fast food–consuming couch potatoes who simply watch sports rather than play and read diet books rather than eat right. Our portions are larger than ever as we eat, smoke, and drink our way into early graves.

Nothing short of outlawing our fatty diets or sedentary lifestyles will work. Since Congress could never go this far, we know who will: the lawyers! Remember those class actions? Fatty foods, alcohol, and other noxious substances are already on their list. But they may have gone too far. Attorney Roger Carrick wants warning labels on chocolate! He has pushed the California attorney general to sue for this remedy. He professes concern about the carcinogens lead and cadmium present in minute quantities in the finished product. "I don't believe there is anyone on the planet that doesn't believe these are serious issues. You've got a very reasonable debate about the harm coming from chocolate," Carrick tells us.

Our various consumer safety agencies have enough on their plates. They are running very fast but getting nowhere. Sometimes they run into one another. If a company meets an FDA standard for some health claim, it must still seek review from USDA before asserting it to the public. These warring agencies can create amazing havoc. While the FDA regulates latex gloves as a "medical device" and approves their use by healthcare professionals, OSHA is hell-bent on outlawing them. In September 1997 the FDA reported that nearly 15 billion powdered natural rubber latex medical gloves were in use. "Less than one allergic reaction of any kind is reported to the FDA for every 49 million gloves used. The vast majority of the reported reactions are not serious or life-threatening and are treatable with sensible clinical intervention." Data collected by the Centers for Disease Control also shows no occupational link to latex allergy. Yet OSHA keeps trying to label this product a "hazard" because a small, and I mean *small,* percentage of the population is allergic.

When David Kessler headed the FDA under President Clinton, he unintentionally summed up his agency's biggest concern: "If members of our society were empowered to make their own decisions about the entire range of products for which the FDA has responsibility, then the whole rationale for the agency would cease to exist." That reminds me of Clinton's response to a push for tax cuts in 1999.

When told he should give money back to the people, he replied, "We can spend it better than they can." So the government regulates our food, our teapots, and our bath seats. But this caretaking doesn't hold a candle to the intrusion by the two remaining agencies we should examine.

The real regulatory monster for most employers is OSHA. Created in 1970, this enforcement agency now attempts to regulate every aspect of health and safety in the workplace. The goal is not only daunting but also ludicrous. Despite thirty years of (over)diligent rule making, the agency itself estimates that 80 percent of American workplaces are not in compliance with the law.

Without question, the agency has contributed to the decline in certain work-related fatalities since its inception. For example, brown lung disease caused by inhalation of cotton dust has been virtually eliminated in the textile industry. Here was a clearly identifiable problem in a targeted industry with a feasible solution. Today, however, OSHA regulates everything from ladder length to the size of warning bells on boats.

With only a few thousand inspectors for millions of companies, most problems go unnoticed. The 1999 report *Reinventing Government: The Safety Challenge* revealed that "2,200 employees and a $350 million dollar budget have the daunting duty of protecting 100 million people at more than 6.5 million work sites. If required to inspect every work site, agency officials say, staff could only do so about once every 80 years."

Examinations usually are triggered by serious injuries or death. Fines may be issued, but they are regularly reduced on appeal. Given this imbalance, it would seem that a cooperative, incentive-based relationship between business and government would be most effective. As with citizens, most law-abiding behavior by companies is voluntary, arising from the desire to cooperate and keep things running smoothly, not because of fear of punishment. The most important ingredient for compliance is a reasoned approach to problems and a fair, evenhanded manner of dealing with violations. Unfortunately, this is not OSHA's track record.

Business owners complain that one inspector might tour a company finding no violations while another might write up a dozen. The rules, encompassing thousands of pages, are virtually unknowable. Disgruntled workers can instigate an inspection for purposes of harassment, and voluntary testing and disclosure often are punished rather than praised.

Despite the countless rules, nine of OSHA's most frequent violations are administrative in nature, and about half of all citations are for paperwork problems. A former chairman of the OSHA Review Commission, Edwin G. Foulke, handled citation appeals and has written a check list for businesses facing inspection. Of six recommendations, five deal with updating paperwork and designating personnel as compliance officials or safety teams. Only one bullet point suggests that owners should "conduct a survey of your work site to find and correct possible safety violations."

It makes sense that a worker should have access to proper instructions about the use of equipment on the job. However, contractor Eamonn McGready, with twenty-seven volumes of safety rules and procedures in his construction office, thought it reasonable that the instructions for welding respirator masks be kept with those masks in his company trailer. Unfortunately, the inspector disagreed. The regulations said the instructions should be "available" to the workers, and the seventy-five feet between the welders and the trailer did not meet that criterion. Despite the fact the welders knew how to use the masks, the instructions were close by, and the condition was immediately corrected, McGready was fined $1,000. A small sign on his company door appeared. "Warning: If you think OSHA is a small town in Wisconsin, you're in trouble."

Over 6,000 workers die from work-related injuries every year, more than 6 million are injured, and about 500,000 experience job-related illnesses. What is the correlation between OSHA's work and these numbers? Has there been any improvement over the years because of its existence? Some argue yes, but until recently, it has been anyone's guess.

The administration's record keeping over its first two decades was abysmal. Job surveys shed little light on the nature of reported injuries or illnesses, how they happened, and what job was involved. There was no comprehensive count of workers dying on the job or how such deaths occurred. In 1987 the National Academy of Sciences "suggested" that OSHA revise its survey, implying the data being collected was not adequate as a basis for designing safety and health programs to prevent serious injuries on the job.

Not until this methodology was revised in 1993 did the numbers become meaningful. Finally information was gathered on serious non-fatal incidents that included: the occupation, age, and gender; the nature of the disabling conditions; how they occurred; and the time away from work. Until then such portentous OSHA pronouncements like "roofing work entailed the greatest risk of falls to a lower level" were the norm. I can certainly see why billions of dollars were spent to come to that conclusion.

Interestingly, highway incidents have been the number-one cause of workplace deaths for some time. Truck drivers topped the accident list with 15 percent of all fatalities, although truckers account for less than 2 percent of the nation's workforce. About 19 percent of these drivers are self-employed so we must ask just how OSHA regulations can affect this sector. Falls were the second most frequent cause followed by workplace homicides. I wonder how the regulation about "no robberies on the job site" reads.

OSHA may not be good at information gathering, but it sure can write up violations. In 1995 President Clinton said, "If the government rewards inspectors for writing citations and levying fines more than [for] insuring safety, there's a chance you could get more citations, more fines, more hassle and no more safety." Chance? Make that a sure thing. Note this "corollary" between enforcement and safety. Between 1994 and 1996 the number of OSHA citations dropped by 62 percent, yet in those two years, workplace injuries and illnesses dropped to the lowest rate in nearly a decade.

Congress uses the number of inspections and volume of fines to measure the agency's performance. The agency has no incentive to help businesses evaluate their safety and health programs or improve performance in these areas. In the words of one executive, the agency is simply a "traffic cop looking for rule violations." Labor lawyer Arthur G. Sapper summed it up nicely when he said, "OSHA is not your friend. It's not there to help you. It's there to boss you around."

In January 2000 OSHA crossed the line in dramatic fashion. The agency proposed to regulate home safety for the 20 million telecommuters who worked at least part time from their houses. Remember Riley the hazardous collie? The political truth behind this move was pressure by the unions to halt the work-from-home trend. This rule seemed to be a good way to do it.

Although thwarted in this effort, OSHA wasn't finished. In the final days of the Clinton administration, the agency came out with another gem. It issued a 1,600-page final rule requiring employers to enact programs to protect workers from repetitive-motion injuries. This rule emerged despite the voluntary measures that had reduced such injuries by about 22 percent over the past five years.

The sides lined up in predictable fashion. Organized labor supported the new workstations, redesigned facilities, and tool changes to prevent injury. Business interests screamed their disapproval, challenging the science and overall costs. Walter B. McCormick, Jr., of the American Trucking Association noted that the regulations would cover even excessive road vibrations or prolonged sitting. While OSHA estimated a business cost of $4.5 billion and savings of $9 billion from reduced medical expenses and workers' compensation, some business groups argued that initial compliance could cost over $120 billion.

Both were right *and* wrong. Certain injuries are avoidable with new equipment and training, but the expensive regulations will cost a fortune. What happens if an employee develops a strain from play on the weekend but aggravates it at work? How many repetitive motions are considered to produce damage? How do doctors confirm back pain, tendonitis, or carpal tunnel syndrome? Medicine is still quite vague in these areas, but companies were supposed to comply with the rules. Companies had to encourage early reporting and provide substantial compensation for such injuries. Not surprisingly, they expected associated costs to rise.

I was overcome by scientific enlightenment as I perused some of the congressional testimony dealing with the subject of ergonomics. First, a litany of costly studies was introduced, revealing that (Shock! Surprise!), "heavy loading and high occupational physical demands predicted future back pain." The National Academy of Sciences weighed in on this to add a bit of legitimacy. The majority of its "75 scientists and other workshop participants agreed that 'There is a higher incidence of . . . injury . . . and disability among individuals who are employed in occupations where there is a high level of exposure to physical loading than for those employed in occupations with lower levels of exposure.' " I wonder how much the academy was paid to come to such conclusions. I am not making fun of hardworking Americans with back problems. I have three herniated discs myself. Just remember while you work toward April 15 that your tax dollars are paying for our regulatory personnel to deliver such numbingly obvious conclusions.

Speaking of tax dollars, we should finally address our country's most hated agency, the Internal Revenue Service. After several attempts in earlier years, Congress finally secured a federal income tax in 1913 through the Sixteenth Amendment to the Constitution. The first income tax affected only the richest 5 percent of households. The entire code was twenty pages long. It wasn't until about 1978 that Congress really began manipulating the tax laws to favor the big-money interests. For those who believe the Democrats are looking out for the little guy, note that this tactic was honed during a time when they held both the White House and Congress.

The 1997 Taxpayer Relief Act, an ironic title, added 800 amendments, 290 new sections, and 36 retroactive provisions to the Tax Code, which is now twice the length of *War and Peace*. The accompanying regulations are about four times as long. Altogether, we now have over 36,000 pages of federal tax laws. What good has this done? It has provided cover! The countless "reforms" have pushed the tax burden onto lower- and middle-income filers while creating myriad tax breaks, subsidies, and grants for the elite. The loopholes are invitations to unprecedented cheating and tax avoidance for the well informed. The hypocritical rhetoric churned my stomach. The 1997 act was pitched as "middle-class" relief and sprinkled with child and education credits, but its essence was the capital gains cut and corporate tax breaks handed to the rich. The complexity of the Tax Code was increased, to the joy of accountants and lawyers, providing even more ways around both payment and enforcement.

The choice to prosecute and punish tax cheaters is a prerogative of authority, and the big guys usually skate. If action *is* taken, a quiet settlement is the most likely outcome. On the other hand, if you want to get someone, what better tool than the tax laws? Noncompliance always can be discovered in this swamp of regulation. There's even a violation classified as "involuntary noncompliance." What a great catchall: "I did it but I hadn't a clue."

Most of us could fit in that category as IRS statistics prove. In 1999 the agency provided almost 9.8 million incorrect answers to taxpayers who called in to the agency hot line, according to Texas congressman Dick Armey. By 2001 the Associated Press was reporting that one-quarter of the 70 million taxpayer calls were answered incorrectly. That's over 17 million calls. One year H&R Block gave the same tax packet to forty-four experts who responded with forty-four different returns. As one expert stated, "If noncompliance can be found under any law, what protections do we think all this legal detail is providing?" It is making the system more arbitrary, more corrupt, and ultimately more dangerous to the law-abiding citizen who is most vulnerable to pursuit.

In 2000, 44 percent of the audited federal returns were those filed by poor Americans seeking earned income tax credits. There are certainly cheaters in this bunch, but the amount of unpaid taxes from this entire category hardly holds a candle to the amounts owed by the tiny group at the top that escapes enforcement. Take the case of Alec Wildenstein. He is the subject of an entire chapter in the eye-opening book, *The Great American Tax Dodge* by Donald L. Bartlett and James B. Steele. Despite living in Manhattan for nineteen years, birthing and raising his children there and doing business as an American corporation, Wildenstein & Company, Inc., he had never even filed a tax return. As the authors report, "No one in Washington or New York noticed. Or cared. Under ordinary circumstances, even the complex tax returns of the very wealthy that are filed go unchecked."

Unfortunately, his wife spilled the beans during their ugly divorce. Court papers revealed that the couple's personal spending exceeded $25 million in 1997 and 1996 alone. Alec protested he owed no taxes. He said he was a Swiss citizen and didn't even have a green card to work in the United States. His only job, according to documents, was as an "unpaid personal assistant" to his father, netting a mere $175,000 a year.

The authors estimate that every law-abiding taxpayer is probably paying, on average, about $3,000 in annual taxes to cover the amount the big guys are evading. They conclude: "Over the last three decades, America's elected officials have turned a reasonably fair tax code into one crafted for the benefit of those who give the largest campaign contributions, enjoy the greatest access, hire the most influential lobbyists, or otherwise exercise power beyond that enjoyed by average citizens. Congress and the White House have auctioned off the tax code to the highest bidders at the expense of ordinary individuals and families." Amen.

Without question, tax laws are the largest source of political corruption in Washington. Those 150,000 pages of regulations that interpret the code are, to a great extent, payoffs. Loopholes, exceptions, and deductions buy votes and reward contributors. Of the 67,000 lobbyists working inside the Beltway, a majority labors for tax breaks for their clients. They don't want equity, they want favors, and they're getting them.

Bartlett and Steele recite a litany of such "favors" over the years. Senators lauded the fairness of the Tax Reform Act of 1986, as they quietly paid off big contributors right and left. The usually well regarded Senator Daniel Patrick Moynihan called the legislation "a profound statement concerning the requirements of citizenship and the ethical basis of the American republic." He then plugged in "at least a half dozen custom-tailored tax breaks including the following: 'In the case of a taxpayer which was incorporated on February 17, 1983, and the five largest stockholders of which are doctors of medicine, any royalties of such taxpayer from products resulting from medical research shall be treated in the same manner as royalties from computer software are treated.' " Bartlett and Steele explained, "That cut the tax bills of five doctors who were the principal owners of a Rochester, New York, company that sold vaccines to pharmaceutical companies."

This behavior is now commonplace in every tax bill passed on Capitol Hill. Better yet, Congress has figured out if you write in these breaks with an automatic expiration date, say every one or two years, contributors have to keep paying to get those provisions renewed. The amount of money a particular congressman or senator rakes in is usually commensurate with his or her ranking and committee appointments. Members of the House Ways and Means Committee and Senate Finance Committee do particularly well. It is a real racket. As for the nation's lawyers and accountants, they make a financial killing maneuvering around each new piece of tax legislation. Complexity works right into their hands.

Despite the increase in most corporate annual profits, the amount paid by companies continues to diminish, while the little guy carries more of the burden. In 1999 corporations paid 2 percent less in federal taxes than they did the year before, which was less than they paid in 1997. Remember Enron? Not only did that company receive $250 million in new tax breaks in the 2001 GOP tax bill, it had already avoided paying *any* federal taxes in the last four out of five years.

It's also the little guy who gets whacked for failing to pay. As Senator Charles Grassley noted, "One of the [IRS] agents said, 'we were told to go after the little guy. They do not have the resources to fight it.' " Yet the big guys and corporations are the ones who owe the real dough. As with any other government agency or department today, it's a numbers game with the IRS. Don't go for the big tough cases; instead, audit a large number of tax returns to improve agency statistics.

Bartlett and Steele interviewed a career examiner, Maureen O'Dwyer, who told them of pressure to close cases within a set time frame to meet agency goals, regardless of the outcome. These agents are judged on meaningless numbers, not legitimate outcomes. In her congressional testimony on tax enforcement, O'Dwyer described the arbitrary and corrupt behavior of IRS examiners and managers. One citizen without representation got hit with every penalty imaginable, while an influential defendant who appeared only through counsel was let off the hook. She made it clear that this "favor" was done because the auditor wanted "a tax appointment outside the service. By this decision he bonded with two men he saw as wealthy and powerful and in a position to recommend him for some future job opening. . . . Other even more senior level executives do the same. . . . They network and make friends in preparation for careers outside the service. Their sense of morality has been eclipsed by their personal ambition." (We'll talk about this "revolving door" in a minute.) Even worse for O'Dwyer was the reaction of our representatives. They apparently attempted to cut her off, dismissing her charges entirely.

Joe Citizen slaves well into May each year simply to pay his tax bill while corporations buy their way clear. The government, in the meantime, complains endlessly about the need for more money. I think I've figured out why: It keeps losing it. Have you heard the one about the federal agency that "misplaced" so much money it cannot be audited? It sounds like a bad joke, but there are eleven such agencies, to be exact. In 1999, of the twenty-four big federal agencies, only thirteen could provide reliable enough financial records to undergo an annual audit.

The Pentagon hasn't submitted a report capable of being audited since at least 1992. In his GAO investigation, Senator Fred Thompson noted that the monies this agency couldn't account for in 1999, $2.3 trillion, exceeded the entire federal budget that year. Multiply this by fifty-four agencies and just imagine what financial atrocities have been concealed in the past.

On July 19, 2001, Defense Secretary Donald Rumsfeld sent senior Pentagon officials an internal memo calling for an overhaul of the agency's financial operations (including the award of a $100 million contract to an outside firm to evaluate the steps being taken to make sense of defense finances). The undersecretary of defense and the Pentagon's chief financial officer, Dov Zakheim, said, "If this were a private company, we would have been bankrupt years ago." Things haven't improved much. Early in 2002 the Pentagon was reporting about $700 billion in undocumented accounting entries, down from $1.3 trillion at the beginning of 2001. Robert Borosage made this analogy in a *Washington Post* op-ed piece: "The Pentagon remains the largest source of waste, fraud and abuse in the federal government. Its bookkeeping makes Enron look transparent."

That is the state of affairs throughout our federal government. No one knows how much is being spent on what. Fraud and mismanagement are rampant. Rules are formulated to fit lobbyists' agendas. Even the cost-benefit approach that was supposed to inject some reason into the regulatory arena ends up as nonsense. The Office of Management and Budget (OMB) spends millions calculating meaningless numbers that ultimately will conform to the desires of the dominant political powers.

According to William Greider in his heartbreaking work *Who Will Tell the People:* "The practical result is a lawless government—a reality no one in power wishes to face squarely since all are implicated. . . . The classical sense of law is lost in sliding scales of targets and goals, acceptable tolerances and negotiated exceptions, discretionary enforcement and discretionary compliance." Sadly, this ambiguous, nebulous environment is not an accident but intentional. Elected officials duck their responsibilities and avoid the tough issues by delegating to agencies. Those agencies grind slowly, succumbing to lobbyists, litigation, and grandstanding politicians. If they act "improperly," the courts get involved or Congress holds hearings . . . and so it goes. High-powered attorney Lloyd Cutler summed it up for Greider when he said, "The professional lobbyists and lawyers prefer to live in this world where there are so many buttons to push, so many other places to go if you lose your fight." Greider concluded, "If the power to decide things is located everywhere then it really exists nowhere."

But nature abhors a vacuum. What fills that void is a bit of corporate anarchy. With the political system rendered impotent, the targets of those rules can go about their business virtually uninterrupted.

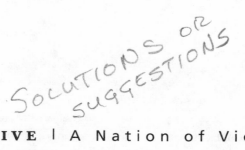
SOLUTIONS OR SUGGESTIONS

FIVE | A Nation of Victims

Lady Justice might throw in her sword if she examined some of the attitudes about responsibility that are evidenced by our laws today. Certainly the civil docket demonstrates that you can find someone to blame for just about everything, from an unexpected gopher hole to a bad golf shot. Our regulatory laws protect us against boiling teapots and smoking candles. But, judging from the defenses and verdicts in cases around the country, the criminal courts are trying hard to catch up.

"Yeah, I did it, but it's not my fault." How many times have we heard that excuse in recent years? Law, particularly criminal law, is supposed to demand accountability for transgressions deemed violations of our social contract. The legislature then passes rules reflecting these agreed-upon values. Do not steal, abuse, or kill, for example. A range of penalties is assigned for violations, and it is up to the judge or jury to decide where along a punishment continuum the conduct falls. But first society must demand that the actor be held responsible. Someone who is judged legally insane should go to a psychiatric hospital. Someone who commits a crime in the throes of passion should receive consideration at sentencing. These variables can mitigate punishment, but they are not reasons to abdicate responsibility.

Yet today we often ignore old-fashioned norms as the measure of behavior. Instead we examine conduct through the eyes of the perpetrator, asking whether the actions were reasonable given his or her background, upbringing, attitudes, and prejudices. Instead of varying the punishment, we vary the definition of or even eliminate the crime.

The media has helped foster this mood with plenty of help from camera-hungry attorneys eager to make their reputation on some high-profile tragedy. From Dan White's 1979 so-called Twinkie defense (depression aggravated by too much junk food) in his trial for the murders of San Francisco mayor George Moscone and Harvey Milk, to the Menendez brothers' excuse asserted by defense attorney Leslie Abramson that the parents "set in motion a series of events that eventually killed them," the premise that we are no longer responsible for individual conduct has gained strength in our courts. Following the 1992 riots in south-central Los Angeles, Damien Williams was tried for the aggravated assault on truck driver Reginald Denney. Williams was caught on video bashing Denney's skull with a concrete block, complete with a victory dance. During trial, the defendant was portrayed as a member of an "aggrieved class" of African American males. Defense counsel argued that Williams was entitled to engage in a "political" act, albeit one that almost killed an innocent passerby. The jury bought it, finding Williams guilty of only one misdemeanor.

Then there was the outrageous acquittal of O. J. Simpson. Stripped of its rhetoric, his defense was simply that the white cops of L.A. are inherently corrupt and it is time to punish them. African Americans have been victims long enough. After all, former detective Mark Fuhrman lied about having used the "n" word several years before Nicole Brown Simpson's murder. That must prove something. The fact that O. J. Simpson was married to a white woman, living in a wealthy white neighborhood, and protected regularly by starstruck cops who covered up his prior spousal abuse went right over the jurors' heads.

During my stint at ABC's *20/20,* I covered the story of a young black woman who had utilized posttraumatic stress disorder (PTSD) as a defense against murder charges. Her attempted robbery of a girl to obtain her leather coat became the flashpoint for homicide. There was no question the defendant's short life had been gut-wrenchingly traumatic. In her fifteen years, she had suffered child abuse and rape and was surrounded by family violence. She probably had seen as much torture and degradation as many battle veterans (who have on rare occasion been successful with the PTSD defense), but does this justify the execution of another child who refused to relinquish her coat? Even though the trial judge rejected the proposed defense and imposed a life sentence, the girl's attorney was flooded with calls inquiring about this new twist on the wartime syndrome.

Some defenses seem downright laughable but are delivered by counsel with a very straight face. A few years ago a murder case on Shelter Island in New York brought this response from the defense attorney. Learning that Lyme disease (which is caused by a bite from an infected deer tick) may result in depression and psychosis, the sharp litigator told the press that "apparently, it may be a viable defense, but it remains to be seen if my client was afflicted with the problem, and whether it played into the scenario as it unfolded." He had no idea if his client had the disease, but it offered a great excuse in a community with a bad tick problem. The attorney went on. "The major defense is that my client did not intend to kill the deceased"—despite the fact he walked into the man's house and opened up on him with a twelve-gauge shotgun. "The key question is what was my client's state of mind and what if anything affected his thinking." Maybe he was just having a bad day.

Even the terror attacks on the World Trade Center provided fodder for defendants and their attorneys. In a New York murder case that occurred shortly after the attacks, the accused offered what was termed the "9/11 defense." He was charged with killing a Middle Eastern man in a fit of rage after the victim allegedly applauded the tragedy. When I interviewed his counsel and asked about the exact provocation, he said the deceased had said something to the effect that "he could understand the motivation for the actions and that the U.S. carried some responsibility for the obvious hatred expressed by the hijackers." What had to be pried out of the lawyer's mouth was the fact that these two men were longtime business partners who were having some serious disagreements. Remember—timing is everything!

Dan White was convicted not of murder but the lesser included charge of manslaughter and received five and a half years in prison with time off for good behavior. The first Menendez trial resulted in a hung jury, O. J. was acquitted in the criminal case, and Williams, despite the horrific video of his brutal attack, received a misdemeanor slap from the jury. In every one of these cases, the perpetrators were portrayed as victims. Their suffering, regardless of the origins or remoteness from the act in question, excused their behavior. I'm sorry, but *people* kill people, not a "political event," an abusive childhood, or too much sugar in the bloodstream. All of these cases seem to assert that there was no crime at all, no breach of ethics, no violation of social responsibility. Increasingly, we are accepting the notion that everyone is entitled to—no, endowed with—inalienable rights to a great childhood, a permanent job, loving parents and spouses, and a world free from discrimination or pain. To waive responsibility because of political pressure, the women's movement, or minority discrimination is wrong. Empathy is one thing, but excusing criminal, even murderous conduct is quite another.

In his speech "Defining Deviance Down," Patrick Moynihan suggested that Americans are either so unwilling or so unable to deal with violent, destructive antisocial behavior that instead we accept it as normal. We "define deviance down" to avoid the expense and pain of curing, punishing, or expunging it. We have created the Blame Game.

One of the gravest consequences of this trend is the effect on our children. Kids must learn responsibility for the choices they make at an early age. We blather about the importance of this value yet we behave otherwise. While demanding responsibility from our children, we reward those who transgress. We are reaping what we've sown.

Examine the national debate following each school shooting. Commentators focus on where the teachers went wrong or why the defendants fell victim to social pressures. The gun lobby, parents, teachers, and, of course, television, films, and video games may have varying degrees of culpability in a given case. Satanic cults are thrown in regularly for good measure. What usually is missing is the concept of personal responsibility that must reside with the shooter.

After the Jonesboro shooting in March 1998, where two boys killed five and injured eleven, Arkansas governor Mike Huckabee had this to say: "It makes me angry not so much at individual children that have done it as much as angry at a world in which such a thing can happen." He saw these children as the norm in modern society. To Huckabee they were not the transgressors but the victims.

The first anniversary of the Columbine shooting prompted much soul searching on this question. Uniquely, *Time* magazine tried to assemble facts rather than engage in more finger-pointing. Interestingly, profiles of a string of young killers did not lead to external blame for their behavior. These "children" did share certain characteristics. Many were cruel to animals as very young kids. They lit fires. They displayed obvious emotional disturbances. They had an early fascination with guns and easy access to weapons. Sadly, they all telegraphed their intentions to others, including their parents, classmates, and teachers, but they were universally ignored. Note, however, what they did *not* share: an obsession with violent video games, music, or any of the other external factors we keep highlighting in these discussions. Each case had its own peculiarities, but the common characteristics were internal psychological displacement from an early age, not external stimuli.

We keep forgetting that millions of people are exposed daily to the same factors we blame for a minuscule number of horrific events. Instead, we write more laws based on these episodes. Legislators now regularly name laws for victims, like Megan's Law or Stephanie's Law—the better to make the evening news. The original crimes are horrific, but they often encourage an emotional response and knee-jerk support rather than an appropriate prescription for some broader problem.

Zero tolerance in the schools, liability lawsuits against teachers and cops, and twelve-year-olds sentenced to life in adult prisons are but a few of the "remedies" enacted following high-profile events. It is easier and more psychologically appeasing to abdicate responsibility than to place it squarely on the actors involved and at times the families and friends who ignored obvious warning signs.

Such excuses have invaded the highest levels of society. Take President Clinton. He lied under oath and obstructed justice. While the Senate gave him a pass on all charges, federal judge Susan Webber Wright stepped up to the plate and called a foul by finding him in contempt. For his part, Clinton suffered the indignity of a House impeachment while the rest of us endured a national nightmare. The Senate decided against the ultimate punishment, but it did so in a cowardly way. Many members refused to label the president's conduct for what it was, instead blaming the circumstances (It was about sex) or the investigators (It was a right-wing conspiracy) or human nature (Everybody does it). We can differ on the proper punishment, but we should not equivocate on the crime. Yet this political behavior just mirrored mainstream attitudes on personal responsibility.

The consequences for society are tremendous. A democracy is based on the (legitimate) rule of law, not the whim of man. If we excuse compliance because of our innumerable idiosyncrasies, then no rules apply. We have permitted an individual standard for each of us rather than a reasonable standard for all. It is Heisenberg's uncertainty principle and the Hobbesian war of all against all rolled into one. Social organization is thrown out the window and anarchy reigns. For the nation's well-being and our own, we must restore personal responsibility in the law and let justice and mercy handle the rest.

We abdicate our responsibility in other ways. Rather than establishing broad general guidelines for judging the reasonableness of an act, which would require us to take a stand on how the "average" citizen or cop or criminal should behave, we write ever more minute rules to accommodate each new event and personality. Even worse, we expect the people who are affected to know and obey these ever-changing interpretations rather than use their experience and judgment to make rational decisions. This situation has become exasperatingly clear in the world of regulatory law, but the concept infects our criminal laws as well.

Ask the cop on the beat. One day Miranda warnings are to be given upon arrest. The next, some judge says they are required as soon as you focus on a suspect. Then another court decides that if someone blurts out a confession before you can read the warnings, in fact before you say anything, the confession is inadmissible. We've reached the point that a spontaneous admission of guilt has been deemed involuntary, thus invalid. Here's an actual scenario for you. Give someone his rights; he hires an attorney. After consultation with counsel, he decides to tell you about the crime. Unfortunately, he does so when the attorney is *not* present. His right to counsel was "indelible," the court ruled. An adult apparently cannot waive counsel without counsel being present for the waiver. How in the world could a cop expect that ruling? What nonsense.

As Judge Harold Rothwax wrote in his wonderful book *Guilty,* "The criminal justice system has become a sporting event in which the defendant has a sporting chance to evade society's punishment." That was never the intent. The rationale in the *Miranda* case was to prohibit physical or serious mental coercion in the obtaining of a confession. Now, as in every other aspect of life, the law presumes we are idiots. If the cops do anything halfway clever in eliciting a confession (like appealing to a defendant's conscience by simply stating that the parents of a murdered child should be able to recover and bury her body before Christmas . . . to which the suspect voluntarily responded, "I'll show you where she is"), some court will rule this a violation of the defendant's rights (and it did).

Similarly, we must now treat smart and stupid defendants (not, please note, the mentally handicapped) equally. As with employment and education laws, that doesn't mean what you think it says. Just as teachers must accommodate each child's particularities rather than provide appropriate instruction to the class as a whole, police cannot give a standard instruction to all citizens but must modify it for every unique characteristic they might encounter. Once again, the reaction of the "reasonable man" is not the guide to appropriate police behavior. Instead the question is whether the police behavior was reasonable given the defendant's emotional or intellectual makeup. To accommodate court rulings, cops are wise to play to the lowest common denominator, giving the same breaks to a genius that they might give to a complete fool.

In reviewing cases, judges also seem to put themselves into the minds of each defendant rather than setting general standards for the police. Justice Thurgood Marshall once said, "No sane person would knowingly relinquish the right to be free from compulsion." Thus we now approach every interrogation, as Justice Warren Burger lamented, as an "act of poor judgment by a vulnerable person outmaneuvered by the police." That's crazy. If a suspect receives his warnings, is treated with respect and not physically abused or browbeaten, a little outmaneuvering to get the facts is not an infringement on his rights.

The exclusionary rule is another bogey that haunts reasonable policing. What if an officer receives an anonymous call that a man in a green cap and a plaid jacket standing on the corner of Vine and Main is armed with a gun? He cannot stop and pat the man down. The courts have said that a very specific but anonymous tip is insufficient to justify a brief intrusion. Any weapon recovered at the time would be inadmissible. Let's say a telephone call tells police to go to an apartment where a little girl is possibly being held against her will. If the tenant (and perpetrator) isn't home, the girl may not have the right to let you in. If she tells you he raped her and threatened her with guns that are located in the closet, you'd better not look in there. Rules are rules if you can figure them out. (The courts eventually decided that the cops *could* enter and rescue the child, but they could *not* look in the closet without a warrant.)

Not long ago the New York Court of Appeals disallowed the introduction of a bag containing four high-powered handguns and 150 rounds of ammunition as evidence. Apparently an underage runaway literally dropped this at the feet of a Port Authority cop. Testimony revealed that the officer was a trained firearms expert who could see the bag contained weapons by the clear outlines protruding in the thin cloth bag. The court, however, ruled there were insufficient grounds to open the sack.

A few years ago two officers were patrolling a drug-infested neighborhood in the wee hours of the morning and noticed several people loading large duffel bags into the trunk of a car. When the officers approached, the individuals fled. The cops gave chase and stopped the suspects. Sure enough, the bags were filled with drugs. Sounds like good preventive police work, doesn't it? Not according to New York federal judge Harold Baer, Jr., who suppressed the evidence and the subsequent taped confession. Baer said that "running from the police" was a normal reaction in that community and should not give rise to any suspicion or search. He threw out the evidence and dismissed the case. What planet was he on?

A PRO-CRIME JUDGE

His ruling promoted a national uproar. When editorials suggested his ouster, Baer reversed his decision, justifying the retraction as based on "new evidence." This fresh information was simply corroboration of the events by another cop. In his reversal Baer quoted John Marshall: "Because the strongest advocates of 4th amendment rights [which prohibit unreasonable searches and seizures] are frequently criminals, it is easy to forget that our interpretations of such rights apply to the innocent and the guilty alike." In colloquial terms, that is called "CYA" (cover your ass).

National attention quickly faded without any meaningful look at the culprit here—judicial rule making. Lawyers and judges continue to second-guess the most intense, spontaneous policing decisions at a time and place far removed from the streets.

The reasonableness standard is disappearing. Remember the O. J. Simpson case? The state had to fight tooth and nail to get testimony about the initial search of O. J.'s Rockingham estate into evidence. The defense argued that there was no probable cause to jump the gate and investigate, despite the murder of two people, including O. J.'s ex-wife, just blocks away, the blood on Simpson's Bronco parked outside his gate, the blood trail leading toward the front door, which was visible from the street, and the fact that no one answered the buzzer when the officers rang the house. Attorney Johnnie Cochran and his team used this episode to begin planting the notion that police had already fingered Simpson for the crimes and were beginning to set him up.

You be the judge. Here are the questions to ask: Was there an emergency at the time? What was the degree of police intrusion? Was it in proportion to the allegations? What was the danger presented? Finally, was the officer's behavior under these circumstances a reasonable exercise of police powers? Under a general reasonableness standard, there should be no doubt that this entry was appropriate. However, the defense presented unique reasons that it said should prohibit the conduct under Simpson's unique circumstances. Simpson was a black man married to a white woman, so naturally white cops would be prejudiced against him, his celebrity status would make them want to arrest him for the glory, they had to get in to set him up, and on and on. This is absurd.

One of my favorite and very telling stories was reported in *Washington Monthly*. In our nation's capital, there are so many law enforcement agencies that no one seems to know who has what territory. According to reporter Nancy Beiles, "That's why it took two civilians to stop Francisco Duran firing on the White House late last year—the Secret Service were patrolling the grounds, the Park Police the sidewalk, and the MPD [Metropolitan Police Department] the street. Before the different officers could figure out who had jurisdiction, two civilians had disarmed Duran and wrestled him to the ground."

Criminal law now reinforces the notion that cops are better off simply responding to crimes after the fact. Don't take any initiative. Don't use common sense and experience. Don't try to stop something before it escalates. Answer those 911 calls, file a report, and wait for the next summons, but remember catch-22. If you don't check or if you fail to follow through when that reasonable officer would have done so, the city and police department (actually the taxpayers) may be liable for damages in a civil suit.

We may be lucky if most cops can perform even these more limited tasks. Discrimination rulings require police departments to hire the incompetent, illiterate, and even those with juvenile records. Walter Olson documents this and other outrages in *The Excuse Factory*. He tells of a Boston police force applicant who lied about his past psychiatric history. Of course, the city fired him when they learned of this. We don't want someone with a history of mental problems on the street with a gun . . . or do we? At least the lie was disqualification enough . . . wasn't it? After all, police officers are called on to swear truthfully to many things, including their testimony in court. The judge thought otherwise and, as Olson relates, the court "reinstated him with back pay and damages for emotional distress. It said Massachusetts handicap-rights law prohibited employers from taking into account job applicants' medical history, including mental health treatment"; would-be cops were no exception. Since the city had no business taking past hospitalization into account, it had no business asking about it. And since it had no business asking about it, it also had no right to act on the basis of responses to its question—a sort of employment-law version of the exclusionary rule. As Olson notes sardonically, "If a question is improper, a job applicant needn't answer it truthfully; it's known as the 'right to lie.' "

The absurdities continue and apparently apply to the physical conditioning of recruits as well. Olson pointed out an exposé in *New York* magazine that noted some police recruits had fallen into the "almost inconceivably unfit first percentile"; that is, from a physical standpoint, they were "worse than 99 percent of others their age and gender." As he elaborated, "cops without the physical ability to catch or subdue suspects by force, of course, might have to resort to using their guns. Some New York City officers were found to lack the strength to pull the trigger of their standard-issue revolvers. After lawyers argued that women and minorities might lack the familiarity with firearms allegedly typical of white male recruits, Pittsburgh agreed to give more tries to those who failed a silhouette-target test, thereby establishing bad aim as another legally protected category." While our nation's capital was hiring virtually every breathing applicant, Congress bravely drew the line at Mayor Marion Barry's suggestion to "hire by lottery." I don't want to digress into more horrors of employment law, but I couldn't pass up the chance to note how these ridiculous rulings endanger those of us who rely on police protection.

No responsibility in the courts, on the streets, or at the job—sounds pretty good? Just remember, if someone is cutting you slack on your qualifications or performance, the people you rely on may be skating as well. Next time you hear someone blame his or her incompetence on outside forces or you find yourself passed though levels of bureaucracy only to be told "Our rules don't permit that," ask yourself: Is it worth it? Are we really getting away with anything?

Note how a bit of reason can enter the game when the rule makers are personally threatened. Shortly after the September 11 attacks, the Justice Department suddenly backed away from its support of a plaintiff's suit against the Philadelphia transit police that was seeking to weaken fitness standards for employment. Given the critical role our police and firefighters played under the most extreme conditions, these Justice lawyers decided that just maybe certain physical requirements were appropriate. However, the chief counsel for the Public Interest Law Center of Philadelphia called this a "slap in the face of women" and a retreat on civil rights issues. I seriously doubt anyone saved by the heroes in the Pentagon or the World Trade Center would agree with that assessment.

SIX | Our Criminal Laws
Are a Crime

The way we manage our lives has been forever changed by the perception of rampant crime. It creeps insidiously into the most benign activities. We all recognize the dark thoughts that appear each time we send our children off to school, head to the parking lot after dark, or double lock our doors before retiring. Halloween has all but disappeared as a joyous, mischievous romp through darkened neighborhoods. Who in his or her right mind would risk a little necking at the lake or overlook? Even camping in remote regions is not undertaken without trepidation. It is not the animal but the human predators we truly fear.

The fear that permeates our homes and streets is palpable. It is fear of each other and fear of our kids. Male relatives don't cuddle their little nieces and nephews to avoid possible misinterpretation. Teachers don't touch students for the same reasons. In fact, it is wise to ignore small children entirely if they are not your own. The other day my husband and I finished playing golf only to find a car idling behind ours as we prepared to leave. The driver must have run into the golf shop or clubhouse. My husband started to slip into the front seat to move the vehicle forward a few feet so we could leave when he noticed a child buckled in a safety seat in the back. We both laughed but simultaneously called out to another foursome a few feet away "We're not kidnapping anyone . . . just moving the car!"

There is fear of the police, particularly in minority communities, and mistrust of the legal system that was designed to protect us. Despite marked reductions in police brutality, complaints about cops are soaring. Perceptions about the racial origins of crime deepen chasms that we seem unwilling and unable to cross. The scales of justice seem to tilt not from the weight of evidence but from money and status. Concerns that once shadowed lives in the inner cities now follow us all, through urban areas and affluent suburbs right into the most rural communities.

We are spending billions on private security services, more than is spent on all our local, state, and federal police. In 2001 the National Association of Security Companies reported that there was almost three times the number of private security guards as public police officers. Add the rest of our protections—locks on the doors, bars on the windows, security systems in the home and office, steering wheel restraints and other antitheft devices in cars, and the insurance for everything—and you have a $200 billion-a-year industry. Don't forget the panic buttons in hand, whistles around our necks, fingerprinting our children, crime watches in the neighborhoods, and entire communities built behind walls complete with guards at the entrances. The list goes on and on.

As we lock ourselves away, the police and courts, spurred on by politicians, are turning the key on criminals at an extraordinary rate. We have soared past other nations in the number of people we incarcerate, with about 2 million now behind bars. The prison industry is building new facilities as quickly as legislators can fund them. Between 1980 and 2000 state spending on prisons nearly tripled, and according to the Justice Policy Institute, by the year 2000, one out of every fourteen state dollars was spent on prisons. Taxpayers shell out about $40 billion a year on this warehousing industry. Sentences are lengthening as mandatory punishments take decision making away from our judges. Tough parole laws mean we spend millions of dollars for medical care on an aging prison population. This amount will grow exponentially in the coming years. The overall cost to this country for actual crime and our fearful response is beyond calculation.

In 1997 the Justice Department proudly announced that the violent crime rate had hit its lowest level in twenty-five years. Conservatives applauded harsh sentencing and increased policing for this downturn. Others hinted that the strong economy during this period had the greatest effect. By 2001 those statistics leveled off and began to inch up again. Nothing had changed in the policing or sentencing strategies. The economy, however, had taken a sharp downward plunge, putting countless individuals at the low end of the earning scale out of work. None of this empirical data matters to the politicians. Their rhetoric on crime and justice hasn't changed in decades.

It is time to get angry about the state of criminal justice in this country. We rant about the malfunctions of the system but fail to recognize that the origins of most problems are often the very laws we enact and the manner in which they are implemented. We must scrutinize these rules and their consequences by asking some very basic questions:

- What are the real social, political, and economic costs of these programs?
- Do we fund the right policies with dollars and support staff or opt for the politically popular course of action?
- Have we inhibited responsible law enforcement by the explosion of rules governing police officers, corrections officials, and judges?
- Are our trials a search for truth or a sporting event?
- Are our courts becoming de facto legislatures, creating rules and laws without the consent of the governed?
- Should we be using criminal sanctions to direct our moral choices?
- Most important, are we truly safer, freer, and more cohesive as a nation as a result of our criminal justice approach?

For decades, our representatives have delivered empty buzzwords and created bogeymen to justify unnecessary criminal laws and increased law enforcement spending and to win our votes. The political mileage has been tremendous, but the economic and social costs are devastating.

Remember the 100,000 new police officers President Clinton promised the nation? The cops sure liked this, as did their unions. The voters applauded the apparent increase in protection, but local governments were a bit more restrained. Why? This federal legislation delivered credit for attacking crime to the national sponsors, but they didn't shoulder the real responsibility for making things happen. As is often the case, after the applause died down, the local and state agencies were left with the bill. This program only funded the initial hiring of more officers. Someone else would have to pay to keep them working. Additionally, no one considered the extra support staff that must accompany increased arrests to keep the system running smoothly. Where were the new judges, court personnel, district attorneys, public defenders, probation and parole officers and corrections officers? Who was going to pay for those employees, the space for them to work, and the new jails and prisons to house the growing number of arrestees?

Clinton scored big points through this largely symbolic gesture. The impressive numbers deflected further inquiry into the actual long-term effect of this program. In the same way, numbers more than results propel almost everyone in the justice system. Cops know they're being judged on arrest numbers rather than on crime prevention. Courts are measured in the same way. The question is not "How much justice did you dispense today?" Instead, disposition numbers are tallied. Assistant DAs are evaluated on their backlog or the severity of the sentences they obtain in plea bargains or before a jury. Corrections officers are rarely concerned with rehabilitation. Instead, they want the job security that comes with more prisons, more inmates, and longer sentences.

National politicians point to more laws and tougher sentences as their positive contribution in the fight against crime. There are now fifty-two federal crimes for which you can get the death penalty! While there is no correlation between the number of federal crimes and the degree of public safety, legislators pretend there is. However, there is a definite relationship between the federalizing of more crimes and the expansion of federal control over the states and individual citizens.

This trend is obvious in the area of civil and regulatory law, but did you know the Commerce Clause has become a key to increase federal police power? Article 1, Section 8 of the U.S. Constitution reads in part: "The Congress shall have the power . . . to regulate Commerce with foreign nations, and among the several states, and with the Indian tribes." This clause has become the justification for most federal expansion; it seems almost anything can be pigeonholed as a national economic concern. Take a gander at Bard College president Leon Botstein's editorial on education from the *New York Times*. Defending federal intervention in education, he asserts, "Contrary to the claims of some, there is no constitutional objection to a larger federal role. The framers did not specifically exclude education from the federal agenda."

Huh? I thought every power not specifically delegated to the federal government belonged to the states. Silly me. Botstein goes on: "If one wants a clear constitutional basis for rethinking the federal role, look to the interstate commerce clause. The Internet has made it plain that information and knowledge cross state lines. If that argument seems a bit too clever, consider that since we live now in the so-called global economy, contingent on scientific knowledge and high levels of literacy, should not education be deemed essential to the national defense and foreign policy? There are many precedents that can permit a 21st century America to abandon 18th century practices." And thus, via the Commerce Clause, Botstein arrives at a national education policy.

How does this argument apply to criminal law? Well, in 1971 the Supreme Court held that a local loan shark was subject to federal conviction although there was no evidence he crossed state lines. Because his behavior was part of a class of activities that Congress said affected commerce through organized crime, it was a federal case.

A more recent attempt actually failed. In the Christy Brzonkala case heard by the Supreme Court in 2000, the plaintiff was seeking federal damages against her alleged attackers for the act of rape. Christy never went to the police with her charges. In fact, she waited several months to go to Virginia Tech University to request an administrative hearing. Unsuccessful there, she turned to the 1994 Federal Violence Against Women Act to pursue her case.

The dispute revolved around the question: Who has the power to punish for the crime? Brzonkala's advocates argued that rape is a form of discrimination. Furthermore, because any injury to a woman from this crime could affect her economic freedom (as she might limit her movements from state to state out of fear), the federal government can use the Commerce Clause to justify its intervention. Women's rights advocates were furious when the Court rejected this analysis, but one defeat does not assure victory for the states. The argument is now open for further refinement. I expect we will hear it again.

The notion that gender-based crimes should be categorized as discrimination and trigger the Commerce Clause exceeds my comprehension. Under this rationale, all crimes—those against men, children, the elderly, minorities—for whatever reason, would become civil rights violations and require coverage by federal law. We might as well abolish local cops and courts and create a federal police state.

At last count there were over 3,000 federal crimes. An American Bar Association Task Force reported in 1999 that "whatever the exact number of crimes that comprise today's 'federal criminal law,' it is clear that the amount of individual citizen behavior now potentially subject to federal criminal controls has increased in astonishing proportions in the last few decades." The federal regulations that carry some sort of civil or criminal penalty increase by about 10,000 the number of criminalized rules we must obey.

Already the civil rights laws have allowed the federal government to circumvent the notion of double jeopardy. Few voices will be raised for an unpopular defendant and a politically unacceptable verdict, if federal prosecutors try him or her again. This happened in the Rodney King case in California and in the Abner Louima charges against Officer Charles Schwarz in New York. In this latter case, the Court of Appeals reversed Schwarz's first conviction on insufficient evidence. Now the federal prosecutors are taking a second bite. Amazingly, the prosecutors are also pursuing two perjury counts against Schwarz for testifying he did not escort Abner Louima to the precinct bathroom and did not witness any assault. If this is perjury, then any denial of one's own guilt could become grounds for prosecution.

I accept the rationale that state and federal governments are "separate sovereigns" and thus can each pursue criminal violations. Sometimes in history it has been necessary for the nation to appropriately chastise a recalcitrant state by conducting its own proceeding. But without some fundamental wrong apparent in the state trial, such as corruption or intimidation, the rule against double jeopardy should be respected. Writer Jimmy Breslin took the risk by labeling the federal trial of Lemrick Nelson for the murder of Yankel Rosenbaum as "flat-out double jeopardy." Nevertheless, Nelson went down. I have absolutely no sympathy for Nelson, but remember, if the federal government can take a second shot at unpopular defendants, it has the precedent to use this tactic against others.

The federal government has an even better opportunity to gain control of and expand the criminal law in times of national emergencies. We have been seduced by the notion that law will save us from harm. As a result, we abdicate freedom in the hope that we will be protected from unpredictable or dangerous behavior. After September 11, it became almost unpatriotic to challenge increased security measures, regardless of their effectiveness. If more wiretaps and search warrants are now necessary, so be it. By the way, let's create a special court for this outside the authorized system. If limitless detention of unnamed suspects is necessary, who cares? That could never happen to you or me.

Did you know that your face now appears on tape and film all day long as you walk past secure buildings, ride in most any elevator, do business at the bank and ATM, shop in stores, and, of course, park in a public garage. Citibank alone records about 250,000 ATM transactions a day. The 2001 Super Bowl crowd helped test facial recognition technology that is coming to an airport near you. Maybe your local police department has already joined the 80 percent of our 19,000 U.S. police departments that now use some form of closed-circuit television system in their jurisdictions, according to a 2001 survey by the International Association of Chiefs of Police. We know about the cameras catching tollbooth cheats, but how about the Hollywood cops that snap the license plates on cars driving through a certain drug-infested area and then drop a note to the owner about the sighting?

In Washington, D.C., the police are now linking hundreds of government video cameras to get a running show of much of the city. The federal government has poured millions of taxpayer dollars into developing this technology, which can not only zoom in on your credit card from several hundred feet away but includes listening devices on light poles allegedly to locate the source of gunfire in dangerous neighborhoods. I guess they'd never tape anything else.

To date, the Supreme Court still examines our "expectation of privacy" to see if some action has violated our rights. That expectation is clearly diminishing as you move away from your front door. Some communities and businesses have invited police to set up cameras to increase security. It will be hard for any of those people to ever complain that their privacy was violated.

If you are a law-abiding soul who has no objection to being watched, would you mind showing up in someone's homemade videotape? The British have had several best-sellers in their country apparently compiled from both public and private security cameras. As you can imagine, there were some shots you wouldn't want to show the kids. Big Brother is already here.

Don't forget the thought police. The hate crime movement is getting downright scary. These laws make a defendant's thoughts and beliefs an element of the crime. Without some overt statement at the crime scene, this mental state can be very hard to prove. Do we want to call a defendant's friends and family to inquire about what sort of things he or she said in the past about a particular group? Should we suppress free but objectionable speech with this threat of punishment for such expressions? Do we assume bias if the victim was gay or female or African American? Why or why not?

A few years ago an actor was charged with assaulting a tabloid re-porter. The actor said the journalist had been following and harassing him. He finally responded with his fists and was charged with a misde-meanor assault. The warring parties agreed to a six-figure settlement and were ready to walk away. But the DA wouldn't let them. What happened? The prosecutor discovered that the reporter was gay. Learning this fact, he added a hate crime charge to the list and opposed the dismissal of the criminal case. The DA said the seriousness of the beating was one factor (although booked as a simple misdemeanor) and, here's the catch, "because a hate crime has been alleged as well." The state attorney would have to attempt to prove what the actor felt as he threw the punch. Was it because the reporter was gay, or be-cause he was obnoxious? Either way, would that make the injury more severe?

I do not condone any crime, certainly not the harassment or at-tack of a targeted group. Why, however, is a crime against gays, women, or minorities more heinous than one against a straight white guy? Every single victim of crime has a unique status. The attempt to use criminal law to highlight some social or political agenda is terribly misguided. If the purpose is to help a group that suffers disproportion-ately, the *Detroit News* printed a good suggestion. When the Michigan State House passed two bills letting judges "double the fines levied against criminals who victimize the young, the elderly or the dis-abled," the paper's editorialist responded. "If the real purpose of these bills is to deter crime against our most vulnerable citizens, the Legisla-ture [should] increase the penalties for crimes against men or blacks, the poor or taxi drivers . . . in fact persons aged 65 or older are the least likely to experience violent crime." Where is our equal protec-tion under the law if certain groups are singled out for special safe-guards? Remember, any aggravating factors in a crime can be used to justify the higher range of punishment. Hateful behavior should be considered in the sentencing phase. The primary reason for the rash of hate crimes statutes is political, not pragmatic.

The British are leading the way in criminalizing our speech. Their 1999 McPherson Report suggested criminalizing the use of "racist lan-guage" in private as well as public. It also proposed defining a "racial incident" as any incident that is perceived to be racist by the victim or other person. This is not too far-fetched given the extremes to which our workplace harassment laws and politically correct constrictions have taken us. My modern-day hero Walter Olson warns: "Consider for example the continuing expansion of American harassment law, which, in the view of some legal authorities, has made it legally hazardous while in an irritable mood to snap 'Idiot!' at one of your co-workers or classmates, since the epithets might contribute to a hostile environment for mentally disabled colleagues." If the use of the word "niggardly" in a Washington, D.C., budget meeting can get you fired, and the city councils of San Diego and Boston are banning the word "minority" as disparaging, how long might it be before we criminalize such expressions?

Rules at all government levels permit myriad transgressions into our individual space in the name of safety. If there are too many bars producing too many intoxicated drivers in a particular area, the law permits roadblocks and Breathalyzers for passing motorists. These activities are just minor intrusions for major protections, right? But how far should we go? Although drug roadblocks have not been upheld, an even greater invasion has accompanied the search for narcotics. Racial profiling on the nation's highways has finally gained national attention. "Driving While Black" is a well-known offense among African Americans, but it was the statistical revelations about minority stops on the New Jersey Turnpike that brought the crackdown on this practice. In the spring of 2002 the New Jersey police argued that more minorities were shown to speed on the turnpike, but this justification for the stops came long after the original explanation that this was simply intelligent drug profiling.

Not all profiling is an abuse of police powers. If a rape victim describes her attacker as a white male, early twenties, five foot nine, brown hair with a mustache, and an obvious limp, it would be entirely appropriate for officers to stop and question any men in the target area resembling that description. But this is very different from stopping every black or Hispanic traveling down a freeway because minority dealers sometimes use that road to transport drugs. Black women are stopped at the airports far more than any other group of Americans, yet they are less likely to be carrying drugs than white men or women. Is the accidental capture of a drug mule or dope smoker through these tactics worth the countless breaches of personal freedom it takes to make the arrest? Of what social value is the imprisonment of this one person when hundreds must be stopped in the process?

We narrowly escaped the latest technological intrusion thanks to the Supreme Court. In a case in 2001, law enforcement authorities tried to justify a search and drug bust that resulted from an external "heat" scan of a defendant's home. While out playing with their new high-tech toy, some cops pointed the heat-sensing radar at the defendant's house. The infrared sensor showed higher temperatures radiating from below the roof than in the rest of the house. Police obtained a search warrant and found the resident was using heat lamps to grow marijuana. Once the heat escapes from your house, police argued, it is in the public domain. Why shouldn't they be able to measure this output and search accordingly? (Be careful, the human body gives off heat, and adultery is still illegal in some states.)

The Court said no and overturned the conviction, but the division between the justices was disturbing. The sanctity of our homes was protected by a single vote. The 5 to 4 split united conservatives Antonin Scalia and Clarence Thomas with Stephen Breyer, Ruth Bader Ginsburg and David Souter, while Sandra Day O'Connor, Anthony Kennedy, and William Rehnquist sided with the dissent. Liberal Justice John Paul Stevens had no trouble with the intrusion and objected to Scalia's condemnation of the search. When Scalia went further and expanded the ruling to any future technology capable of "seeing" through walls, Stevens was irate, but this may be a good thing. Police would like to use X-ray vision! New technology can scan people walking down the street and identify items like guns under their clothing. I wonder what else might be examined.

The body is being invaded in other ways. A few years ago the Medical University of South Carolina established "an innovative effort to deal with a sad aspect of child abuse." The innovation? Pregnant women would have their urine screened. If drugs appeared, they could be prosecuted. The objective, protecting children, is worthwhile, but the fallout for our civil liberties is treacherous. I held my breath when the Supreme Court issued its ruling in the case. The law was shot down, but how did that legislation pass in the first place? This unprecedented invasion of privacy invited a frightening array of laws in its wake.

Why not institute alcohol screenings? Fetal alcohol syndrome is a devastating consequence of excessive drinking during pregnancy. What about legal drugs ingested by prescription? If they help the woman but harm the fetus, whose interest prevails? What if a woman undertakes dangerous but legal behavior that harms the baby? I recall my mother ordering a female horse trainer off our farm after she caught her riding a young colt during her eighth month of pregnancy. Mother told her to either quit riding till the baby came or move her horses. That was a rational response. But what if the trainer had been hurt? Might she have been prosecuted for child abuse if the baby was injured? If not, why not? Recently courts have allowed children to sue their mothers for personal injuries occurring before birth. (Cynics look at this as a great way to collect on the family insurance.) It is not much of a leap to criminalize the conduct.

A variation on this train of thought has been upheld. At twenty-two years of age, Regina McKnight suffered from a low IQ, was unable to hold a job, and was addicted to cocaine. Then things got worse. She gave birth to a stillborn child. Although there were traces of cocaine in the infant's system, doctors did not agree this was the cause of death. That did not matter to South Carolina prosecutors, who charged McKnight with homicide by child abuse, or the jury, which convicted her after only fifteen minutes of deliberation. This sick, pathetic woman is now serving twelve years in the penitentiary.

In 2001 Latrece Jones of Chattanooga, Tennessee, was convicted of criminally negligent homicide in the death of her two-year-old son. What did she do? She let him ride in her lap while sitting in the front passenger seat of a car. The airbag deployed when an accident occurred and the impact killed the little boy. Car seats are now the law, but how could we compound her loss of that child with such charges?

In Glendale, Arizona, police don't wait for an accident. They set up roadblocks to check that children under five years old are in those child safety seats. Drivers who violate the law receive citations. "We have sobriety checkpoints for DUIs trying to get drunk drivers off the road," Sergeant Greg Dominguez said. "Why do we do that? Because they are killing people. It's the same with people who don't put their kids in car seats. These kids are dying." This could be a good excuse for a lot of things.

Laws do more than protect kids; they target them as well. In the effort to make our schools safer, criminal law is increasingly the tool. The zero tolerance movement has created a litany of absurd yet tragic results. A Tweety bird key chain is defined as a weapon and gets a young girl suspended for two weeks. A twelve-year-old boy in Iverness, Florida, stomps his foot in a puddle, splashing others, and he finds himself whisked to jail for two hours. Forget playing cowboys and Indians or cops and robbers. Using the thumb and index finger to simulate a gun will get a kid in serious trouble. One young honor student was handcuffed and removed from school simply for drawing pictures of weapons. Of course possessing them is another story. Despite hundreds of laws regulating firearms, these weapons are readily available. Get caught in school with one and you will likely suffer no more time off than you would for that key chain.

There is a profitable side to infringements on liberty. Taking a tip from Amtrak, bus companies and airlines now leak passenger information to the Drug Enforcement Administration in exchange for 10 percent of any forfeiture profits gained in a subsequent drug bust. The police in Cedar Rapids, Iowa, are using financial incentives on a teen hot line. "Teens who call about classmates they believe to have alcohol, drugs, or weapons on school property get $50 if the police recover anything." Home or car owners might have no connection with a crime occurring on or in their property, but they can still lose these items if they are linked however tangentially to a crime. According to a story in the *Albuquerque Tribune/Nando Times,* that city's local council passed a bill in 2000 that permitted the taking of someone's house if the neighbors complained about repeated teenage parties while the owner wasn't home.

Many sheriff and police departments count on such property forfeitures to help pay the bills. When state governments tried to dedicate these funds to things like education or healthcare, the agencies worked a scam with the feds. The local and state boys would do all the work on a case, then give credit to the federal agencies, which then collected the forfeiture money or property. Washington would then kick back monies to those departments, bypassing the state's requirements and filling police coffers. This scam can have a very unjust influence on who is targeted and what is seized during an arrest.

The criminal law has been compromised across the board. We all recognize there is rich justice and poor justice and that this affects the system in many ways. Since there is no way to try more than a fraction of cases filed in the courts each year, plea bargains move most suspects through the system without much fuss. Most criminal attorneys are familiar with the term "misdemeanor murder." The term refers to stabbing that occurs after a night of drinking in the projects or a shooting in some disreputable bar. When these cases appear, few in the system care about either side. Shuffle them through and move on to the next.

We have looked at the way judges and jurors rewrite the long-standing rules of responsibility when it comes to high-profile cases. However, even the well-to-do usually should avoid the insanity defense. The law in most states is so restrictive that only a minuscule number of truly crazy defendants would qualify. The case of Andrea Yates is an excellent example. This Houston woman committed one of the most heinous offenses imaginable: She drowned all five of her children, then called the police and waited to be arrested. As the facts unfolded, a dramatic portrait of mental illness emerged. A literal baby machine, she became pregnant a fifth time despite lingering depression after the birth of her fourth child and a psychiatrist's warnings against having another baby. She was simultaneously caring for her extended family including a father with Alzheimer's, living with a controlling husband, home-schooling her children, and trying to handle an unbalanced psyche. Just before she committed the murders, she was taken off some powerful antipsychotic and antidepressant drugs that were being combined and prescribed at very high doses.

As I sat in the courtroom watching Yates, I thought that anyone could see she was desperately ill. Yet the archaic insanity standard in Texas says that despite any mental disease or defect, if she knew the difference between right and wrong, she was legally sane at the time of the crime. During the trial it was apparent that Andrea Yates knew she had killed her children. She knew it was legally and morally wrong. However, even the state psychiatrist, Dr. Park Dietz, said she really seemed to believe that by drowning her children she was saving them from eternal damnation and sending them to heaven. Her personal right and wrong, her struggle between God and the Devil, guided her that tragic day.

Despite his findings that she was psychotic and possibly schizophrenic, Dietz would not say whether Andrea Yates actually was sane. He would only say that she knew the difference between right and wrong. The jury agreed and convicted her of the murders. They rejected the death penalty in favor of the mandatory life sentence, but I wonder if they did her any favor.

I suggest the doctor could not say Yates was sane because he knew what any modern psychiatrist knows: The ability to distinguish right from wrong is not the measure of someone's sanity. It seemed appropriate in the eighteenth century, when the definition was written. Today we keep this rule because it is politically popular, not because it is legally sound. When John Hinckley was acquitted by reason of insanity for the shooting of President Reagan, we witnessed a wholesale toughening of this defense. As so often occurs, one notable event can cause the legislature to rewrite an entire statute, whether it is called for or not.

Our prisons are now brimming with the mentally ill. Ken Silverstein wrote a piece for *Mother Jones* in October 2001 that highlighted a number of cases where everyone—prosecutors, judges, and jurors alike—agreed the defendants were "crazy." They didn't fit the technical definition, though, so "off with their heads." The case of Daniel Colwell was particularly disturbing. He had been diagnosed as schizophrenic and manic depressive, had warned his sister to tell police he intended to kill, kept telling doctors and law enforcement officials to kill him, and finally shot two people to achieve that end. The state, thus far, is complying. Although the Georgia Supreme Court acknowledged that he "likely suffered from a mental disease," he was competent to be executed because he "clearly understood the nature and object of the proceedings" and could "participate in his own case."

The solution to this dilemma is relatively easy but requires a rewriting of the law. The biggest fear citizens have is that the criminally insane will be released back to the street by some lenient psychiatrist if we don't lock them in prison. The Court should be allowed to explain to a jury the commitment process that accompanies a finding of insanity, or we could just have our verdicts read "guilty but insane" rather than "not guilty by reason of insanity." The judge could then assign the defendant to the appropriate mental facility for incarceration rather than a prison, and the state would retain jurisdiction.

As Justice Benjamin Cardozo said, "Justice is a concept by far more subtle and indefinite than is yielded by mere obedience to a rule." We are certainly ignoring this truth in the application of our insanity laws, but the worst abuse is elsewhere. If Cardozo was right, then justice has been virtually eliminated from the sentencing process.

Cops select the charges they wish to file. The DA then chooses which crime to prosecute and what punishment to pursue. However, the supposedly impartial arbiter in the court, the judge, is now hamstrung by myriad rules that dictate a defendant's sentence. For years various groups have complained about disparate punishment. If one person gets five years for burglary and another gets nine, is that just? It may well be once all the circumstances are considered. But because this process is subjective, there could always be some stealthy discrimination floating in the judge's brain. After all, here is a job that actually relies on subjective criteria and analyzes it with wisdom and experience, very untrustworthy stuff these days. So without thinking it through, officials in the federal system and many state jurisdictions decided they could do better. They would create a method of sentencing that would withstand all criticism of disparity.

The result? Most criminal court judges have been effectively neutered. Between mandatory sentences and federal sentencing guidelines, we might as well have computers on the bench to dispense punishment. We can insert the particular crime, the number of gunshots or the weight of the drugs, and out pops a sentence. As long as it's consistent with others, it doesn't seem to matter if it is fair or just.

Some of the gravest wrongs in recent years have resulted from such rule book sentencing. The certification of juveniles to stand trial as adults is one example. As children became more and more violent in the 1990s, our reaction was to lower the age at which they could be prosecuted under adult laws. Decisions about prosecution are invariably political, as district attorneys gauge the emotional reaction of a community before deciding how to proceed. If convicted in adult court of, say, murder, the juvenile gets no special consideration. Suddenly we have twelve-year-olds sentenced to mandatory life without parole. People argue that this measure is necessary to prevent some little sociopath from walking out of juvenile detention at age eighteen, whether rehabilitated or not.

As with the insanity cases, there is an easy solution to the dilemma—the dual-track program that some states have instituted for such offenders. These juveniles are tried under adult laws but remain in the custody of juvenile facilities. If by age eighteen (or twenty-one) they still represent a threat to the community, adult supervision and the traditional prison system takes over. A judge can review sentencing as needed to adapt to the particular defendant and is given the discretion to make this call.

Our drug laws are a particularly perverse example of sentencing gone awry. A welfare mom deals a little crack to feed her kids. She can't flip some big dealer to the district attorney, so she faces the judge and gets the max while the really bad guy does a deal in the back room for a few names and stands before the court with a reduced charge. No matter the circumstances, if the drugs you are busted with weigh a certain amount, you are looking at long hard time. I'll talk more about the insanity of these laws in the next chapter.

Sadly, harsh punishment does not stop with the mandatory minimums that apply to drug convictions. The expansion of the three-strikes laws is another example of a knee-jerk reaction to violent crime. If you have two prior felony convictions and are convicted again, good-bye. Washington was the first state to enact the three-strikes provision. Crimes like drunk driving, promoting prostitution, and petty theft have all triggered the application of this penalty. Small-time burglars or thieves caught lifting a bottle of aspirin or package of cookies went to prison for life. This was not supposed to happen.

The law was passed in response to the early release of dangerous criminals—armed robbers, rapists, and the like. Instead of addressing the underlying problems of prison overcrowding and lenient sentencing of truly serious offenders, the legislature drafted an inflexible law that eliminated all judicial discretion. Nowadays prosecutors must reclassify or drop charges, even negotiate pleas to inapplicable offenses to circumvent the unjust results of this law. In other words, officers of the court must effectively lie to ease their conscience.

Taxpayers must pay to house such inmates for life. By the time the three-strikes penalty is applied, most of these crooks are middle aged and moving out of their criminally productive years, while the younger, more violent hoodlums get plea bargains and another chance on the streets. Statistics estimate we'll spend close to $700,000 over the lifetime of a prisoner who is fifty or older. Entire geriatric units are being designed to house our aging inmates, they are essentially nursing homes with bars.

We spend in the seven figures just to try most death penalty cases through the appellate process to completion. Most inmates sit on death row between eight and fifteen years before execution. In terms of dollars, this penalty is a real waste of money. More than that, I don't understand how we can insist so desperately on measurable equality in our courts and still uphold the death penalty. Supreme Court Justice Harry Blackmun expressed my personal feelings about the death penalty in an eloquent dissent penned in 1994: "From this day forward, I no longer tinker with the machinery of death. For more than 20 years I have endeavored . . . along with a majority of this court, to develop procedural and substantive rules that would lend more than the mere appearance of fairness to the death penalty endeavor. Rather than continue to coddle the Court's delusion that the desired level of fairness has been achieved . . . I feel morally and intellectually obligated simply to concede that the death penalty experiment has failed."

The death penalty is a perfect example of the passions and prejudices that govern rule making. The stated purpose of this law is to deter violent behavior and exact social retribution. The only strong argument for the death penalty is the moral one: the biblical logic of an eye for an eye, and there is no convincing argument for someone who truly believes it is just to take one life for another.

So rather than debate moral absolutes, let's examine the goals asserted by death penalty advocates. The first one is deterrence. The old adage "Guess he won't do that again" certainly applies to the recipient of that lethal injection. As for his death intimidating others who might act similarly, research shows otherwise. Study after study demonstrates that the death penalty has absolutely no deterrent effect on the criminal class. Murderous behavior is driven not by rational contemplation about consequences but by the passion or evil of the moment or the universal sense of invincibility. Interestingly, many murderers have admitted that if the idea of their execution had entered their minds, they might be more prone to kill witnesses rather than leave survivors to tell the tale.

If there is no deterrence value to the death penalty, we should ask if the punishment is applied fairly and equitably. The answer is a resounding no. Repeated studies demonstrate that poor minority defendants are most likely to face this ultimate punishment, usually with the services of a public defender or court-appointed attorney. The quality of death penalty trial counsel is often poor, and the money for a serious defense is almost nonexistent. I remember one attorney who frequently topped the list of "most appointed" by criminal judges in Dallas. His motto? "I may not be good, but I'm fast." Most defense attorneys realize the state is not going to waste the time and money to pursue a death penalty case that doesn't present a good opportunity for victory. District attorneys are still elected in this country and do not want to lose high-profile cases. Often there is a political element to the decision to pursue the death penalty; the story probably hit the papers in a big way or a notable victim was involved. A DA likely will offer a plea if the case appears difficult to prosecute, even if the facts of the case are horrifying or the defendant is brutally unsympathetic. In any case, the formidable powers of the state usually are rallied against an underpaid, often inexperienced defense lawyer who hasn't the time, resources, or experience to handle the trial. A more egregious and distressing example of the selective enforcement of the law can hardly be imagined.

If a defendant has even a minimal understanding of the proceedings and can "assist" with the defense (always liberally construed by the courts), then incompetence is out. We know that if this person has a cursory notion of right and wrong, then insanity is out. So what about the retarded?

What does this classification mean? Is it a particular IQ level? Must the condition exist since childhood? Consider the case of Ricky Ray Rector, the inmate whose execution tough-on-crime presidential candidate Bill Clinton left the campaign trail to oversee. He had been essentially lobotomized by a self-inflicted gunshot wound years before. Accustomed to saving his dessert until bedtime, he carefully set it aside after his last meal before heading for his death. As he made the last walk, he told the guard he would probably vote for Clinton in the fall election. How could this man have helped in his own defense? Although the prisoners on death row have been deemed sane, mental illness and retardation are rampant among this group, as they are throughout our prisons.

If this case evokes no sympathy, what about someone's actual innocence? The *Herrera* case decided by the Supreme Court in 1992 held that "innocence was not sufficient justification to stop an execution." Even the most conservative columnists are beginning to cringe at this idea. George Will, columnist for the *Washington Post,* concluded in 2001 that "many innocent people are in prison, and some innocent people have been executed." On January 31, 2000, Illinois governor George H. Ryan declared a moratorium on executions after one too many prisoners was released from death row for procedural irregularities or evidence of innocence.

Anthony Porter spent sixteen years on death row in Illinois before Northwestern University students uncovered evidence implicating another man in the murders for which he was found guilty. Once coming within two days of execution, Porter was freed in 1999, joining twelve others released in that state since 1987. Similar calls for a halt to the death penalty have occurred in other states, even on the federal level, but have thus far been denied. As Senator Patrick Leahy has said, "People of good conscience can and will disagree on the morality of the death penalty, [but] we should all be able to agree that a system that may sentence one innocent person to death for every seven it executes has no place in a civilized society."

Amazingly, many supporters of the death penalty point to the release of innocent people as evidence that the system works. They ignore the unique circumstances, even luck, that surround these reversals of fortune. A law class wants a special project and takes on a defendant's case. The students are not saddled with the regular practice of law while they toil long hours to retrace a case history, reinterview witnesses, and retest forensic evidence. They may wish to save a life, but they're also after class credit. What if another case, not Anthony Porter's, had caught the professor's eye? Porter would be dead by now. What about the many cases that have no forensic evidence to retest in our latest frenzy over DNA? We could retest every DNA sampling in which there were forensic questions and still not address the majority of death penalty convictions. Unfortunately for some defendants, there is no DNA left at a crime scene. In many older cases, collection procedures were less than ideal. The storage of such material over years has left much to be desired. Are we to assume that the percentage of innocent prisoners is less in such cases? On what basis?

The Innocence Protection Act of 2000 was introduced in Congress to address problems in the administration of the death penalty. Naively, legislators seem to think that improving representation will cure the many flaws in this punishment. It cannot cure the overzealous law enforcement community that may conceal exculpatory evidence or the discretionary application of this punishment against the poor and minority community. Certainly we can chart the percentages of blacks, whites, and Hispanics, but where does that leave us? Shall we have quotas for the needle? While we can and should increase the quality of defense counsel, that alone will not provide more funding to investigate and try these cases.

The growing numbers of panels and commissions convened to study the death penalty is testament to its failure as a means of achieving justice. More rules, more supervision, more universal application will not cure the flaws. I believe, as do many others, that the variables in criminal prosecutions are simply too great to eliminate the inequities surrounding this penalty. Furthermore, I do not believe the problem can be addressed by legislation. For those who believe we can, I say, Present your statute for debate. Until then the death penalty will be the ultimate example of selective enforcement sanctioned by our "justice" system.

While there are fifty-two federal crimes for which the death penalty applies, Timothy McVeigh was the first to be executed under one of them. Most federal convictions are in the more traditional categories. The sentencing, however, is anything but traditional. As in many state courts, mandatory punishments also bind federal judges. A very clever system of sentencing guidelines requires the court actually to plot a defendant's "criminal history category" along with the "offense level" on a graph. Point values are determined by giving a number to things like "level of involvement" (did the defendant lead five or more people: +4; manage five or more: +3; lead or manage fewer than five: +2).

The following paragraph, courtesy of *Fear of Judging* by Kate Smith and José A. Cabranes, comes from a U.S. Sentencing Commission staff memo circulated in 1995. It explains how to calculate the number of criminal history points to be assigned to a prior sentence of three years imposed on a defendant twenty years ago.

> First, it appears that Sec. 4A1.1(a) requires assignment of three points to the prior sentence because the sentence imposed exceeded one year and one month. However, Application Note 1 in the commentary to Sec. 4A1.1 contains some limitations on the application of this guideline, including the applicable time period in which convictions can be counted. According to this application note, this conviction would not be counted, unless the sentence was imposed within 15 years of the commencement of the instant offense or the term of imprisonment on the sentence extended into the 15 year time period. This requires a determination of the date of release from imprisonment to determine whether or not the sentence is counted. However, before a final determination can be made, Application Note 1 to Sec. 4A1.1 references eight additional places in Sec. 4A1.2 for further definitions and instructions that impact application.

Although the section goes on and on, I'll stop now. You get the point. This is ludicrous. Not only does the dreaded discretion reside with prosecutors and other law enforcement officials, these officials are the very individuals who provide the information that a judge uses to plot a sentence. They can manipulate the outcome through their characterization of the criminal history and offense.

Finally, studies have shown that the application of all these rules and laws and procedures still results in disparity of sentencing from district to district around the country. As Stith and Cabranes said, "The federal sentencing guidelines of today are based on a fear of judging; they attempt to repress the exercise of informed discretion by judges. Instead . . . the judge is supposed to perform an automaton's function by mechanically applying stark formulae set by a distant administrator." They then recited this dire prediction from a federal judge: "[The guidelines] tend to deaden the sense that a judge must treat each defendant as a unique human being. . . . It is quite possible that we judges will cease to aspire to the highest traditions of humanity and personal responsibility that characterize our office." Like every other use of human judgment, judicial discretion is now inherently suspect as a guise for inequality.

In the meantime, justice is accomplished by doing what is fair and right in a given circumstance, not what is identical in each category of cases. Our depiction of Lady Justice shows her with a sword in one hand and scales in the other. Her blindfold does not insure that everyone is treated the same. Instead, it insures that a meaningless distinction, like status or color, will not dictate the outcome. Every event, every crime is unique and should be analyzed and weighed individually. "Let the punishment fit the crime" means taking each perpetrator, injury, victim, and fact pattern into consideration when assessing the penalty. All of this, however, applies to the manner in which the lady wields her sword. She should still demand we be responsible for our conduct.

As a footnote here, let's not forget our more civilized white-collar crime. In the *Monthly Review,* George Winslow noted that as early as 1972, the U.S. Chamber of Commerce estimated that white-collar crimes cost the economy some $40 billion a year, about seven times what the FBI claimed was stolen by street criminals. Today global crime is a huge problem, but because money laundering benefits "legitimate" businesses, the government has essentially ignored it. Just ask Texas senator Phil Gramm. As head of the Senate Banking Committee, he did more than any other senator to prevent the regulation of offshore money laundering before September 11. Suddenly we found that terrorists are funneling cash in the same way, and the politicians have to take notice. We have yet to see what, if anything, they will do.

Tax fraud by multinational corporations and wealthy business elites bilks government agencies out of tens of billions of dollars in revenue. Bond fraud by major financial institutions significantly increases the costs local governments must pay to borrow money. If our officials were trying to help the American people, they would do something about this. I will get to political corruption shortly, but suffice it to say that corporate interests have suppressed the prosecution of white-collar crimes despite the fact that a single white-collar criminal can cost the nation billions and injure tens of thousands of people.

There is one category of crime, however, that displays all of my concerns about the criminal justice system in one neat package. Next to the Tax Code, the war on drugs has been the most abused exercise of legislative and legal authority in the country. For well over a decade, experts have been shouting that the drug war has failed. From Ralph Nader to William F. Buckley, both liberals and conservatives echo this conclusion, not because they want to legalize narcotics but because the cure has been far more damaging than the disease.

Let's selfishly start with our tax dollars. David Boaz of the Cato Institute offered these sobering numbers in a piece for *USA Today Magazine*: "Drug enforcement cost around twenty-two billion dollars in the Reagan years, another forty-five billion in the four years of the Bush Administration, and [ran] about sixteen billion a year in federal spending alone" during Clinton's tenure. He noted: "When drug use goes up, taxpayers are told the government needs more money so that it can redouble its efforts against a rising drug scourge. When drug use goes down, taxpayers are told that it would be a big mistake to curtail spending just when progress is being made. Good news or bad, spending levels are maintained or increased."

In a nutshell, despite the decades of domestic battling and the billions of tax dollars expended, illegal narcotics are everywhere. The quantity and purity of street drugs is at an all-time high, and the price remains low. In the mid-1990s the White House reported that "we have yet to substantially influence either the availability or purity of cocaine and heroin in the U.S." About that time William F. Buckley published his article "The Drug War Is Lost." He described our achievements as "a plague that consumes an estimated $75 billion per year of public money, exacts an estimated $70 billion a year from consumers, is responsible for nearly 50 percent of the million who are today in jail, occupies an estimated 50 percent of the trial time of our judiciary, and takes the time of 400,000 policemen." No one listened.

As noted earlier, the United States retains the ignoble distinction of housing more prisoners than any other country in the world, having doubled our residents since 1996. Sure enough, almost half of the inmates are serving time for nonviolent drug-related offenses despite admissions like the one from Clinton's drug czar, General Barry Mc-Caffery, who repeatedly stated, "We cannot incarcerate our way out of this problem." However, we can certainly exacerbate it. The social costs include a widening of the racial gulf, the destruction of countless families, and the weakening of certain civil rights. Cops have been given an impossible mission. The temptation of easy money has corrupted many in law enforcement, corrections, even the military. Our courts are overwhelmed, and prison building is one of the largest industries in the country.

In the face of obvious defeat, we get more laws that ratchet up arrests, punishment, and incarceration rates. Property forfeitures without conviction, perjured testimony in the courts, a war in Latin America: There has been no limit to the extent to which we have pressed a losing case.

In this blind pursuit, we have ignored the basic questions about any policy or law.

- What are the problems we seek to solve?
- What are the goals?
- Can they be achieved through legislation and laws? Who is protected and who is punished?
- What are the costs, and ultimately, who benefits?

Let's examine these questions and see how we fare.

From the outset, the stated goals of a drug-free society were unachievable. Throughout recorded history, man has used intoxicants to alter his condition. Some psychedelics and other mind-altering substances are still central to various religious practices, such as the use of peyote in certain Native American rituals. Laws will not eliminate this inherent behavior. They may influence choices, but rules alone do not alter the social and moral choices that people make. When asked why they do not take drugs, most people describe health concerns, moral scruples, or personal dislikes. Religion, peer pressure, and community attitudes influence these decisions. Rarely is law mentioned as a reason for abstinence. Furthermore, any good capitalist knows that with demand comes supply. Our porous borders and innovative citizenry will thwart interdiction efforts.

Finally, hundreds of thousands of people die every year from alcohol, tobacco, and prescription drug abuse. Less than 1 percent of this number will succumb to illegal drugs. The hypocritical distinction our government makes between one poison and another weakens its moral authority to enforce the law.

Since the 1860s, our government has used a variety of techniques to attack drug use. First came taxation, labeling, and reporting requirements, and then came control of the international opium supply. Despite a move in the 1880s to criminalize drug taking, only scattered laws were passed. It was not fear of crime that ultimately propelled legislation, it was political pressure on the part of religious and temperance groups. The first inroad was easy. The habits of "nasty" Chinese immigrants were targeted with a ban on the importation of opium in 1887.

The Pure Food and Drug Act of 1906 had a reasonable task. It simply required the labeling of any over-the-counter medicines that contained "habit-forming" drugs. During this period, the weary housewife still could purchase her cocaine-laced pick-me-ups in the local drugstores. By 1912 nearly every state and many municipalities had regulations controlling the distribution of certain drugs. This civil approach reduced addictions through education, not incarceration.

Then the politics seriously changed. In 1914 Congress passed the Harrison Act, making the possession of narcotics illegal. Suddenly the medical and social approach disappeared and users became criminals. One of the prime targets at the time was marijuana. Viewed as a "black" and "Hispanic" drug, it was easily banned.

With the advent of the beatniks in the 1950s, drugs became more evident in the white population. The climate was ripening for a severe drug crackdown. When the youth of America rebelled in the 1960s, the simplest explanation for this cultural upheaval was the use of illegal narcotics. Blind to any contrary theories or positions, our government pressed the law enforcement approach to this problem, and cost was no object.

The accompanying political fury led to irresponsible, even dangerous laws. New sentencing legislation filled our prisons. New York governor Nelson Rockefeller took the lead in 1973. Under his revisions, the penalty for possession of four ounces or more of a narcotic drug became fifteen years to life. That mandatory minimum sentence is higher than the minimum for rape and is equivalent to the sentence for murder, arson, and kidnapping. Under federal law, the minimum for a first-time offender convicted of possessing one gram of LSD or five grams of crack cocaine is five years without parole, yet there is no federal minimum for rape. From 1980 to 1989 the average sentence for federal drug offenders more than doubled. By 1993 drug sentences averaged eighty-four months. This sentencing increase occurred despite the fact that drug use in the regular population has been steady or declining since 1982 and the percentage of hard-core users remains static.

The war against marijuana is even worse. Both Richard Nixon and Jimmy Carter established blue-ribbon commissions to study this drug. Both groups issued the finding that pot was no more harmful than tobacco or alcohol. Given the political climate, such facts didn't matter, and the reports were buried. During an interview for my ABC drug special in 1996, former drug czar Bill Bennett acknowledged that marijuana is less harmful to adults than alcohol or tobacco. Realizing what he'd said, Bennett quickly recited the negative effects on children, such as short-term memory loss and lackadaisical behavior. Additionally he argued that higher THC levels in today's "new and improved" marijuana had increased its potency and thus its effects. Yet to use the term "addict" for pot smokers is ludicrous in all but the most extreme cases. Marijuana is not physically addictive, and psychological addiction is almost unheard of. Serious criminal conduct is rarely associated with the use of marijuana, and there has never been a death associated with smoking pot. Over 450,000 die each year courtesy of the government-subsidized tobacco industry, and countless individuals lose their lives to alcohol-related diseases, crimes, and accidents. However, the political power possessed by these industries insures that Congress will never criminalize these cash cows.

Throughout the war on drugs, our number-one rationale has been to protect "the children." We want to raise intelligent, productive members of society and fear that drug use will destroy that mission. Since the vast majority of baby boomers now running our businesses and government have experimented with narcotics, I'm not sure this concern is legitimate. Let's see: Clinton didn't inhale, but Al Gore, Newt Gingrich, Bill Bradley, and George Pataki did.

Modern teens are more knowledgeable and more capable of

acquiring narcotics than ever before. According to the 1996 National Household Survey on Drug Abuse, 44.9 percent kids had tried pot, 1.8 percent had tried heroin, 7.1 percent had tried cocaine, and 3.3 percent had tried crack (79.2 percent of the kids had tried alcohol and 63.5 percent had smoked cigarettes, and of the 10 million underage respondents who consumed alcohol in the previous month, 4.4 million admitted to having five or more drinks on the same occasion). Today estimates are that almost 15 million people use illegal drugs each year, about 7 percent of the population over age twelve. Of these "recreational" users, somewhere between 6 and 10 percent will move on to serious, chronic use.

This percentage is the *very same number* statisticians cited forty years ago. All the laws, harsh sentences, and undercover cops haven't changed the percentage of hard-core addicts in the country one iota. Depending on the definition of addiction (some agencies actually include anyone using a drug just once a month), this number has remained stable over forty years, ranging between 2 million and 4 million people. These are the individuals who consume the bulk of intoxicants and almost 100 percent of all heroin sold on the streets. The ever-increasing availability of "hard" drugs—cocaine, crack, and heroin—has not elevated these figures over time, nor has smoking marijuana by so many kids become a "gateway" to these narcotics. If increasing availability of "hard" drugs or marijuana as a "gateway" drug were true, the number of addicts in the country would have soared in the last three decades.

We have made a conscious decision to continue to criminalize marijuana despite the rejected gateway theory, the contrary medical evidence, and the lack of any correlation with serious crime. If we were to ignore purely political objections, legalization of marijuana seems the only sensible answer. Its use might increase initially, just as drinking surged after the lifting of Prohibition, but the Netherlands experiment challenges this notion. The legal consumption rate among its teens is actually lower than here at home where it is a crime. At a minimum, we should decriminalize the use of this drug immediately.

Currently Europe is continuing its downward scaling of marijuana offenses. According to a European Union (EU) report in 2001, many member states consider cannabis use as normal or mundane rather than deviant. For example, in Spain, Italy, and Portugal, there are no criminal sanctions for possessing any drugs for personal use. Law enforcement focuses on dealers and traffickers. Belgium followed suit by decriminalizing possession of marijuana for personal use. Luxembourg lets cannabis users off with a fine. In Denmark, Germany, and Austria, the law says that people caught for the first time with drugs should not be punished. In the Netherlands, the law prohibits possession of cannabis, yet tolerates it under certain circumstances (as in the cannabis cafés). The British government is currently considering reclassifying marijuana as a Class C, instead of the more serious Class B, drug. If this happens, people who possess cannabis for personal use would no longer be arrested.

If this occurred in the United States, hundreds of thousands of people currently jailed for marijuana use and small-time dealing could return to their lives as taxpaying citizens. We should permit the use of marijuana by doctors and researchers, as its medical benefits have been clearly established. The social benefits and savings in law enforcement costs would be tremendous. In fact, if marijuana were removed from the list of targets, the scope of this drug war would become manageable. We could focus on the small number of hardcore addicts and the serious crime resulting from the trade in heroin and cocaine.

Heroin is horribly addictive, but the pure pharmaceutical variety causes no long-term physical disease, like cancer or cirrhosis, when taken in small, regular doses. When an addict gets past the horrors of physical withdrawal, it is the psychological craving that remains. To avoid the agony of withdrawal, many users must spend most of their lucid hours chasing the drug or the money to buy it. Most addicts ultimately resort to criminal behavior. A few years back I interviewed several individuals participating in a British heroin maintenance program. They received enough heroin each day to avoid crashing but not enough to "get high." They didn't have to hit the streets or commit crimes to get their fix. They were going to school or working, and every one of them was planning for a drug-free future. The goal was complete withdrawal, but it was a gradual weaning that included rebuilding the life they'd abandoned because of their addiction.

According to an EU report on its drug problem, by 2000, the British National Health Service was providing over $20 million worth of heroin annually to at least one hundred licensed doctors for its maintenance experiment. Studies showed a 75 percent drop in the theft rate among addicts in this program. The Netherlands and Switzerland also are prescribing heroin and have seen a drop in crime.

History and literature are replete with cocaine addicts, from Sigmund Freud to Sherlock Holmes. Recently various pipes were discovered from 17th-century England. Testing revealed the residue of both marijuana and cocaine. Although we have yet to discover the reason, some frequent users do not seem to become addicted. In that 1995 Federal Household Drug Survey, only 3 percent of those who had tried cocaine were using it as often as once a week. However, consistent use of this drug and its hellish offspring, crack, is devastating to the body and mind. The tremendous physical and psychological strain of the rush and crash eventually will ravage the habitual user. The additional immediacy of crack with its quick highs and lows stimulate both a violent pattern of behavior and a constant search for the next fix.

But truthfully, the vast majority of dangerous drugs that are abused are available by prescription. As with tobacco and alcohol, the pharmaceutical industry and medical profession would just as soon avoid this discussion. According to the American Medical Association (AMA), about 6 percent of the nation's doctors, dentists, and pharmacists make a nice living by dishonestly or negligently prescribing medication. However, selective enforcement sends only a few dozen of these culprits to court each year. If prosecuted, they usually receive probation, and about three in four keep their licenses. The case of California doctor Eric C. Tucker is a good example. State narcotics officers got wind of his entrepreneurial sideline, began scrutinizing his prescriptions, and finally arrested him in 1991. They found that more Dilaudid (an opiate derivative known as drugstore heroin) was coming out of his office than out of County USC Medical Center, the West Coast's largest public hospital. One prescribed pill costs about two dollars while on the street it brings fifty times that amount. After dispensing hundreds of thousands, if not millions, of tablets, Tucker pleaded guilty to two counts of prescription fraud and (thank God) lost his medical license. He was sentenced to eight days in jail.

Hundreds of millions of prescription pills flood the black market annually, producing fortunes for dealers, but this abuse receives little attention. Special agent Walter Allen III of the California State Bureau of Narcotics Enforcement explained the lack of criminal enforcement. "There's just no glory in it . . . no guns, no piles of coke and no bundles of cash to stack up for the TV cameras."

So given the selective targeting of drugs like heroin and cocaine, how are we doing in the fight? One day headlines proclaim victory,

"Cocaine use slows," only to be overshadowed by the next day's announcement, "Heroin use surges." This seeming success followed by subsequent failure is actually quite predictable. Since 1885 cocaine then opiate waves have consistently succeeded one another. As Herb Kleber, the head of the National Center on Addiction and Substance Abuse (CASA), noted, "All drug cycles carry the seed of their own destruction." Heroin use surges slowly until many addicts burn out, kick the habit, or die. A shorter cycle of stimulant use, methamphetamine and cocaine, then begins. This is a rougher ride and crashes more quickly, and then the cycle begins again.

Additionally, drug entrepreneurs are quite innovative, keeping our legislators and enforcement agencies on their toes. The 1960s gave us LSD and other hallucinogens. In the 1980s it was crack. We are currently panicking over the designer drug Ecstacy, a drug Merck patented in 1914. Like other stimulants, Ecstacy works by flooding the brain with serotonin. Its prohibition has, predictably, spurred popularity. Ecstacy is pouring into the country, and the drug is readily available in nightclubs, at rave parties, and on the street.

A National Drug Use Forecasting study in the mid-1990s found that about 72 percent of men and 64 percent of women had drugs in their system at the time of arrest. Today this number exceeds 80 percent. If our drug policies are having an effect, why is this number going up? Drug czar McCaffrey knew where his bread was buttered and continued to advocate tougher penalties and more prisons. In his last days in office, the general finally told the truth when he said, "Science is teaching us this is a medical illness." At last—and too late.

By the way, a Newswire report in April 2002 said that twenty-three states, five cities, and Washington, D.C., have detected an increased demand for alcohol and drug treatment since September 11, according to a new survey conducted by CASA. "The rubble may be almost cleared away, but the lingering effects of September 11 and its aftermath are far from over," said Joseph A. Califano, Jr., CASA president and former U.S. Secretary of Health, Education, and Welfare. "It is imperative to provide treatment for individuals who have turned to alcohol and drugs to cope or have relapsed from sobriety, so that they do not become the second wave of victims of our national tragedy."

Interestingly, the report said that areas farther away from New York stated different reasons for the increased abuse. For example:

"Arizona attributed its increase to the passage of Proposition 204 in October, which enlarged the population eligible for state health services, including substance abuse treatment, Hawaii cited a drop in tourism after September 11 and concern about the job market as reasons for the increase and Houston attributed its greater need for substance abuse treatment to the fall of Enron and the slump in the airline industry." No matter. Given that these people seem to represent a different class of abusers, I would suggest that social standing is at least part of the reason for Califano's national plea. "The double whammy of the terrorist attacks and difficult economic conditions makes it essential for the federal government to provide increased funding for drug and alcohol treatment," he said. "Congress and the Administration must pay as much attention to providing individuals with the services to rebuild their lives as they are to providing resources to rebuild physical facilities." Why don't we hear this more often?

After the effect of drugs on our children, we worry most about drug-related crime. As a pragmatist, I want the biggest bang for my buck. We are wasting limited resources by targeting the wrong crimes and the wrong people. Most drug users commit property offenses, such as theft or burglary. Narcotics capitalists commit most of the vicious drug-related crimes, including the homicides. Robert Silbering, former chief narcotics prosecutor in New York City, confirms this: "People have a misconception that drug users use guns to support habits, but it's usually the dealers who have the guns." The dealers stay relatively sober, the better to prey on children and take accurate aim at those who would threaten their enterprise. Users are more likely to be slumped in a stupor somewhere. When roused, they might write bad checks or steal your stuff, but most of the violence comes from entrepreneurs.

The dealers make the money and create the addicts, who then fill our jails at the taxpayers' expense. Do the big guys worry when some politician ups the ante for trading in the black market? A momentary lag in supply simply *increases* their profits. If you take one dealer out, another will replace him. In fact, many lieutenants snitch on their leaders to create an opening for advancement. Police Chief Nick Pastore in New Haven, Connecticut, once told me: "If this country ever considered legalizing the drug trade, the first group to lobby in opposition would be the dealers." Our policies insure their continued profits.

To build prisons, our human warehouses, we are diverting precious resources from other needs. California is currently spending more to house its criminals than teach college students, and its corrections lobby is one of the most powerful in the state. Prison construction has become one of the major growth industries in the country. Makes you proud, doesn't it?

Whom are we locking up? Nearly three-quarters of those sentenced under our mandatory drug laws have committed nonviolent offenses, like larceny or small-time drug dealing. Over one-third of the federal drug convicts have no prior criminal record. These inmates are not likely to be the big-time dealers we should target.

Where are all the traffickers? The big cheese usually can rat out friends, get a reduced sentence, and be out in no time. If you do happen to get seriously snagged but have good connections and make the right contributions, you can even get a pardon. Just ask Carlos Vignali, busted for operating a huge cocaine distribution ring. His wealthy father started spreading cash to various politicians as soon as Carlos was imprisoned. Hillary Clinton's brother, Hugh Rodham, was hired at considerable expense to pursue a pardon in the final days of the Clinton administration. Sure enough, Vignali received his reprieve. Officials in Colombia were outraged. After all the finger-pointing at the Colombian drug trade, we're letting big dealers and money launderers off with presidential pardons?

Of course, if you are rich or famous, that doesn't hurt either. It seems your punishment will match your wallet and your publicist's Rolodex. Talk to Darryl Strawberry. It took over ten years of arrests before Strawberry received his first drug conviction. In February of 1999 the star hitter tested positive for cocaine while on probation for the same drug. His probation officer recommended the following: "an enhancement of his after-care program with urine testing, weekly therapy sessions and continuing AA and narcotics anonymous meetings." There was no mention of jail time.

In September of 2000 Strawberry was arrested for blacking out while driving, running through a stop sign, and rear-ending another car. He later admitted ingesting sleeping pills and painkillers before getting behind the wheel. Then on October 25, 2000, he slipped away from his treatment house, smoked a bit of crack, and downed some Xanax. The recommendation was thirty days in jail, then back to the private clinic to complete his two-year probation. In March 2002

Strawberry was charged again with probation violation. Imagine the reaction if his name was Joe Smith and he never pinch-hit for the Yankees in a World Series. Ol' Joe would have been locked away for years a long time ago. For Strawberry, the debate was never about prison; it was always about his future in baseball. Just before the most recent conviction, George Steinbrenner, the owner of the Yankees, had hired him to counsel young ballplayers about the dangers of drugs and other temptations!

How can we show so much compassion for a millionaire ballplayer accused of domestic violence, smashing cars, and soliciting hookers while doing lots of dope, then lock away others who have done far less? The answer is easy. Money and influence buys probation and therapy for whatever ails you. If you're lacking in these, bring your toothbrush and plan on a long stay behind bars.

If you're at the bottom of the food chain and don't have names to flip to the DA, forget it. Check out the number of women doing long stints for helping their pusher boyfriends or simply trying to feed their kids. Either through loyalty or ignorance, they can't or won't deliver helpful information, so they serve decades while the big boys (and their boyfriends) are out in a matter of months. Two years ago actor and activist Charles Grodin publicized four cases involving New York women sentenced under the draconian Rockefeller drug laws. These women, all mothers, had each served more than ten years for transporting small amounts of drugs in exchange for much-needed cash.

One of these women, Angela Thompson, was arrested in 1988, at age seventeen, for selling two ounces of cocaine to an undercover officer. She was following orders from her drug-dealing uncle, her legal guardian at the time. With no criminal record, she received the mandatory minimum sentence of fifteen years to life in prison. Shortly after her incarceration, Thompson gave birth to a son who was placed with her sisters. In reviewing this case, former State Supreme Court justice Jerome Marks said, "This is one of the great injustices that I've run across. I was a judge for twenty-two years and I never had a case where a youngster seventeen years of age, with no criminal background at all, ends up doing fifteen years to life."

Judge Marks had no choice with her sentence. The legislature had decided judicial discretion was bad. Why rely on those who handled these cases every day? Our politicians, in all their wisdom, could set penalties for us. Marks was so outraged, he actually filed the first clemency petition for Thompson in 1996. It was rejected. The second effort succeeded, and she was released in January 1998.

The female population in our prisons and jails has increased 600 percent in the last twenty years, faster than the rate of men entering the system. By the end of 1995, 828,100 women were under some form of correctional supervision, including probation and parole, with over 130,000 actually behind bars. By 1999 Amnesty International reported that over one-third of the U.S. female inmates were imprisoned solely for drug possession. That's possession, not trafficking.

Seventy-five percent of these women have children, and of those, two-thirds have children under age eighteen. Studies show that when men go to prison, their family support system remains steadfast. When the women are locked up, boyfriends and husbands disappear. So what happens to all those children? If the kids are lucky, a grandmother is around to pick up the slack. All too often they are sent to foster care. Families are destroyed and taxpayers are tapped not only to warehouse these women but to care for their kids. Today foster care in New York can cost up to $20,000 per child per year. Add in the annual prison expense, and one small-time drug bust will cost about $40,000 per year for just one mother and child in "the system." You do the math.

But of course we're helping these women along with all the men, right? The answer is no. Training in woodworking, auto repair, or telephone solicitation doesn't insure much long-term opportunity upon release. Higher education, the most powerful weapon against recidivism, is almost nonexistent. Again, not wanting to appear soft, our politicians have eliminated the Pell Grants that once funded college courses for inmates.

Most convicts leave prison with nothing more than a few dollars and a bus ticket. We expect these people to leave the best crime schools in the country with virtually no useful training, education, rehabilitation, or transitional help and become productive, law-abiding citizens. And who is waiting for them? Drug dealers, pimps, and other criminals often greet new parolees at the bus station to recruit them or abscond with their pocket money. Invariably parolees return home with absolutely nothing to discourage further criminal behavior. In fact, some might argue we have practically insured they will resort to the same behavior that sent them away in the first place. For many, the return to prison is a relief.

In Ted Koppel's 1999 report "Women in Prison," he followed the progress of a paroled addict, Denise Jones. She quickly applied for welfare and began receiving $474 a month. Going home was not an option as drugs were an ongoing problem for other family members. She signed up for Section 8 housing and applied for jobs but received no offers. Soon she failed her mandatory drug testing and was sent back to prison. Her comments were not surprising. "I don't like to say it, but when I was in prison, I didn't have anything to worry about . . . 'cause I know how to do time. Then when you are out there everything is on you, everything, a lot of pressure . . . sometimes I just feel like giving up . . . I really mean it."

Koppel ended his program with an admonition. "Fixing a problem early on can be expensive; dealing with it later on can be exorbitant. Drug rehab programs can be expensive. Serious vocational training programs can be expensive. But the constant recycling of tens of thousands of American women through our prison system is exorbitant; and it is getting worse."

Sadly, we know what works, we just aren't doing it. With some 2 million Americans behind bars and up to 80 percent of this number abusing drugs and alcohol, rehabilitation programs can decrease addiction, crime, and the spiraling costs of incarceration. Yet only about one in six inmates receives any kind of treatment, usually consisting of cold-turkey withdrawal and the admonition to "Just say no." This is not very effective, since any corrections officer will tell you that if you want drugs in prison, they are available. Creative smuggling is rampant, as is corruption within the corrections ranks. Only a fraction of our inmates—about 2 percent—undergoes any serious rehabilitation, yet the best programs cut the rearrest rate and save money. Thus far our national leaders just say no, instead giving most of our tax dollars to the politically powerful prison industry for bricks and mortar, not programs.

So why don't we treat addicts while they're a captive audience? For starters, drug treatment is initially more expensive, adding $10 to $20 a day per prisoner. This makes it a tougher political sell. What the officials don't tell you is what therapeutic drug experts like Dr. Lewis Yablonsky calculate: "With real treatment, we could cut our prison population in half over the next 25 years . . . and save billions of dollars." Continued therapy, as a condition of parole, would increase savings and further cut the rearrest rate by up to 20 percent. But thus far these programs are very rare.

Let's get selfish about this. Depending on the state you live in and the quality of the prison facility, it costs somewhere between $20,000 and $50,000 a year to incarcerate an offender. The cost to build a prison cell is upward of $90,000. On the other hand, the relatively new drug courts that divert new offenders to rehabilitation averages less than $2,000 annually per person for treatment.

A RAND Corporation study estimated that for a 1 percent reduction in annual cocaine consumption, we would need to spend (in 1994 dollars) about $783 million more in the source countries (Colombia or Peru), $366 million more for interdiction (stopping drugs at the border), and $246 million more for domestic enforcement, plus the added cost of incarceration—or we could spend $34 million for treatment. More simply, treatment was found to be about seven times more cost-effective than law enforcement, ten times more cost-effective than interdiction, and about twenty-three times more cost-effective than source control. It's your money. You choose.

Here are the facts. The legal distinctions between various intoxicants are not supported by the harm created, the addictive character, or the destructive behavior resulting from use. Our laws have had little effect on the consumption of narcotics. Punishment alone will not deter use. Children continue to experiment with drugs, predominately marijuana, despite the mantra to "Just say no." Virtually the same percentage of the population becomes addicted to narcotics today as in the 1960s. Science has concluded quite rightly that drug addiction is a medical, not a criminal, problem. Obviously, the goal of a drug-free society is impossible.

The application of criminal law to this problem has been terribly destructive. The penalties for use fall disproportionately on the small-time user and dealer, often in minority communities, rather than the serious traffickers or predominately white users. The imprisonment of nonviolent users has cost billions of dollars and destroyed countless families. Law enforcement has been diverted to this task to the detriment of public safety and our constitutional rights. The corrupting influence on police, corrections officers, and the court system has been substantial. Finally, interdiction to stem supply has proven a costly and utter failure, negatively affecting international relations particularly with our neighbors to the south.

As to who benefits, the answers are easy. Politicians have had a hobbyhorse to ride in every election, diverting attention from problems they would rather not address. Expenditures for our burgeoning drug war industry have kept prison contractors and corrections lobby-ists ecstatic. The growing economic importance of this prison-industrial complex has proven profitable for other industries. Major defense contractors supply police departments with high-tech weapons and surveillance equipment. Wall Street firms collect lucrative fees for issuing bonds for new prisons, and wealthy investors collect tax-free in-terest on the bonds, which can triple the cost of building a $90,000 cell. Phone companies and health maintenance organizations aggressively bid on lucrative contracts to provide inmates and prisons with services. Private companies that run prisons will soon have more than $1 billion in revenues a year.

Law enforcement provides employment for 1.7 million people, and many soldiers work on the Pentagon's $1 billion-a-year war against drugs. In the private sector, there are countless securities guards, and about 100,000 people find employment in the $124 billion-a-year re-lated legal services industry. Not surprisingly, this prison-industrial com-plex, now a powerful voting block of several million voters, staunchly supports law-and-order politicians.

The federal government has had an excuse to tighten control over state activities by effectively nationalizing drug laws and police action in the country. Constitutional rights have been willingly abridged, and, for the conspiratorially inclined, a race war has been maintained. Finally, the military has an ongoing justification for injecting U.S. forces into the internal affairs of other countries.

Law professor Steven Duke reviewed our accomplishments in a brilliant piece in *National Review*. He said of the drug war, "If the pur-pose is to make criminals out of one in three African-American males, it has succeeded. If its purpose is to create one of the highest crime rates in the world—and thus to provide permanent fodder for dema-gogues who decry crime and promise to do something about it—it is achieving that end. If its purpose is de facto repeal of the Bill of Rights, victory is in sight. If its purpose is to transfer individual free-dom to the central government, it is carrying that off as well as any of our real wars did. If its purpose is to destroy our inner cities by mak-ing them war zones, triumph is near."

Despite the irrefutable evidence, President George W. Bush is fol-lowing his predecessors' worthless playbook. His drug czar, John Wal-ters, had served in Bush Sr.'s administration and remains a steadfast law enforcement and punishment advocate. In fact, in May 2002 Walters told the *Wall Street Journal* that the five-year, $929 million anti-drug media campaign has been a failure. The ads may have actually tempted some kids to try marijuana. Nevertheless, Walters wants the next $180 million installment so he can direct his own new and improved commercials. Duke rightly suggests that to continue on this path with full knowledge of the consequences is to effectively make such damning results part of the policy.

In 1967 the bipartisan Crime Commission reported that it "has no doubt whatever that the most significant action that can be taken against crime is action designed to eliminate slums and ghettos, to improve education, to provide jobs, to make sure that every American is given the opportunities and freedoms that will enable him to assume his responsibilities." Much like "eat less and exercise" to lose weight, we ignore such obvious remedies in favor of the self-serving arguments of politicians and enforcement industries. Only by acknowledging the enormous economic and social expense of the current approach and recognizing the ultimate savings in money and social capital will we rise up and support alternative methods of addressing our criminal justice problems.

EIGHT | The Toxic Politics of Money

How did we reach the point where laws and rules govern our every move? Worse yet, how did we create a society where politicians, lawyers, and bureaucrats are running the show? The bad news is things are getting worse. The good news: It has happened relatively quickly and still can be reversed.

While there is plenty to say about excessive litigation or legislating from the bench, it is not in the courtroom but in the halls of Congress where the primary and most insidious corruption of our system of laws has occurred. If you were to remove all campaign finance abuses from the political system, elected officials still would have the authority to make and manipulate laws. This power can foster tyranny in the noblest legislator. Attorneys have always dominated elected positions, but they merely share responsibility with other officials for the power grab that has transformed America in barely eighty years.

Until the twentieth century, the federal government was primarily concerned with military affairs. If our borders were secure, the interior workings were left to the states. Thomas Jefferson believed that "the state is a source of corrupt power and ultimate tyranny" and must be guided and controlled by an active citizenry. Although the founders realized that national security was by necessity a federal function, the Second Amendment permits, at the very least, state militias. Domestically, however, Jefferson and his associates deemed that most governing should occur and be paid for at the state and local levels.

This intention was made clear in Article I, Section 8, of the U.S. Constitution. That provision, known as the "General Welfare" clause, reads in part: "Congress shall have the power to lay and collect taxes, to pay the debts and provide for the common defense and promote the general welfare of the U.S." This article strictly limits the power of the federal government and was honored as doing so for well over a century.

The first appropriations bill passed by Congress consisted of 111 words—not pages. The military and debt retirement from the Revolutionary War were the main expenditures. Requests for charitable spending were rejected. As James Madison said in 1794, "I cannot undertake to lay my finger on that article of the Constitution which granted a right to Congress of expending on objects of benevolence, the money of their constituents."

Members of Congress tried to challenge this philosophy, so in 1798 Thomas Jefferson reiterated the extent of national authority. "Congress has *not* unlimited power to provide for the General Welfare, but *only* those specifically enumerated." He penned those words to remove all doubt as to Congress's limitations. That his meaning was clear was still evident thirty years later, when Senator William Drayton of South Carolina said, "If Congress can determine what constitutes the General Welfare and can appropriate money for its advancement, where is the limitation by carrying into execution whatever can be affected by money?" He realized that once the government was turned loose, free to use our money to woo and win favor, there would be no stopping it.

In 1913 Congress manufactured the key to unlock its own power. After it had struggled with the issue of a federal income tax since the Civil War, it enacted the Sixteenth Amendment to conclude the debate and create a new source of national revenue. Until then Congress's power to spend was limited by its restricted power to tax. In 1912 the government derived 45 percent of its revenue from duties on imported goods and 42 percent from taxes on tobacco and alcohol. By 1921 these sources accounted for only 17 percent of government monies; the rest came from the income tax and other new assessments on rich individuals and corporations. Once our representatives opened this vault, a new activist philosophy emerged. In 1931 Representative John O'Connor of New York expressed the change when he said, "I am going to give the Constitution the flexibility as will enable me to vote for my measure anything I dream of value to the flesh and blood of my day."

The Great Depression absolutely devastated this country. No one doubted the need for emergency action and extraordinary expenditures to try to stem the economic ruin. By necessity, President Franklin

D. Roosevelt expanded federal control to attempt a national rescue but grabbed far more power than he needed. The Supreme Court was an unwilling partner, ruling in *United States v. Butler* (1936) that "the power of Congress to authorize appropriations of public money for public purposes is not limited by the grants of legislative powers found in the Constitution." This had been Alexander Hamilton's interpretation, the notion that Congress had the power to tax and spend, provided only that the "General Welfare" was served (whatever Congress deemed that to be), although Thomas Jefferson had soundly rejected that concept. With this ruling, our legislature could apparently appropriate money at will and pacify or accommodate whomever it pleased.

The Supreme Court was under tremendous pressure from the president as FDR alternately threatened to ignore its rulings and spark a constitutional crisis or pack the Court with his appointees through a Judicial Reorganization Plan. He even talked about a constitutional amendment to reduce judicial authority and strengthen the national government. He told his advisor Harold Ickes at one point that if any more New Deal legislation was ruled unconstitutional, he'd ask Congress whether he was to "follow [its] mandate or the mandate of the Court." With legislative support, he would then "carry out the will of Congress through the offices of the U.S. Marshals and ignore the Court."

The political pressure brought to bear on the justices proved sufficient, and soon previously rejected legislation was passing their review. These rulings gave credibility to this executive and legislative power grab, but it was achieved through political blackmail. FDR succeeded in overthrowing constitutional restrictions on the national government—a revolution of sorts—with barely a skirmish. Nevertheless, popular opinion was on his side. The country needed things to be accomplished, and our willingness to suspend founding principles was clear. Unfortunately, the expedient became entrenched, and the federal government garnered the means to extend its powers far beyond the founders' intentions. Whether another Court will someday restore the balance is unlikely.

So, by the 1930s, Congress had the laws and the funds to usurp authority from the very people this country intended to empower. The seeds were sown for a divisive political system wherein the giving of largess and the manipulation of rules would insure national control over the freedom and will of the people. Pork-barrel politics became the real law of the land, and we have been paying for it ever since. Even more than the wasted tax dollars, it is the enormous social cost that is draining our country, as a seemingly infinite number of special interests now squabble over federal favors. Of course there are the corporate and labor interests, but citizens are caught up as well as seniors, children, minorities, the disabled, and more, all fighting for a piece of the pie.

As Congress expanded its influence into every cranny of our lives, it discovered the real power of laws, rights, and entitlements. The dispensing of legal benefits or exemptions (or the threat of losing them) is much more persuasive to an interest group than a mere appropriation of money. It is also far more insidious and harder to expose. The misuse of the law as a means of delivering political favors now surpasses the cascade of campaign cash as the most corrosive influence on Capitol Hill. (The two are, of course, intimately connected.)

We have reached the point that almost no federal action is deemed improper. A few years ago Supreme Court Justice Anthony Scalia asked Clinton's solicitor general, Seth Waxman, to name a single activity or program that the modern-day Congress might contemplate that would fall outside the bounds of the Constitution. Waxman had no answer. As our tax dollars subsidize everything from social research and sugar sales, to overseas advertising by McDonald's and federally funded self-esteem training, spending is rarely challenged as overreaching.

Liberal politicians have long supported the expansion of federal authority. Let the national government do it, they believe, as if officials inside the Beltway are immune from petty, bigoted squabbling that often typifies the state houses. How times have changed. During our country's earliest days, the great debate between Thomas Jefferson and Alexander Hamilton went far beyond congressional powers. The former believed in a true democracy (some might call it liberalism), versus the more aristocratic, conservative bent of the latter. Guess who wanted the states to retain dominance? As Joseph Ellis writes in his extraordinary biography of Jefferson, *American Sphinx,* "It was the people against the elites, the West against the East, agrarians against Industrialists, Democrats against Republicans . . . the voice of the 'many' holding forth against the 'few.' "

The New Deal administration completely reversed this position.

Roosevelt and his Supreme Court corrupted the General Welfare clause and allowed the federal government to intervene at will, all the while invoking Jefferson's name as the "apostle of freedom." Ellis describes this appropriation as "one of the most inspired acts of political thievery in American history, since the growth of federal power during the New Deal represented the triumph . . . of consolidation over diffusion. The New Deal was in fact the death knell for Jefferson's idea of a minimalist government."

Today the Republicans, the so-called elitists, are calling for state's rights and a more limited federal government. Unfortunately, their disingenuousness is laid bare when you examine the areas in which they are perfectly willing to ladle out largesse to win friends. The GOP will increase rules and loopholes permitting business subsidies, tax write-offs, and exemptions for their favored supporters. They stymied efforts to regulate offshore banks or prosecute white-collar money-laundering operations. As noted earlier, it will be interesting to see how they respond to the call for financial controls to help stop terrorist networks. In the end, Republicans are not attempting to deregulate our lives. They merely assemble a different litany of regulations and preferences for "their side," just as the Democrats do when they're in control.

While pundits and citizens still argue about philosophical differences between the major parties, divergence occurs mainly in their social agendas. The Democrats increase discrimination or disability enforcement, while Republicans create the Marriage Protection Act or put gag rules on abortion doctors and limitations on the distribution of contraceptives. We are distracted by their public arguments over domestic spending as each side promises goodies or threatens cuts that affect individuals and families. Class warfare is a tremendous smoke screen for the real beneficiaries of congressional affections.

What is rarely discussed is the parties' shared agenda. Behind the platitudes and winning smiles, both sides are catering to the single group that keeps incumbents in power: corporate America. As Ralph Nader reminded us in 2000, the only difference between presidential candidates Gore and Bush was the relative velocity "with which their knees hit the floor when the big corporations knocked on the door." The real two parties in this country are simply "the serious contributors" and "the rest of us." Only about 10 percent of citizens actually put any money into our political elections. The real dough comes from the top 10 percent of the top 10 percent! In one night alone, dueling fund-raisers in Washington, D.C., raised $40 million for the two major parties during the last election. This amount did not come from Mom and Pop writing $25 checks.

Looking at contributions of both hard and soft money, we see amazing parallels. The very same corporations sponsor the national conventions to the tune of millions of dollars. They wisely hedge their bets by contributing heavily to both sides in each election year. Leading up to the presidential primaries in 2000, a *Business Week* article looked at where support was shaping up. Of the 389 top CEOs who had contributed thus far, seventy-seven of them donated to multiple candidates. Fifty-two picked contenders in both parties. Ellen S. Miller, executive director of Clean Campaign, offers this explanation. "This illustrates the investment theory of politics. These donors think 'no matter who wins, we'll have our hand in his pocket.' "

The Center for Responsive Politics has concluded that every major industrial sector except for communications/electronics now favors the Republican Party. Yet every sector gives to the Democrats as well. For example, agribusiness donated $69 million to Democrats from 1990 to 2000, and energy/natural resources gave them $64 million during the same period. This is not chump change.

The distribution of monies is always linked to the party currently controlling Congress. Giving also waxes and wanes with the particular legislation on the table. Industries always step up the contributions when their interests are immediately at stake. Check out the agribusiness contributions before the vote on the 2002 farm bill or look back at the communications money that poured in during the two years leading up to the 1996 Telecommunications Act.

Through enormous subsidies, tax breaks, and government contracts, the two major parties please these patrons while expanding the federal apparatus and controlling our taxpayer dollars. The fight they stage for the general public is meant primarily to pacify and distract us.

There is ample proof for this charge. Before 1900 most federal dollars went to military needs. Throughout the twentieth century, social engineering took the lead, retaining the military theme through labels like the "war on poverty," the "war on crime," the "war on inflation," and the never-ending "war on drugs." Today we have a new fight, "global economic warfare." Our democratic principles are regularly sacrificed in the name of global superiority of American business, not American ideals.

Anyone who followed the Chinagate scandal during the Clinton years knows this statement is true. Let's examine the factors that contributed to this outrage. Robert Mosbacher, Commerce secretary during the senior President Bush's administration, labeled the Commerce Department as "nothing more than a hall closet where you throw everything you don't know what to do with." His successor in the Clinton administration knew better. Ron Brown was a specialist when it came to fund-raising. He took an agency on the verge of extinction and turned it into an amazing money machine for the Democrats.

Bill Clinton immediately implemented Brown's great idea to retail access to the expanded Department of Commerce. Sales of sensitive equipment have occurred off and on for years through agency and presidential waivers. What Bill Clinton achieved was a grander shift of power. He transferred approval of these technology sales from the Pentagon, Defense, and State departments to the Commerce secretary. In today's world, where high-tech decisions carry enormous economic consequences, imagine the corporate frustration at the roadblocks established by our security agencies. Companies argued that if they couldn't sell sensitive technologies to the world, someone else would. True enough, but trade agreements between Europe and the United States during this time restricted certain high-technology and military sales to questionable or dangerous markets. Until the United States blatantly violated these agreements, only cheaters were profiting. Maybe those nations were a bunch of rogues, but so what? At least we were not complicit in selling out our own national security interests.

But as the biggest kid on the block, we make the rules, or at least our companies do. Businesses pay and the rules bend and break. In 1992 Bernie Schwartz of Loral gave only $12,500 to Clinton's election campaign. Then he allegedly decided that Chinese rockets were cheaper vehicles for his satellite launches. However, when one of those rockets exploded with a Loral satellite aboard, Loral decided the Chinese needed a little help. The restricted technology that China needed had what is known as dual-use capabilities. While an invoice may reflect the intent to use items for benign civilian purposes, the hardware is easily converted to more malevolent uses.

Schwartz did not give up on his plan to launch in China. By 1996 he and Loral were the number-one soft-money contributor to the Democrats. The siren call of these campaign contributions was simply too great. The Pentagon and Defense departments took a backseat, and Schwartz got his waiver to export the technology.

The Chinagate issue that proved the rallying cry for conservatives was the sellout to foreigners—Chinese communists no less. All that finger-pointing worked to keep the focus away from the real culprits, corporate America and their friends in high office. While about $1 million in contributions may have come in from China, hundreds of millions more filtered in "legally" from American businesses. Our corporations wanted this expansion at least as much as the Chinese and were willing to pay for those lax restrictions and weak oversight.

In 1998 the criminal division of the Justice Department cautioned that another Loral waiver to launch in China might hurt the ongoing investigation. Nevertheless, the president approved the deal, saying later "I can assure you it was handled in the routine course of business." Yet in January 2002 Loral announced it would pay the federal government $14 million as a civil fine to end the Justice Department investigation into whether it had acted illegally in 1996. The Pentagon's report ultimately found that sensitive technology involving missiles was transferred to the Chinese. While denying that this actually helped the Chinese military, CEO Bernard Schwartz said, "Loral accepts full responsibility for the matter and expresses regret for its failure to obtain appropriate State Department approval."

Now fast forward to the fall of 2001 and the collapse of mighty Enron. This is the most outrageous example yet of corporate America's ability to manipulate Capitol Hill for profit. It is fascinating to listen to politicians and pundits on both sides of the aisle cover for Washington's malfeasance. This is just a financial scandal, they say. There were no payoffs, no bribes. Where are the legislative fingerprints of Kenneth Lay or Andrew Fastow?

The pundits say this despite knowing that it is practically impossible to prove an illegality no matter how much it stinks. As Clinton legal advisor Lanny Davis wrote in his book *To Tell the Truth,* there is always some plausible public rationale for the passage of any law. Anything can be justified so that the exchange of money and influence for political results becomes mere coincidence. Davis wrote about a private discussion among White House staffers during the Chinagate scandals. Some people were worried about the apparent improprieties being exposed. Others just laughed. They knew no hard proof would be forthcoming. No one hands cash under the table anymore—well, almost no one. Such crass behavior is no longer necessary. There are too many PACs, special interest groups, and soft-money outlets that can filter illegal contributions.

As a lawyer, I'd like to offer at least a circumstantial case documenting Enron's serious influence in our nation's capital. The facts that Enron was George W. Bush's largest contributor in the 2000 election and its CEO a longtime friend and supporter don't necessarily prove anything. That President Bush, as Texas governor and then from the White House, vigorously supported the energy deregulation effort that made this company a global player is not stand-alone evidence of corruption. Vice President Dick Cheney relied on Enron executives to help formulate our nation's energy policy, even meeting privately with these people. While this presents an ethical question, Cheney argued that it does not violate the Federal Advisory Committee Act, which requires open meetings and public records. Ah, the old it-may-look-bad-but-it's-legal defense! (Cheney's stonewalling of the General Accounting Office about these meetings has not helped his case.)

Our secretary of the army, Thomas White, came from Enron with millions of dollars in the company's stock options. It must have been coincidence that he exchanged many phone calls with its executives during the meltdown. Trade Representative Robert Zoellick was another Enron draftee now on the president's team. The company says its calls last fall to various cabinet members never included a word about its troubles. Yet Clinton's treasury secretary, Robert Rubin, has publicly admitted calling the current treasury undersecretary, Peter Fisher, to suggest a bit of help for Enron.

To really understand the influence, we must look back in time. Enron's relationship with the Bush family goes back decades. As early as 1988, when his father was president, George W. Bush was calling Argentina on the company's behalf. By 1992 Bush administration energy officials were helping out with what would be the 1992 Energy Policy Act, which required utilities to accommodate Enron-generated electricity.

As the Democrats took control in 1993, Enron snapped up some serious Republican talent. Five weeks before leaving the Commodity Futures Trading Commission, Wendy Gramm (wife of Senator Phil Gramm) pushed forward a ruling that exempted many of Enron's energy contracts from regulation. She not only joined Enron's board but also headed the audit committee. Well-respected leaders like former secretary of state and treasury James Baker and former commerce secretary Robert Mosbacher threw their weight behind the high-flying company to help with the international deals.

The Democrats were now on top, but Kenneth Lay was working both sides. In 1993 he was already golfing with President Clinton in Vail, Colorado. That year his company was exempted from some tough regulations in the Public Utility Holding Company Act of 1935. By 1997 Enron had hired the former boss of the very man at the Securities and Exchange Commission (SEC) who could approve a critical exemption that Congress had denied the year before (due in part to the SEC's objections). Sure enough, Enron got what it needed, relief from the Investment Company Act of 1940. This paved the way for the off-the-books partnerships and debt shifting overseas that disguised its financial downfall while enriching a lot of people.

Remember Commerce Secretary Ron Brown? His "advocacy center" within the Commerce Department had federal agencies, from the CIA to the Pentagon, helping Enron with energy deals in the Philippines and India. Ted C. Fishman, a contributing editor to *Harper's,* wrote a piece for *USA Today* describing the chastising our ambassador to India received in that country's press for alleged pressure he put on their government on Enron's behalf. Fishman notes that after leaving government employment, Ambassador Frank Wisner joined the board of an Enron-controlled company.

The World Bank described Enron's Dabhol project in India as "not economically viable," but our taxpayer-financed (politically controlled) agencies were more than willing to invest. In fact, according to the *Washington Times,* "the Clinton administration provided more than $1 billion in subsidized loans to Enron Corp. projects overseas at a time when Enron was contributing nearly $2 million to Democratic causes." Only one of twenty international projects Enron proposed between 1993 and 2000 did not receive government assistance.

Enron's Indian project "received hundreds of millions in assistance and guarantees from the Overseas Private Investment Corporation (OPIC) and the Export-Import Bank." Ultimately the project failed, costing investors millions of dollars, but not before making a few Enron executives seven-figure profits. You and I still are on the hook for several hundred million more, as OPIC, a federal agency, insured the project. As late as October 2001, Cheney was still discussing the Enron issue with India's foreign minister.

By 2000 Enron was worried the Clinton administration was considering increased oversight of its dealings, so it raided Clinton's staff. While still a senior official at Treasury, Linda Robertson was being courted by the company. She was still the department's liaison with Congress. Lo and behold, when the Commodity Futures Modernization Act of 2000 emerged, energy trading was exempt from the very regulation covering other traders, and Ms. Robertson was heading up Enron's Washington office.

During this time, Lay and Enron became George W. Bush's largest corporate contributor. The company's law firm, Vinson & Elkins, wasn't far behind in the rankings. While Governor George W. Bush was passing an Enron-pleasing energy-deregulation plan, a German company, Veba, found the company's finances to be so weak that it canceled a merger. Several major accounting firms and banks were privy to this deal and knew the outcome. Neela Banerjee writes in the *New York Times*, "Vega concluded that Enron had shifted so much debt off its balance sheet accounts that the company's total debt load amounted to 70 to 75 percent of its value as expressed in debt to equity ratio. In March 1999, debt rating agencies would have probably calculated Enron's debt level at about 54.1 percent, based on the information that the company disclosed in regular reports to the SEC." Clearly there were many lenders and Wall Street types that knew Enron was in trouble long before the summer of 2001.

In the meantime, the Republicans won the White House. Lay was there, attending the president's Inaugural Day luncheon. The parade of Enron employees, advisors, and lobbyists who joined the Bush administration was astounding. Larry Lindsey, Robert Zoellick, Thomas White, Clay Johnson, Ted Kassinger, and Laurence Thompson were all placed in senior positions. The former head of the Texas Public Utility Commission was Lay's pick to head the Federal Regulatory Energy Commissions (FERC). He is there now. Another Enron supporter, Nora Brownel, is a member as well.

In the spring of 2001, Kenneth Lay was at the first of Enron's six meetings with Vice President Cheney, an unprecedented one-on-one visit between the two men. The company's desire to break up monopoly control of electricity transmission networks became part of the Bush energy proposals. Lay apparently chatted with Cheney the day before the vice president announced the administration would not support price caps on electricity during the California energy crisis. The Enron memo delivered to the vice president during those April talks shows that numerous company policy suggestions made it into the Energy Task Force recommendations. Investigating congressman Henry

Waxman wrote to Cheney saying "there is no company in the country that stood to gain as much from the White House plan as Enron."

As trouble descended on the energy company, Attorney General John Ashcroft had to recuse himself from any investigation due to the large campaign contributions he had accepted during his Senate career. Although his deputy attorney general Larry Thompson was a member of a law firm that represented Enron before his appointment, Thompson took over the investigation. The entire U.S. Attorney's Office for the Southern District of Texas also recused themselves, as did many of the judges in Houston. Senator Phil Gramm was more than helpful to Enron as head of the Senate Banking Committee. He received almost $100,000 in contributions from the company while wife Wendy made thousands more serving on the company board. Gramm has supported both Enron's energy derivatives and the lack of regulation for same. However, he has decided not to run for reelection.

Enron insiders made off with hundreds of millions of dollars in the company's final months. CEO Kenneth Lay's predecessor, Jeffrey Skilling, made at least $20 million on stock between January and August of 2001. Lay himself banked at least $200 million in salary, stock, and other compensation in his last three years with the company, including $16 million in stock he sold after receiving a whistleblower's memo warning of the impending troubles. Just days before the bankruptcy, select employees received $50 million in bonuses.

Unfortunately, the working stiffs hadn't a clue the company was about to go belly up. Their leader (and most financial analysts) was still telling them to buy. For a time during those last days, they couldn't sell their stock even if they wanted to because of a change in the company's retirement plan administrator. Besides these employees, dozens of national and international businesses have been exposed to tremendous losses. Of course we know who picks up much of the slack in those cases—we taxpayers.

In a *New York Times* editorial, Bill Keller writes: "Did Enron buy political influence? Please. That's not the way things work in Washington. Enron bought access. Money just got it in the door to make its case. (The case it made probably went something like this: If the government does things Enron's way a lot of people will get very rich and they will be very, very grateful to the wise leaders who made it all possible.) If you're asking whether the Bush Administration did favors for Enron, sure it did—and, by the way, so did the Clinton Administration, and both parties in Congress. . . . I'd say Enron's campaign donations, about $6 million over the past dozen years, paid off better than most of its other investments."

What about Arthur Andersen and the regulatory sellout to our big accounting firms? I shuddered to read this quote from Democratic senator Joseph Lieberman: "Knowing what I know now, I presume almost everybody would have been advocating tougher standards for the accounting profession. Just looking back it seems so self-evident that an accounting firm should not be both auditing a company and receiving consulting fees from it, because there is an inherent conflict of interest." Lieberman's confession wasn't persuasive. As Enron had, the big accounting firms had stuffed campaign coffers for years. When that wasn't enough, they made superficial changes to ward off meaningful reform.

Philip B. Chenok was the president of the American Institute of Public Accountants (AICPA) for fifteen years. He wrote a history of the organization in which he proudly talks of thwarting political challenges by increasing contributions and lobbying efforts until "no legislation that affected accountants was drafted without our input." During the Clinton administration, the agency got its liability exposure reduced. When the head of the SEC, Arthur Levitt, tried to restrict dual consulting and accounting by these firms in 2000, they rallied their friends on Capitol Hill who threatened Levitt's budget until he backed off. I find it hard to believe Lieberman missed out on all this.

By the way, Harvey Pitt, Bush's new head of the SEC, spent twenty years as a private attorney working for the Big Five accounting firms and the AICPA. When he proposed a new accounting oversight board in January, Congressman John Dingell noted, "It sounds like it was drafted by Arthur Andersen."

A reporter for *USA Today* came to the same conclusions in April of 2002: "Don't expect Congress to push tough reforms. As with industry, lawmakers rushed in with nearly three-dozen pieces of legislation, and plenty of vocal outrage, about the failings Enron exposed. So far, however, nothing has made it into law, although many of the reforms under consideration have been discussed for years. In fact, few expect any sweeping reforms will ultimately be enacted." The reasons are obvious. "In large part, that's a reflection of the power of the special-interest money that floods congressional campaign coffers each year. The accounting profession, for example, coughed up more than $12 million in campaign contributions since 1999. If permanent reforms are to be imposed on the accounting profession, lawmakers will have to resist the lure of money themselves, which is not likely."

As I hand over this copy, Enron has dropped from the headlines only to be replaced by WorldCom and at least a dozen other major corporations now under investigation for everything from careless accounting to outright fraud. President Bush and Vice President Cheney are being confronted with their timely profits in Harkin Energy Corp. and Halliburton Co. respectively. The House and Senate have begun marking up Corporate Reform bills, which undoubtedly will be watered down before passage. Look for criminal penalties to soften and accounting oversight to weaken.

These scandals embody just about every element of my thesis. They demonstrate a system of government that now passes laws designed by contributors and their lawyer lobbyists, exempts those it chooses, and selectively enforces against others as the mood and politics dictate. They show the revolving door between government and the private sector that twirls so fast it makes me dizzy. What is finally revealed is a two-party system that has but one client now, and it is *not* the American people.

Corporate influence over our political process is growing at the same time these companies are redefining their allegiances. Today's business fortunes exist primarily in an international power structure that serves not a country or a people but the entities themselves. Nowadays, where do most corporate interests lie? How about in their offshore accounts, their international divisions, and their overseas markets? These companies are global. They owe their prosperity not to any one nation but to the world marketplace. They will bribe our politicians, exact favorable rulings, and then plow their profits overseas. Jobs move south, taxes go unpaid, and all the while the companies manipulate the system right under our noses. With pockets bulging, our politicians play along. Even with our most basic security issues, leaders now behave as if this nation's fate resides on Wall Street, not Main Street. To judge from our political behavior, it seems that all we need are successful businesses, not naive principles, old-fashioned ideals, or even a united people.

Robert Kaplan pointed out in a fascinating piece in *Atlantic Monthly* entitled "Was Democracy Just a Moment?" Of the world's one hundred largest "economies," over half are corporations, not countries. While the 200 largest companies employ less than 1 percent of the world's workforce, they account for about one-third of the world's economic activity. The five hundred largest corporations represent at least 70 percent of world trade. Is it surprising that the needs of such an overwhelming force now dominate world politics? If economic success is at stake, corporations feel free to create the social and environmental havoc necessary to succeed. Just as in the days of the old company town, entire communities are subject to upheaval if businesses require it. Cities are rebuilt or torn down, universities restructured, plants relocated, and property rights eliminated—whatever it takes to fuel growth and elevate those stock prices. All too often these goals have little to do with preservation of a community or a state or even the nation.

Years ago robber barons like Andrew Carnegie and John D. Rockefeller bought their share of politicians and sold out American workers in their efforts to monopolize businesses, but they didn't sell out their country. Their assets remained primarily at home. To the extent that they paid taxes, this government benefited. Additionally, their philanthropy returned much to the nation. The libraries, schools, museums, foundations, and hospitals they established are a legacy and recompense to the civilization they plundered. Today many corporate barons leave devastated communities, jobless workers, and polluted cultural and environmental landscapes as evidence of their commitment while taking home astronomical salaries and bonuses.

In 1998 *Harper's* editor Lewis Lapham wrote a two-part series on that year's World Economic Forum in Davos, Switzerland. This is the annual meeting of anyone who is anyone in the global arena. CEOs, government leaders, media bigwigs—all go to hobnob and set the world agenda. Lapham described the attendees' struggle over "post-modern capitalism": "Politicians were by definition untrustworthy, belonging to one of only two familiar types—light-minded demagogues stirring up crowds, or pesky legislators constantly bothering people with demands for bribes. Markets might have their flaws, but government was worse. Political interference wrecked the free play of natural distribution, and government never knew how to manage anything—not roads, not dairy farms or gambling casinos or capital flows. All would be well, and civilization much improved, if only politics could be manufactured in the way that one manufactured railroad cars or tomato soup."

Uneasy references were made to human dislocation and discomfort occurring in the name of global competition, but no one wanted to discuss the subject. When John Sweeney of the AFL/CIO spoke up, he mentioned the unmentionable. While acknowledging the feats of modern business, he questioned how the enormous new wealth served more than the upper echelon. He described America, saying "one child in four is in poverty, schools are a shambles, as are hospitals and roads." Unless the profits generated by the global economy were more evenly distributed in America and around the world, the theme of the conference, "Priorities for the 21st Century," would be better titled "The Four Horsemen of the Apocalypse," Sweeney said.

Latham noted that Sweeney's remarks would have been but "a pebble into a well of indifference" if it weren't for the man who followed him onto the podium, an example of wealth incarnate, the currency trader and financier George Soros. His words were every bit as somber: "Only fools believe in the conscience of markets." And yet the conscience of markets is now driving political decisions.

This attitude certainly defines our government today. For example, Big Oil wins out no matter who controls Capitol Hill. When President Bush took office, his opponents threatened to throw themselves on the tracks before they would allow drilling in the Arctic Preserve. Six months later that legislation passed the House with plenty of Democratic support. As of this writing, the legislation has been defeated, but I'm not letting down my vigil. The very liberals who scream for conservation crumble when the Big Auto companies protest higher gas mileage requirements for their popular SUVs. While it is estimated that Arctic drilling would produce about 42 million gallons a day (years down the track), a current (and very doable) mileage increase of only three miles per gallon in SUVs would save the nation 49 million gallons a day *right away*. You do the math! It is all a sham: Play the part for the cameras, but vote your reelection pocketbook.

The oil companies share the political favors with the other big corporations. There are about 125 business subsidy programs in the federal budget, implemented by every single federal agency. Under Bill Clinton's watch, these giveaways continued to escalate. He left office having recommended another 10 percent hike for these subsidies in the 2000 budget. According to Stephen Moore of the Cato Institute, "Corporate welfare in the tax code and federal budget costs in excess of $100 billion a year . . . and most of these subsidies are direct outlays to Fortune 500 companies." Many of the largest, like General Electric, Westinghouse, and Rockwell International, are getting ten, twenty, even thirty or more annual grants from different agencies. Yet each of these companies have profits of at least half a billion dollars a year.

The grants include direct subsidies here at home. Remember the annual ethanol debate? In the face of token opposition, Archer Daniels Midland Co. (ADM) has sustained this subsidy, garnering over $3 billion for itself thus far, by investing only $3 million in political contributions in the 1990s. That's a nice return on your money. Since the ethanol costs more to produce than it sells for, we also give a tax credit to producers on top of the subsidy. Bottom line—this and other giveaways to ADM add up to about $400 million a year; this to a company with annual sales of around $14 billion.

What about tobacco? We continue spending tax dollars to subsidize this product while simultaneously spending money to target the industry in federal lawsuits. Why aren't tobacco farmers being allowed to sink or swim in the current climate? Make no mistake, the farmers should be able to grow and market their perfectly legal product if they choose, but the government should not subsidize Big Tobacco on one hand and sue it on the other.

U.S. Representative Bob Etheridge, a member of the House Agriculture Committee, said at the end of 2000, "Our tobacco farmers deserve an opportunity to thrive, not just survive." These comments were made in conjunction with letters and pleas he issued to the big tobacco companies to file purchase intentions that matched the previous year's tobacco orders. No one noticed the 2001 Presidential Commission report on the tobacco "crisis" that blamed the government's current policies of price supports and quotas for "produc[ing] a situation in which more people are involved in tobacco production than the system can support."

As we write these checks, tobacco companies are increasingly moving their operations overseas. Their profits increase while the farmers see their revenues decline. So what do we do? Funnel more money to the poor farmers. Good grief. It is one thing to use tax dollars to help farmers transition out of what we profess to be a dying industry (no pun intended). It is another thing entirely to use our money to underwrite the continuing success of this crop.

Tobacco, however, is a bipartisan cash cow. You would expect Republican Jesse Helms of North Carolina to push for these farmers, but until tobacco became a political hot button, House Minority leader Richard Gephardt was the fourth highest recipient of industry money from 1986 to 1996, despite the fact that his state has no significant tobacco interests. In 1998, after pledging to wean himself from such funds, Gephardt still voted *against* killing $48 million in tobacco subsidies. (He continues to favor the big sugar and ethanol producers with huge subsidies and has been rewarded accordingly.) We all remember the Al Gore gaffe, when he campaigned heavily for the tobacco vote in 1988 by telling boyhood tales of planting the crop by hand. By 1992 he was tearfully lamenting the death of his sister from lung cancer. Whatever works for the voters while appeasing industry is the way to play.

As of June 2001, the American Lung Association was giving failing grades to the federal and state governments in the tobacco wars. States have cut appeal bonds for court judgments (making it cheaper for tobacco companies to challenge adverse rulings). They have gleefully pledged future settlement monies for up-front payments. Very cooperatively, states have reduced penalties for selling tobacco to minors while increasing their revenues through higher taxes on cigarettes. The forty-six states that are participating in the Master Settlement Agreement collected an additional $7 billion in cigarette taxes in 2000. Most important, they have used only small amounts of these settlement monies for health and prevention programs. Liz Chandler of the *Charlotte Observer* reported this ditty about her state's use of its award in June 2002. "About 73 percent of the $59 million so far—about $43 million—has gone towards production and marketing of North Carolina tobacco."

Actually, the tobacco settlements are making our federal and state governments literal partners in the industry's success. The settlements are tied to "volume and inflation adjustments." This means the more cigarettes that are sold, the more money states can add to their treasuries. We all know that owners want increased profits, not declining earnings. That same logic applies to cash-hungry politicians. Also, the tobacco agreements protect the large cigarette companies through a complex formula to inhibit competition from smaller companies not part of the settlement. This agreement has created what is essentially a government-sponsored monopoly.

As you can see, there is no incentive to slow production, stop sales, or regulate tobacco. The lawsuits are simply an added source of government money that is most often inserted into general revenues. They are also a great way for the big tobacco companies to control the industry and a tremendous source of fees for a tiny group of litigators.

Philip Morris cringed when its perfectly honest report to the Czech government in July 2001 was made public. The study compared health costs of smoking to the national taxes earned from the sale of tobacco. It is worth noting that the company included costs of secondhand smoking illnesses, although it continues to deny there is such a thing. The report concluded that the nation was making more money on cigarettes than it was spending to treat or bury its citizens. What a deal! Those same numbers apply in the United States, but Philip Morris knows better than to publish that information at home.

There aren't many subsidies that do make sense in a free enterprise system. Products should survive through demand. The government has artificially inflated the price of items such as milk, peanuts, and sugar for so long, we have no idea as to their real market value. Consumers are hit twice by this giveaway, once with our tax dollars for the subsidy, then again through higher prices for the end products.

Are the small farmers really benefiting? Not a chance. Peanuts (now under scrutiny by the FDA as a major allergen) are sold in the United States at nearly twice the world price. According to the GAO, this adds between $300 million and $500 million to the consumer cost for peanut products. Even more outrageous, peanuts are subject to quotas that restrict production. According to Rich Pasco of the American Peanut Coalition, more than two-thirds of the quota owners are in the business of leasing them out to the real growers. (In 1997 there were about 12,000 farms actually harvesting peanuts, but the Environmental Working Group [EWG] database showed 70,000 quota owners.) Essentially this corporate welfare is going to the middleman! Despite promises to eliminate this subsidy, the 2001 farm bill included $3.5 billion for peanuts and over $1 billion for a buyout program. According to the EWG, John Hancock Mutual Life Insurance Company will be the largest beneficiary of this program in the next four years. I'll bet you didn't know an insurance company raised peanuts.

Sugar is priced at two to four times its market value, costing American consumers an additional $2 billion a year. Forty percent of this subsidy benefits just 1 percent of sugar growers. The cost of this subsidy is actually much greater. For example, the runoff from sugar fields has been polluting the Florida Everglades for years. In 1996 Senator Bob Dole nixed a plan to tax Florida cane growers to help restore this area. His big contributor, José Fanjul, would have objected. Instead, Dole let the culprits skate and took $200 million from the general treasury—from you and me—for this program. Please note that while José was one of Dole's finance vice chairmen that year, his brother Alfonso was performing the same task for Bill Clinton.

In 1999 the Department of Agriculture had to accept almost 800,000 tons of sugar in lieu of missed loan payments from producers at a cost of $430 million to the taxpayers. It then spent $1.4 million a month to store the surplus. It couldn't sell the sugar; that would depress prices! Instead, it is chasing away our candy industries rather than let prices find their own market levels. *Time* magazine reported in February 2002 that Brach's "announced last year it would close a large manufacturing plant in the [United States] and shed more than 1,000 jobs"; it will outsource candymaking to Argentina. Kraft Foods intends to close its Holland, Michigan, manufacturing facility for Life-Savers in 2003 and plans to make the iconic candy in Quebec, Canada, where sugar sells at market rates. Not even this loss of jobs can top the influence of the big sugar growers like U.S. Sugar Corp. in Florida or the corn syrup producers like our old friend Archer Daniels Midland.

Once upon a time, these subsidy policies were meant to support the small farmer. With less than 2 percent of Americans still on the family farm, current rhetoric to that effect is simply a bald-faced lie to justify political favors to giant agribusinesses. In fact, of the nation's 2 million farmers, less than one-quarter receive 84 percent of the subsidies; over $60 billion of the $71.5 billion allocated from 1996 to 2000. Obviously most money goes to the biggest farms. According to Agriculture Department records, the average payment for the top 1 percent of recipients was about $550,000 over five years while the bottom 80 percent of farmers averaged less than $6,000 each. We hear nonsense about reform, but from 1995 to 2000, the overall subsidies quadrupled to $32.5 billion. They went up even more again this year. Nearly half the net farm income in the United States comes from federal subsidies.

A few brave politicians tell the truth about this farce, but most of them (on both sides of the aisle) suck up to the corporate lobbyists and maintain these insane programs. The Democrats pretend they're sticking up for Willy Nelson's farmers, while Republicans lie that they're eliminating trade restrictions and regulations. The little guys on real family farms actually protest these giveaways, because such monies simply help fund corporate takeovers of their small parcels. In a *New York Times* piece about the National Corn Growers complaint about low corn prices, Elizabeth Becker asked small farmers what they thought. Tom Buis of the National Farmers Union responded that grain prices are low because the large farmers are overproducing at the taxpayers' expense.

The 1996 Freedom to Farm Act actually proposed serious reform by removing farmers, especially the big guys, from the government teat. That ambitious legislation produced tremendous lobbying opposition, which resulted in a continued escalation of these benefits, particularly to the top 10 percent of farming businesses.

There's food—and then there's jewelry! How about the minerals (gold, silver, copper) located on our public lands? Actually, these materials can still be purchased by industry at 1872 prices! The mining industry produces more toxic waste than any other. It uses about five times the amount of land actually being mined for milling, dumping, and support facilities. Despite the typical rhetoric about saving jobs, the number of people employed in the mining industry is on the decline. Since 1997 Nevada, the biggest mining state, has experienced a more than 25 percent drop in these workers.

Once a claim holder, always a claim holder—whether you mine or not, as long as you pay a $100 annual fee. If you quit mining the land, why not build a home or maybe a golf course on this public land? A 1996 television documentary, *The Last Great American Gold Heist,* found one deed holder who "paid $170 for a patent on some 60 acres outside Phoenix, Arizona, then turned the site into a resort golf course valued at sixty million dollars." Amazingly, the mining industry sector enjoys more benefits and breaks than our oil and gas companies. It beats that group hands down in the royalty department. Companies pay *no* royalties to the government for the extraction of these metals. The truth about this policy was best stated by former interior secretary Bruce Babbitt when he described our mining laws as "one of the most outrageous corporate subsidies" in American history. Even worse, most big mining companies doing business in the United States are foreign owned!

President Clinton signed several mining laws into effect in his final days in office, having been unable to win congressional support given the industry's powerful lobbying and lucrative contributions. (His fellow Democrat, Senator Harry Reid of Nevada, is the industry's biggest supporter.) The laws were intended to produce more accountability for the tremendous environmental destruction caused by mining. The Bush administration is already rolling back these regulations. Of particular concern is the reversal of federal power to block mining operations likely to cause "substantial irreparable harm" to public lands.

The feds are not alone in all of this. Local and state governments get into the business in a big way. Fighting to bring jobs into communities, they offer breaks and subsidies bordering on the absurd. In their award-winning series for *Time,* "What Corporate Welfare Costs," Donald L. Barlett and James B. Steele tell a heartbreaking story of a little-known company, Seaboards Corporation, that, with enormous government help, has devastated virtually every town where it has set up shop. This hog-farming company raises and processes pork. It goes from town to town promising jobs. State and local governments bend over backward to build infrastructure and deliver low-interest loans and long-term tax credits. When Seaboards moves in search of even better deals, it leaves enormous pollution, thousands of displaced immigrant workers, and usually a tax increase or city debt as its parting gift.

Barlett and Steele calculated that from 1990 to 1997, "Seaboard Corp. was the beneficiary of at least $150 million in economic incentives from federal, state and local governments. . . . Local [and federal] taxpayers supplied the dollars not just for the outright corporate welfare, but also by picking up the costs of new classrooms and teachers, homelessness, increased crime, dwindling property values and an overall decline in the quality of life . . . and all this for jobs that pay little more than poverty-level wages." During this period the company stock price went from $116 to $387. The owners' holdings jumped from $125 million to $425 million.

Take a quick glance offshore. Today all the big companies trade overseas through foreign sales corporations (FSCs) labeled offshore subsidiaries. They funnel export paperwork through places like Jamaica or the Bahamas and poof, no federal income taxes on a portion of those profits. Between 1988 and 1998 this fiction cost the government $10 billion in lost revenue. In 1999 another $4 billion escaped the taxman this way. No one believes this tactic is anything but another subsidy for major companies like Boeing, Microsoft, and General Motors, paid for by the American people.

Don't forget the egregious giveaways by the Export-Import Bank, Overseas Private Investment Corporation, Advanced Technology Program, and Market Access Program. Corporate lobbyists defend each plan as necessary for small business or to create jobs for the American worker. The facts demonstrate otherwise.

In defending a funding increase for the Export-Import Bank in the summer of 2001 (long nicknamed the Bank of Boeing), bigtime lobbyists said anything less would hurt small businesses. They pointed to numbers showing that small businesses account for 86 percent of all its transactions, but glossed over the punch line. This large group of small businesses gets only 18 percent of the money. The other 82 percent of the funding goes to only 14 percent of the deals. In fact, just ten companies, including Boeing, General Electric, and AT&T, account for about half of all monies loaned, granted, or guaranteed through this program. As for job creation, over 1 million U.S. manufacturing jobs have disappeared in the last decade. GE alone cut 123,000 jobs between 1986 and 1997.

We know, of course, that companies like McDonald's couldn't survive without Market Access Program (MAP) tax dollars to help sell Big Macs in Moscow. Campbell Soup and Ralston Purina, impoverished as they are, apparently also must receive similar grants to compete overseas. The MAP actually solicits these companies to submit requests for grants: Take my money . . . please.

Surely all Americans are benefiting as these corporations fill the nation's coffers with tax revenues from their profits. Nope. A 1999 GAO report states that in the years between 1989 and 1995, a majority of corporations, both foreign- and U.S.-controlled, paid no U.S. income taxes. This trend hasn't slowed. Pepsico, for example, paid no federal taxes in 1999. The seventeen major cruise lines that are based in the United States and cater almost exclusively to Americans simply register as foreign corporations and avoid almost all taxes. Carnival Corp. earned $2 billion in profits from 1996 to 1999 yet paid less than 1 percent in taxes. After its trade association spent over half a billion in lobbying fees in 1997, the next year it was rewarded with a one-line insert in the federal budget bill that saved the cruise lines $20 million in exemptions from government fees. In the meantime, we read regularly about the pollution expelled from these liners, particularly in the pristine areas around Alaskan glaciers.

In the boom year of 1997, Lindy Paull, the chief of staff of the Joint Committee on Taxation, noted that corporate income tax receipts actually fell by $4 billion (about 2 percent) from the previous year. This was the first decline in corporate revenues since 1990, a year in which the country entered a brief recession. How could this happen? There are several reasons.

Congress has downsized the IRS to diminish the threat of enforcement against the favored (just as it has done with the SEC). While it is still staffed to chase little guys, it hasn't the resources or political support to go after those who can fight back. Of course, with all the breaks for the big moneymakers, most of this tax avoidance is legal.

The Institute on Taxation and Economic Policy issued a report in October 2000 that examined tax returns from 250 of America's largest companies. Tax breaks, subsidies, and grants enable many of these companies to legally zero out their tax bill. Some even produce a negative bill, which means they actually get money back from the government. From 1996 to 1998, forty-one of these companies paid no federal income taxes for at least one year. Under current tax laws, they should have paid $9 billion on pretax profits of almost $26 billion, but instead this group received rebates totaling $3.2 billion. One company, Texaco, reported $3.4 billion in U.S. profits over that period yet received checks back from the government for $304 million. In 1998, twenty-four of these companies received rebates, including such needy names as Texaco, Chevron, Pepsico, Pfizer, J. P. Morgan, General Motors, Phillips Petroleum, and Northrop Grumman. The petroleum industry was the lowest-taxed group during this entire three-year period, with an effective tax rate of 5.6 percent in 1998.

Of all the various tax breaks, almost half the dollars went to just twenty-five companies, with each receiving over $1 billion in benefits. General Electric topped the list, with $6.9 billion in breaks over the three years. (As a footnote, in the last six months of 1998, GE, GM, IBM, and Disney alone spent $8.8 million on lobbyists, according to Public Disclosure, Inc.) The corporate alternative minimum tax (AMT) was adopted in 1986 to make sure these big companies paid some taxes each year. But legislation enacted in 1993 (with a Democratic Congress and president) and again in 1997 allowed the loopholes that have produced the current results. Now the Bush administration wants to repeal the corporate AMT altogether *and* rebate all such taxes paid by companies since 1986.

In the meantime, some companies are simply reincorporating in places like Bermuda so they don't have to focus so much on tax dodges. As James Surowiecki tells us in *The New Yorker*: "If you want to avoid taxes with impunity, hide millions in offshore banks, and contentedly snub the tax authorities of your home country, you need to be something more than an ordinary citizen. You need to be a corporation. You need to be, say, Ingersoll-Rand." He notes that this company was founded in America over a century ago and does a lot of business with the federal government. "Yet when it comes to paying taxes, Ingersoll-Rand is not an American company. It's Bermudan." Of course, no part of this company exists in Bermuda other than a mail drop—"But that is enough to save the company forty million dollars a year." Surowiecki makes a reasonable suggestion. If the average Joe must pay taxes in exchange for the benefits of American life, why don't Tyco, Cooper Industries, and Ingersoll-Rand, among others, have to do the same thing? Because it's the law! Forget any changes. "House Republicans, cajoled by industry lobbyists, tend to equate the closing of any tax loophole with a tax hike," he explains.

Tax breaks account for about half of the corporate welfare provisions. They are the most insidious of the giveaways because of their permanence. While subsidies and grant programs are reviewed regularly, tax provisions usually stay on the books unless someone actually tries to change or eliminate them. Handing checks to companies is more noticeable than the stealthy penning of some confusing tax law that allows preferential treatment and write-offs.

Remember, too, that these corporations are spending outlandish amounts on their upper management. Whether you are a salaried employee or a stockholder, you should be enraged. While real wages for the average citizen remain stagnant, the golden parachutes and stock option payouts have made "billionaire" a common term. How can companies afford this? Ask your congressman. CEOs make much of this money through options to buy their stock at a low price. When they exercise their options (as the share price rises), the company gets a tax deduction for the difference in the price. Better yet, these transactions are not reported as business expenses, so it becomes a benefit on top of a benefit—a write-off for no expense! From 1996 to 1998, 233 of the nation's 250 largest and most profitable companies lowered their taxes from stock options by over $25 billion. The better the company does, the more the stock increases, the more write-offs they get in this category.

CEOs are rewarded for eliminating jobs, moving companies overseas, and holding down wages for American workers. Even the *Wall Street Journal* dared to ask "How rich is too rich?" in recent years. In response to the disparity between workers and corporate leaders, some members of Congress actually proposed giving tax breaks to companies for reducing executive compensation! We're supposed to pay them for cutting salaries? It's shameful.

Forget the mere elimination of the corporate AMT; President Bush and his treasury secretary, Paul O'Neill, have advocated eliminating *all* corporate income tax. Maybe we should just ditch this charade and remove one of the most powerful tools in a legislator's arsenal: the ability to trade tax favors in exchange for contributions.

We could eliminate corporate income taxes in exchange for removing the fiction that corporations are "persons" under the law. In 1886 the Supreme Court made this ruling without debate, thus giving companies the right to due process. Big companies now invoke the Fourteenth Amendment protection far more than any citizen group. As William Greider points out in his book *Who Will Tell the People*: "When corporations commit crimes, they do not wish to be treated as people, but as 'artificial legal entities' that cannot be held personally accountable for their misdeeds. . . . If an individual is convicted of a felony, he automatically loses his political rights. More broadly, ex-convicts are not normally invited to testify before congressional hearings or to advise the White House on important policies. . . . Corporations are 'citizens' who regularly offend the law—both in the criminal sense and in the civil terms of flouting regulatory statutes. Yet their formidable influence on political decisions goes forward undiminished, as well as the substantial financial rewards they harvest from government." This might be a worthwhile trade!

There would certainly be a few more CEOs in prison with this change in status. *Mother Jones* ran a piece by Ken Silverstein in April of 2002 called "Unjust Rewards" that detailed the serious yet blatant violations of regulatory laws by major government contractors like General Electric, General Motors, TRW, and Archer Daniels Midland. While these companies may have paid fines in the millions for EPA or OSHA violations, they were (and are) reaping billions from our treasury in federal contracts. In addition, the crimes of fraud, theft, and negligent homicide pop up regularly.

According to Silverstein: "General Dynamics, the nation's fifth largest contractor, paid the government nearly $2 million in 1995 to resolve charges that it falsified employee time cards to bill the Pentagon for thousands of hours that were never worked on a contract for testing F-16 fighters. Northrop Grumman, the nation's fourth largest contractor, paid nearly $6.7 million in 2000 to settle two separate cases in which it was charged with inflating the costs of parts and materials for warplanes. Yet the two defense giants continue to receive federal contracts, collecting a combined total of $38 billion between 1995 and 2000."

Surely we ban these corporations when they actually defraud the taxpayers? Nope. As with the IRS, the little guys get swept up but the giants are left alone. Silverstein reports that "Some 244,000 contractors are currently barred from government work and almost all are small firms or individuals like Kenneth Hansen, a Kansas dentist banned from receiving low-income patients because he defaulted on $164,000 in student loans. 'We never take down the big guys,' concedes [Steven] Schooner. Formerly a lawyer in the Office of Federal Procurement Policy, he now teaches government-contracts law." How appropriate.

We should note that Bill Clinton took action to remedy this problem—during his last month in office. Upon proof of a pattern of "significant" and "pervasive" abuses, the government could suspend or debar companies and contractors from receiving government work. The business lobbyists were heading to court over this when George W. Bush quietly suspended the rule shortly after taking office. "The Congressional Research Service issued an opinion concluding that the secret suspension of the rule was probably illegal, but the move went virtually unreported by the media." The president revoked the rule completely in December 2001. According to Representative Thomas Davis III, a Republican from Virginia, "There was never any rational basis or need for additional standards, since existing regulations already insure the government does not do business with unethical companies." Right.

Money is certainly one means of buying laws, exemptions, and legislative protection, but it's not the only currency. An official's list of contributors tells only part of the influence story. There is much, much more.

NINE | Lobbyists: The Bandits of Gucci Gulch

Special interests and their representatives are not new in Washington, D.C. Thomas Jefferson warned of these "clubbists" and, by 1831, Tocqueville described "a welter of civil and political associations" in America. The Frenchman didn't see this as all bad in the early stages. He said that large associations, workers, businesses, and church groups actually could facilitate democracy by transmitting general policy concerns to our elected officials. However, he warned, as these associations splintered and the interests became more divergent, the effect would be disastrous. There would be no way for each tiny sector to be heard over the din without something "special" to grab a politician's attention. All too often, that something is cash.

Our elected officials still pretend that average citizens influence their political decisions. They do so to capture our votes, because, quite simply, even their fattest cats get only one ballot. Yet all the while they madly cater to the powerful interests in Washington. Until the Enron debacle shamed them enough, at least in the press, members of Congress had rejected all forms of campaign finance reform under the banner of free speech. As soon as the 2002 reform bill passed, Senator Mitch McConnell took to the airways to promise a court challenge.

Beyond limits on direct campaign monies, our elected officials point to laws that require registration of lobbyists or gift bans as somehow limiting the corrupting influence on government. These rules are just empty form over toxic substance. The system both encourages and supports influence peddling and vote buying. The laws to prevent both are notable for their easy circumvention, not tough enforcement. Do our leaders think we are stupid? Yes.

In 1992 candidate Bill Clinton chastised the Bush and Reagan administrations. "The last twelve years were nothing less than an extended hunting season for high-priced lobbyists and Washington influence peddlers. On streets where statesmen once strolled, a never-ending stream of money now changes hands—tying the hands of those elected to lead," Clinton said.

When he took office, Clinton promised "the most ethical administration in American history." O.K., wipe that smile off your face. In fact, on his first day in office, the new president signed an executive order that barred senior officials of the White House and other agencies from lobbying former colleagues for five years, extending the traditional ban by four years. He was going to stop the rotation from "public service to private enrichment" by enacting an extremely important and effective measure to decrease the incestuous relationship between business and government employees. Only one week before leaving office Clinton announced the repeal of that ban, to a collective sigh of relief from his cohorts. "It had more to do with image than ethics," one advisor said. The president didn't need that image any longer so he simply dropped the charade.

No kidding. While serving as White House counsel, Jack Quinn drafted that executive order, which he now terms "someone else's silly idea." The ban was lifted just in time for Quinn to pull off one of the pardoning coups of the century. Actually, Quinn lobbied for his client, fugitive financier Marc Rich, even before the order was reversed but argued that his presidential contact was permitted under a "little exception." The lobbying ban apparently doesn't include "communicating or appearing with regard to a judicial proceeding or a criminal or civil law enforcement inquiry, investigation, or proceeding." (Notice that lawyers always cover themselves.) This judicial exemption would permit government attorneys to represent the very people or companies they may have prosecuted while in public service! Ethics professor Stephen Gillers says this "exception" was intended to apply only to court cases where some supposedly impartial judge would decide the matter, not to some sweetheart deal between a president and his former counsel. The actual circumstances of the Rich pardon were so outrageous that no one really focused on Quinn's ethics. You may say it's perfectly legal, Jack, but it stinks.

In the final hours of his administration, Clinton delivered the pardon to Rich, a man who eluded prosecution by skipping the country. While Rich bought Israeli support through $100 million in charitable donations, the more interesting trail led through his ex-wife, Denise.

Back in the United States, she funneled enormous sums to the Democratic National Committee (DNC), the Gore and Hillary Clinton campaign, and the Clinton Library. Then she threw in a few luxury furnishings for the outgoing first couple before writing a letter on behalf of the pardon. When asked to testify before Congress, Ms. Rich politely declined, citing the Fifth Amendment against self-incrimination.

The Rich pardon was just one blatant demonstration of influence peddling in the White House. During her Senate campaign, Hillary Clinton met with a representative of four Hasidim convicted of bilking the U.S. government out of $40 million. While she denied any role in their eventual pardon, it is interesting to note that their home community of New Square, Rockland County, in New York voted almost unanimously for Mrs. Clinton, while every neighboring Hasidic enclave went overwhelmingly for Republican Rick Lazio. Just coincidence, I guess.

Influence peddling and political corruption were not invented by the Clinton administration, although there was a certain elevation of the art during those years. Why are the lobbyists so powerful? For one thing, the campaign contributions by industry and organizations insure access. As mentioned earlier, the law now treats corporations as "persons" under many circumstances. This is necessary to permit companies to own property, to enter into contracts, and even to sue and be sued in their name. Yet why should this fiction be used to permit corporate political contributions? Every human being within a group can give as his or her interests dictate, but the only reason to extend that right to an organization is to increase the influence of the entity rather than the citizens who make up that body. Although it will be heresy to many, the elimination of organizational giving would be an enormous blow to political corruption.

A second source of tremendous power among lobbyists is the amazing revolving door between employment with these groups and service in the government. One day you can represent an industry and, the next, work for a senator who relies on that group. You can also leave a high government position for the cushy private sector and be lobbying your buddies the next day (despite formalities to the contrary). Back in 1992, the late Ron Brown, was a lobbyist, Democratic Party chair, and Clinton campaign advisor all at the same time. Then, once Clinton was in office, Brown, as commerce secretary, orchestrated the amazing resurgence of the Commerce Department, to the delight of many former clients. Mark Racicot, former governor of Montana, moved into lobbying as soon as he left office, representing huge clients like Enron, the National Energy Coordinating Council, and the National Electric Reliability Council. His discussion with Dick Cheney about backing off on the EPA clean-air requirements for the energy industry's facilities has become a subject of congressional inquiry on the administration's Energy Task Force. After President Bush tapped him to head the Republican National Committee (RNC), only a huge media outcry caused Racicot to back down on certain influence peddling while heading the party's top organization.

As far back as 1977, the heads of both major parties have worked for other clients at the same time they represented their political organization. Ron Brown was not alone. *Boston Globe* reporter Michael Kranish describes former Republican chair Haley Barbour's assurances when he took over the RNC in 1992. "He pledged to party leaders and on CNN that he would sever his ties to Barbour, Griffith and Rogers. But in fact he never sold his interest in the firm, deriving income from its tobacco, pharmaceutical and other clients. The subterfuge became known to reporters only in the final days of his four-year term, when Barbour's lobbying firm landed a contract representing the Swiss government and had to register ownership and other information under the Foreign Agents Registration Act." Barbour hasn't missed a beat since then and now represents clients like Microsoft, Philip Morris, and airline carriers.

Kranish noted that "although political parties are public institutions in our society, top party officials are not regulated by conflict-of-interest laws and are not even required by law to reveal their sources of annual income. Nor does the Freedom of Information Act apply to them, so whom they meet with, correspond with or telephone is elusive and generally unknown." He summed up these relationships: "Forget those quaint notions that political parties exist to elect candidates. Parties and their chairmen raise hundreds of millions of dollars each election cycle from various special interests that often want something from government. Besides being lobbyist-in-chief, chairmen help to deliver access and other favors to the most generous party patrons."

What about the men and women we actually have elected to represent us? When Bill Clinton reversed his five-year ban on lobbying by former government officials, the prohibition was again only one year, but who's counting? A senator leaves office and promptly joins a lobbying firm. Sit back and watch industry race to that company for assistance. The former official's ability to lobby is allegedly restricted, but it proceeds, I assure you. Ask Jack Quinn. In July 2000 he said that he was still honoring the pledge not to contact the White House on behalf of clients, but he noted that his prohibition didn't stop his associates from doing so. "There are nineteen people in my firm, and the eighteen who are not subject to the pledge because they never signed anything shouldn't be prevented from making a living just because I signed the pledge." Of course Quinn wasn't influencing anything from the wings during this period. Sure.

In 1993 a study by Public Interest Research Group found that of 319 people who left government service that January, 101 went into outright lobbying and another 79 joined law firms that do lobbying. Those numbers are dwarfed by the scale of the present-day switcheroo. More important, it is not the brilliant Treasury Department financier wooed for his talents by some big bank but the power players known for policy expertise and political clout who are the "big gets." Often they are valued by the importance of their contacts and their ability to influence, nothing more.

This swinging door works both ways. Industry officials enter government as fast as federal employees move to the private sector. The really big guys move from corporate heads to administration positions and back; consider Paul O'Neill, Donald Rumsfeld, even Dick Cheney. Both the vice president and the commerce secretary, Don Evans, stepped down from companies in the oil industry. Others shift from government service, where industry has been their big contributor, to a cabinet position overseeing that sector. Energy secretary Spencer Abraham once called for the elimination of the Energy Department. He received more contributions from the energy industry (and the transportation industry) than any other U.S. senator in the year before his defeat, according to Public Campaign. Wisconsin governor Tommy Thompson did very well with the health industry (and big tobacco) before joining the Bush administration as head of Health and Human Services. As close to the president as a cabinet member, the White House chief of staff, Andrew Card, was a former lobbyist for the auto industry. Scott Harshbarger, president of Common Cause, said: "This demonstrates the almost pervasive nature of money and politics. The line gets almost totally blurred. How do you oversee an industry that you have come from or raised money from? At what point are you the captive or advocate of these industries as much as the overseer? These industries give a huge amount of money, so the question is, 'What do they want in return?' " We all know Harshbarger's last query was rhetorical.

Often the more insidious exchange occurs between someone's lobbying or industry work and his or her later service in the agency that oversees or regulates former clients or employers. Rather than simply funneling cash, these people actually get to write the laws for their former and probably future bosses legitimately! President Bush's choices for his agency leaders demonstrates this all too clearly. They trooped over to their new Washington digs . . . right from the industries they were assigned to regulate.

Controversial from the start, Gail Norton was confirmed as interior secretary, returning to the department where she had worked during the Reagan administration under the infamous James Watts. Norton brought back years of additional experience as a lobbyist for various regulated businesses. As Colorado attorney general and in the private sector, Norton actively opposed environmental laws that regulated businesses and individuals. Now she manages the over 400 million acres of public land and much of the nation's water. As Timothy Egan wrote in the *New York Times,* "grizzly bears, major environmental groups and new plans to bring wolves back to the West are out. Local governments in the West, mining and drilling advocates and off-road machines like snowmobiles and swamp buggies are in."

While attitudes about an agency's or a department's emphasis shift between administrations, we should expect appointments to demonstrate some support for the mission of the agency they've been selected to lead. Norton's top appointees all come from the oil, gas, and coal industry lobbies. Her number-two at Interior is mining and chemical industry lobbyist J. Steven Griles. Griles is coming full circle, having also served under James Watts before leaving to service the National Mining Association, Occidental Petroleum, and other corporate interests. In March 2001 then spokesman for the National Mining Association John Grasser called Griles "an ally to the industry." Camden Toohey lobbied for drilling in the Alaskan Arctic. Now he is in charge of that very subject.

Bush's pick for number two at the EPA under former governor

Christie Whitman was Linda J. Fisher, a lobbyist for Monsanto, the chemical giant now moving into agribusiness. Fisher also served in the Reagan administration. The person who will supervise our natural resources including forests at the Agriculture Department is Mark Rey. He circled back and forth as a Senate staffer and twenty-year lobbyist for the timber industry. The president selected Philip Cooney as chief of staff of the Council on Environmental Quality. As a lawyer for the National Petroleum Institute, Cooney lobbied vigorously against the entire concept of global warming. The list continues in this fashion almost without interruption. Remember that old adage about the fox and the henhouse?

The staffing merry-go-round is so blatant that the folks on K Street, home to many lobbyists, try to avoid too many media confrontations on the subject. In a *Los Angeles Times* piece by Edmond Sanders and Richard Simon only two months into the Bush administration, business lobbyists were metaphorically breaking out the champagne. Corporate lobbyist Dan Danner noted he had been invited to the Clinton White House only once in eight years but had been there seven times in the first days of 2001. One trade spokesman who preferred anonymity said, "The whole business of whether big business is dominating this administration is extremely touchy."

To be fair, Bill Clinton staffed positions with his politically favored personnel. Former governor Bruce Babbitt was also the head of the League of Conservation Voters before taking over the Interior Department. The head of the Wilderness Society, George Frampton, became the chair of the White House Environmental Council. However, any honest politician will tell you the power disparity between these public interest groups and big business is astronomical. The former tend to win out not because of money but only when they are able to rally enough of a citizen stink that politicians are worried about voter backlash. What is truly amusing, however, despite protests to the contrary, is how much influence business had throughout the eight years of the Democratic administration.

Bill Clinton was no enemy of corporate America. He repeatedly angered Republicans by usurping their positions on issues. Why do you think he waited until his very last days to enact those ergonomics regulations for labor, the arsenic limitations that offended miners, or the logging and road ban that angered the timber industry? Clinton was able to leave office with his more liberal, environmentalist head held high after eight years of appeasing the industries for his political benefit. So when you read that the Bush administration is now run by business, recognize that such influence has gone from quite good to really great.

While it is not surprising that Republicans and Democrats each fill positions with their people, this behavior simply magnifies the reality that our laws all stem from a private agenda that may have little to do with the good of the country. These agency heads flipflop based on politics, contributions, and the power of special interests, not the needs and long-term interests of the American people. Bill Clinton's political advisor, Stuart Eizenstat, sagely noted, "The law is always up for grabs. That's why Reagan appointed five hundred federal judges. The law is not an inflexible instrument like a cannon that can be lined up and fired. It is a flexible human instrument that responds to political power. That's what having political power is all about for chrissakes."

The spectacle presented by the current Bush administration may be more extreme than usual, but it is predictable. What has happened to the big lobbying firms presents an even more disturbing trend. Once upon a time when you saw a firm's name, you could recognize it as a Democratic group or vice versa. You would expect the liberals to line up with their guys to push that traditional agenda while business and more conservative groups rallied elsewhere. Not any longer.

The big lobbyists-for-hire now all share identical characteristics *and* interests. The powerhouse firms boldly advertise their bipartisan credentials. They have truly become one-stop shopping for all your political influence needs. All pretense of ideological purity has disappeared as Democrats and Republicans throw in together to make the almighty dollar. In 1999 the lobbying firm Clark and Weinstock gave up its GOP exclusivity to take on former Democrat congressman Vic Fazio. The firm's billings jumped 55 percent that year. A principal at the company attributed major new clients like Seagrams, GE, Edison International, Cargill, and others to Fazio's powers of persuasion. Sceptics might attribute this to the new Democratic influence added to it's letterhead.

Nor does it matter which clients you climb in bed with. The tobacco lobby was able to corral former Texas governor Ann Richards, former senator and presidential candidate Bob Dole, and former senator George Mitchell. Foreign countries and corporations also tap into our talent. After his term in office, Clinton's former secretary of defense (and Republican senator) William Cohen wasted no time establishing the Cohen Group with three other former defense officials to "help multinational clients set up businesses overseas and handle problems that may arise." Cohen moved right into offices with the powerful lobbying law firm McDermott, Will and Emery, which represents, among other clients, Pentagon contractor Lockheed Martin.

Just listen to former elected officials talk about their new positions. Bill Paxon left his New York House seat and tenure as chairman of the Republican Congressional Committee to join Akin, Gump, Strauss, Hauer and Feld, once known as a Democratic stronghold. In his first year there, he earned about $750,000. As a representative on the Hill, Paxon said, he spent "a lot of time strategizing on legislative issues, working on the public angles, and trying to keep an eye on the big picture. It's the same downtown"—only for a lot more money. Now that Paxon is cleared to lobby his old chums directly, his value is increasing dramatically.

Paxon now spends much of his time raising money for former colleagues. During the 2000 campaign, for example, his efforts netted millions for the Republicans. Campaign finance reformer Fred Werth-heimer summed it up: "You used to leave Capitol Hill and sell your relationships with former members as a valuable commodity. The new part of the game involves buying your way in by raising large amounts of money for the powers-that-be."

This is how it works. Paxon, a former member of the House Commerce, Energy, and Power Subcommittee, helps acquire a big client, Americans for Affordable Electricity (AAE), as a client for Akin, Gump. (This group included Enron Corporation and other large electricity users.) AAE pays Akin, Gump about $500,000 annually for Paxon's services. Paxon then helps raise campaign money for officials like his buddy Representative Joe Barton, who chairs the House Commerce, Energy, and Power Subcommittee. Of course, Paxon then confers with Barton about the many "issues" facing his clients. All of this is perfectly legal, yet it smells to high heaven.

However, Paxon is just one of hundreds. If you run down the list of retired congressmen and senators, this incestuous employment is the rule, not the exception. Paxon is simply doing what the law allows and making the most of his government experience. As former House Appropriations Committee chair Bob Livingston says, "I was an advocate for my district and my country. Now I'm an advocate for my clients. I don't see a great distinction." You may not, Bob, but others do. K Street is known as "Gucci Gulch" for a reason.

Remember, our former elected officials are just part of the lobbying equation. Don't forget the aides, staffers, and agency lawyers who spin back and forth. While Enron spent about $2.4 million on campaign contributions in the 2000 election cycle, it spent almost that much on big-time lobbyists, including the powerful former aides to both House Majority leader Dick Armey and House Majority whip Tom DeLay. Then there was the fantastic exchange of personnel that occurred between Enron and the Bush administration at this time. Now Harvey Pitt is chairing the SEC after spending years as counsel to the very company, Arthur Andersen, he must now investigate.

As I keep repeating in utter amazement, this is all perfectly legal. Yet the truth behind these relationships is easily discovered simply by following the money. Most significant rules and laws can be tracked right back to the lobbyists and powerful interest groups that fund the politicians who pass them. And don't forget, inaction is just as important as action. When most of the culprits involved in the Enron deal walk away virtually unscathed, and they will, it will be because Congress and the reviewing agencies have intentionally refused to step up to the plate.

Then there are the enormous private organizations that have no need of some lowly lobbying firm. In this sacred realm, there is really no separation between the work of the business and that of the government. When former secretary of both state and the treasury Jim Baker joined the Carlyle Group, he reunited with Frank Carlucci, Reagan's defense secretary, Bush's budget director Richard Darman, and many other friends. He was also joining ranks with those who were once labeled political "enemies," such as Jimmy Carter's domestic advisor, David Rubenstein. Rubenstein described his first meeting with Baker: "Here I was with a man who had helped throw me and other Democrats out of office twelve years ago. We had been brought together by a prominent Democrat [Bob Strauss] fresh from duty in a Republican Administration. It's truly a tale of the way things work in today's Washington." Carlucci echoed this when he said, "We certainly don't look at ourselves as a refuge for former government employees, but I'd be a fool to deny that having a number of high-profile officeholders does provide Carlyle with certain advantages." Yes, it certainly does.

Described in its own literature as "a vast, interlocking, global network of businesses and investment professionals," Carlyle became a multibillion-dollar company within five years of its formation. It needed someone to run a new telecom fund so it promptly hired the former U.S. Federal Communications chairman from the Clinton administration, William Kennard.

When Jim Baker joined the firm, he was under the one-year rule about lobbying at home, but no one said he couldn't do his lobbying abroad. Former policymakers from both sides of the fence represent American businesses one moment and foreign competitors the next. Carlyle even brings in world leaders, including former U.S. president George Bush Sr., former U.K. prime minister John Major, and former president of the Philippines Fidel Ramos.

In a piece for *Red Herring* in January 2002 entitled "Carlyle's Way," Dan Briody wrote: "The Carlyle Group leaves itself open to any number of conflicts of interest and stunning ironies. For example, it is hard to ignore the fact that [Carlyle clients] Osama bin Laden's family members, who renounced their son ten years ago, stood to gain financially from the war being waged against him until late October when public criticism of the relationship forced them to liquidate their holdings in the firm. Or consider that U.S. President George W. Bush is in a position to make budgetary decisions that could pad his father's bank account."

While I'm at this, I might as well bite the hand that feeds me. Many politicians have jumped on the campaign finance bandwagon in recent years as national expenditures reach obscene heights and more blatantly affect the election process. The 2000 election year cycle garnered about $3 billion in hard and soft contributions to the federal campaigns. This figure represents an almost $1 billion increase since 1996. Remember, money buys access and access usually equals influence. For only $25,000 to the RNC, you can meet for dinner each month with the House speaker and committee chairs. The Democratic National Committee's Jefferson Trust entitled $100,000 donors to weekend retreats with leaders, dinner with the president, briefings, and daily reports. Just imagine what the top level of donors, who gave more than $350,000, got in the way of access. A lot more than a night in the Lincoln bedroom, I guarantee.

The McCain-Feingold Bill took a stab at reducing the influence of soft money (unlimited party contributions) and seemingly independent issue ads that were essentially "in-kind" contributions to a candidate. Yet within days of its passage, Republican representative Bill Thomas of California had already offered legislation to weaken regulation of "527" organizations. These groups allegedly are organized for the primary purpose of influencing or attempting to influence the selection, nomination, election, or appointment of an individual to political office. Despite this supposed intent, they are rarely nonpartisan. The 527s can collect unlimited contributions from unions, businesses, and individuals. They are neither fish nor fowl, and with their exemptions from many IRS reporting laws, these groups likely will become great sources of soft money to state and federal candidates.

While the favored get access, what does the average voter get? We get some negative ads, direct mail we don't read, and, of course, a plea for more money. Most political contributions go to salaries, benefits, and other infrastructure of the business known as a campaign. A nice chunk also may go to a candidate's "personal PAC" so that he or she can more directly influence (buy) fellow representatives when their votes are needed. The favorite excuse for the need for all this money is to purchase expensive television advertising, but TV ads represent just a fraction of the overall campaign expenditures.

Why not give candidates free airtime? Every other world democracy does just that. After all, we've allowed the government practically to donate the public airways to companies, which have become monstrously wealthy as a result. Shouldn't these media moguls give back a bit? That was the original bargain as far back as the Communications Act of 1934.

When we handed over the airwaves to our broadcast companies, forgoing billions of dollars for the Treasury, there was an expectation of some public service in exchange. In 1967 the Supreme Court upheld the Fairness Doctrine, which required broadcasters to "provide coverage of vitally important issues of interest to the community" and provide "a reasonable opportunity for contrasting viewpoints on such issues." Since that time, the media and its cohort, the Federal Communications Commission (FCC), have steadily eroded this obligation until it has virtually disappeared. This couldn't have been clearer than when our current FCC chairman, Michael Powell, spoke to the American Bar Association in 1998. "The night after I was sworn in [as a commissioner], I waited for a visit from the angel of the public interest. I waited all night, but she did not come."

Once again, it is all about the money. The TV Bureau of Advertis-

ing examined the relationship between political ad dollars and broadcast reporting in 2000, and the picture wasn't pretty. Political coverage over the airwaves was down about 40 percent since 1988, the last
time the White House was an open seat. An excellent example of the
diminished reporting was the New Jersey Senate primary. New York's
CBS station took in about $4 million in revenue for some 1,200 ads
during this race. In the last two weeks before the vote, the station ran
only eight stories that included two minutes of sound bites while running 100 commercials. Obviously a candidate must buy coverage to
be heard.

Sure enough, TV ad revenues during campaign season are soaring. The TV Bureau of Advertising determined that political advertising in 2000 provided about 9.2 percent of the annual revenues—or
$600 million—for local stations alone. Estimates put total ad costs for
the 2000 election cycle at $1 billion. Not surprisingly, broadcasters ac-
tively oppose any reform that legislates free airtime as they simultaneously diminish meaningful political coverage. In his book *Rich Media,
Poor Democracy,* Robert McChesney wrote, "Broadcasters have little
incentive to cover candidates, because it is in their interest to force
them to purchase time to publicize their campaigns."

Since 1977 the broadcast lobby has defeated about 165 free airtime bills. Between 1996 and 1998 the National Association of Broadcasters (NAB) and five other media outlets spent nearly $11 million to
crush a dozen attempts at this reform. (The NAB's lobbying expenses
in 1999 alone were $4.9 million.) This group stepped up the push as
the 2000 McCain-Feingold Bill gathered steam and was completely
successful in blocking any requirements that broadcasters donate airtime.

McChesney updated his reflections for *The Nation* in January
2002. He noted that the Center for Public Integrity reported that "the
fifty largest media companies and four of their trade associations
spent $111.3 million between 1996 and mid-2000 to lobby Congress
and the executive branch." That this is a good investment is beyond
question. "Explicit government policies and subsidies [permit] the creation of large and profitable conglomerates. When the government
grants free monopoly rights to TV spectrum, for example, it is not setting the terms of competition; it is picking the winner of the competition. Such policies amount to an annual grant of corporate welfare
that economist Dean Baker values in the tens of billions of dollars."

These results cannot be a surprise to anyone. As with the EPA or the SEC, the FCC is also a revolving door for industry lobbyists. Brendan I. Koerner reports for *Mother Jones* that "one former chairman, Dennis Patrick, is now president of AOL Wireless; Powell's immediate predecessor, William Kennard, came to the FCC from the powerful law and lobbying firm Verner Liipfert, known for its influential communications practice. [Remember, he then left the FCC and joined Carlyle.] Powell's chief of staff, Marsha McBride, formerly lobbied for Disney, and Powell's only post–law school job in the private sector was as an attorney at a D.C. law firm where his clients included GTE."

The magazine reviewed FCC disclosure records that set out the agency's daily activities. Of forty-three meetings reported from June 4 to June 7, 2001, thirty-eight of those "ex-parte proceedings" (where only one side of an issue or controversy is present for discussions) "were with lobbyists from AT&T, WorldCom, and other corporate interests." Public interest advocates haven't the money or staff to compete with the communications industry "whose lobbying expenses now stand at roughly $125 million, more than twice the amount spent by defense firms," says Koerner.

What does this industry want? The FCC currently is seriously considering one scary goal. Only two days after the terror attacks of 2001, the FCC voted to "review" the last rules prohibiting virtual monopolies in the area of communication and information. Journalist Mark Crispin Miller, media critic and professor at New York University, describes the nation's prospects: "Unless there's some effective opposition, the several-headed vendor that now sells us nearly all our movies, TV, radio, magazines, books, music and web services will soon be selling us our daily papers, too—for the major dailies have, collectively, been lobbying energetically for that big waiver, which stands to make their owners even richer (an expectation that has no doubt had a sweetening effect on coverage of the Bush Administration)."

These big papers will be partners with the networks that, along with radio, are owned by the big corporations. As *The Week* editorialized in January 2002: "Communications giants aren't interested in airing anti-establishment views. Thanks to the trend toward mega-mergers and conglomerates, they are the establishment. Ultimately, they answer only to the bottom line of dollars and cents, and [quoting Miller] their 'big bosses want big favors from the state' in order to grow even bigger." Miller reminds us, "While such a setup may make economic sense, as anticompetitive arrangements tend to do, it has no place in a democracy, where the people have to know more than their masters want to tell them."

Television, radio, and print outlets are an integral part of a free society. Access to information is critical. It is time to call big media on the money game and demand both increased coverage of important issues and free time for candidates. These changes may hurt ratings as viewers switch to more entertaining programming. They also will also diminish the bottom line for these corporations. However, these are minimal sacrifices for a political system that has given the corporations so much.

Along with the FCC, the Federal Election Commission (FEC) helps perpetuate our current campaign system. Made up of three Republicans and three Democrats, it has long been viewed as an arm of the two political parties. Senator John McCain believes that the FEC "has become an ineffective and toothless commission committed to preserving the status quo instead of enforcing campaign finance reform laws," according to his spokeswoman, Nancy Ives. As the FEC will be enforcing new provisions in the McCain-Feingold Bill, it too must be overhauled. Republican senator Mitch McConnell is not only challenging this McCain-Feingold bill, he intends to oppose any attempt to alter the commission's makeup, saying, "The model for the FEC is the same model used for the Senate and House ethics committees." Now, there's a recommendation.

Pick any government agency. Note its leadership. These people have been selected to push an administration's political point of view. Thirty or forty years ago, appointees at least tried to shed their partisan cloaks in favor of the public interest, but today such magnanimity is gone. We must debunk ourselves of the more noble notions of democratic representation and instead judge all legislation and regulation by its source and its backers. Understanding who wants something and whether they are powerful enough to be heard usually explains new rules in any administration. Most of the other rules can be judged by the political mileage they produce, like Bill Clinton's 100,000 cops and teachers or the latest tax cut allegedly targeted at the middle class.

There is one group that doesn't care who wins or loses in these legislative battles. It's members make money either way. As Tocqueville wrote in *Democracy in America*, "Lawyers in the United States form a power that . . . envelops society as a whole, penetrates into each of the classes that compose it, works in secret, acts constantly on it without its knowing, and in the end models it to its own desires."

In *Henry VI*, Shakespeare wrote that unforgettable line, "First thing we do is kill all the lawyers." We applaud this suggestion today but for reasons he didn't intend. Originally lawyers were perceived to be educated soldiers in defense of freedom. A tyrant would do well to destroy these men. But by the time our nation was founded, such sentiment was in serious question.

As the new government took shape in America, a philosophical battle raged between those who believed in an inherent elite and others who imagined a more inclusive system of power. Federalist Alexander Hamilton had little confidence in the common man. He believed that only lawyers—the "disinterested class"—could properly and impartially run the country. Rather than the merchants, farmers, or businessmen who might have too much self-interest in political outcomes, this "learned profession" with "no vested economic interest to advance" would be nominated as our natural leaders.

The anti-Federalists argued that this group had a clear agenda. As Amos Singeltary of Massachusetts said, "Those lawyers and men of learning, and monied men, that talk so finely, and gloss over matters so smoothly, to make us poor illiterate people swallow down the pills, expect to get into Congress themselves; they expect to be the managers of this Constitution, and get all the power and the money into their own hands, and then they will swallow up all us little folks, like the great Leviathan."

Singeltary was right. The professional class that convinced me to pursue the law has co-opted it instead. We don't operate on a commonsense "reasonable man" standard any longer; instead we have a law for every action and, frighteningly, almost every thought. As we have seen in detail, lawyers have succeeded in expanding control over our lives in the most extraordinary way. Their infiltration has been made easier through the enormous role they play in our legislative process as elected officials, agency leaders, and lobbyists and from the bench as our judges.

Tocqueville warned us of this evolution in the early 1800s, when he witnessed lawyers finding their way to governing bodies like moths to a flame. "In all free governments, whatever their form might be, lawyers will be found in the first ranks of all parties. . . . When the rich man, the noble, and the prince are excluded from the government, the lawyers arrive there so to speak in full right; for they then form the only enlightened and skilled men whom the people can choose outside themselves."

In fact, he predicted danger if lawyers were not co-opted by the system: "A prince who, in the presence of an encroaching democracy, sought to bring down the judicial power in his states and to diminish the political influence of lawyers in them, would commit a great error. . . . It will always be easy for a king to make lawyers the most useful instruments of his power."

Although we like to imagine lawyers challenging authority and suppressing tyranny, Tocqueville recognized their natural affinity for power and structure. "What lawyers love above all things is a life of order, and the greatest guarantee of order is authority. . . . If they prize freedom, they generally place legality well above it; they fear tyranny less than arbitrariness, and provided that the legislator takes charge of taking away men's independence, they are nearly content."

Indeed, lawyers have taken their "rightful" place at the helm, issuing and executing orders in the name of stability over anarchy and structure over freedom. In fact, they now dominate our government. By the mid-1990s both our president and his wife were attorneys, along with 42 percent of the House and 61 percent of the Senate. Add to this the federal regulators, led by lawyers, who supervise over 130,000 employees assigned to churn out and enforce rules (at an annual cost of almost $19 billion), the 70,000 plus lobbyists, mostly lawyers, searching for legal favors and loopholes for their clients; the in-house and private attorneys for every affected business, organization, and agency; and the federal prosecutors prepared to enforce the will of the current administration, and you have a plague of legal locusts. These numbers do not include the countless lawyers and judges involved with the criminal justice system, private litigation, or state and local governments. It would be nice to imagine lawyers as protectors against tyranny, but Tocqueville recognized their true nature.

Lawyers have their finger in every pie. No public policy or personal activity escapes their reach, and the law profession is profiting accordingly. Contacts and political access are the important qualities in a good hire, not grades or legal knowledge. The ambulance chaser has become more sophisticated, roaming the cocktail circuit, television studios, and halls of Congress for profit. In fact, attorneys dominate the ranks of lobbyists.

Many big law firms maintain an entire lobbying division staffed with their most influential partners. When representing corporate and industry clients, they cajole, manipulate, and buy the laws and enforcement their clients need. None other than our current U.S. treasury secretary, Paul O'Neill, has noted this when, as CEO of Alcoa, he dissolved his company's PAC. He told *Fortune* magazine, "What's going on with campaign financing has reached well beyond a reasonable limit. Some people said we'd have a problem with access [to elected officials]. That hasn't been the case." On its website, the Center for Responsive Politics explains that Alcoa employed the Texas law firm of Vinson and Elkins (Enron's primary attorneys) to lobby. "While Bush was still governor of Texas, Vinson and Elkins got a loophole in the state's environmental regulations that will allow Alcoa to continue emitting 60,000 tons of sulfur dioxide annually into the air, solidifying Alcoa's position as one of Texas' top polluters. [This firm] was George Bush's No. 3 campaign contributor, giving him more than $200,000." O'Neill found that access was a snap.

Unless they are employing them, Republicans do not generally win with attorneys. In the 1999–2000 campaign cycle, lawyers and law firms topped the list of all industries contributing to the 107th Congress. This group gave over $29 million, with 67 percent going to the Democrats. Hillary Rodham Clinton led in individual donations from this cadre. During the first six months of 1999, federal candidates received over $4 million from trial lawyers. Nearly one-third of that was from only twelve firms—the twelve law firms that directed the to-

bacco litigation. The $29 million does not include the millions con-
tributed as unregulated soft money

The Association of Trial Lawyers of America (ATLA), ranked by
Fortune magazine as the sixth most powerful lobby group on Capitol
Hill, was number one among the legal/lobbyist donors. Ninety percent
of its contributions went to Democratic candidates. This plaintiff's
group of litigators, petitioning for itself, focuses primarily on preventing tort reform. This area of the law encompasses those wrongful
acts other than a breach of contract for which the law imposes civil liability such as personal injury and medical malpractice cases. The expansion of causes of action and damages and the ability to collect
enormous contingency fees keep this organization busy in the state
houses and on Capitol Hill. As Washington, D.C., attorney John Coale
said knowingly, "With a Democratic Congress, tort reform does not
happen."

These tort lawyers are active in political races at the state and local
level as well. Their effort to develop friends throughout government is
really paying off. In fact, many plaintiff firms are finding themselves
in partnership with elected officials as more states pursue tort litigation on behalf of their citizens. Smart litigators have realized that they
can try big class actions not only for individuals but for the government as well, as seen in the tobacco litigations.

What about the gun companies, lead paint manufacturers, asbestos firms, HMOs, and nursing homes? James K. Glassman, writing
for the *Reason* website, talked of chastising the Michigan attorney general, Jennifer Granholm, at the Democratic National Convention in
2000 upon hearing her threaten a "Smith and Wesson–type thing"
against DoubleClick, the Internet marketing firm. He recalled former
labor secretary Robert Reich warning of this "regulation by lawsuit"
several years ago. Glassman concluded, "It's an old story of a lust for
publicity, for money, for votes at any price, but it is fast making the
nation's system of justice into a tool for government extortion."

Just ask Smith and Wesson about extortion. When the plaintiffs' bar
and government targets an industry, legal principles may go out the
window. The financial pressures, public maligning, and production uncertainty can put a company out of business before any liability is contested. This gun manufacturer bowed to such blackmail when reaching
a settlement with the government two years ago. By agreeing to include safety locks, insure background checks, and take ballistic finger-

prints of its guns (among other provisions), state and local lawsuits were dropped and the federal government declined to sue the company. While the agreement is laudable, the manner in which it was achieved is not. As John Velleco of the Gun Owners of America said, "It has taken the full weight of the federal government at taxpayer expense to put a stranglehold on one of the largest producers of a legal product in this country to force it to change its behavior." Other manufacturers and gun dealers who resented the cave-in promptly ostracized the firm, further damaging its reputation and bottom line. Ironically, in the early 1990s, Smith and Wesson's home state of Connecticut feared the company might fold and put residents out of work. Officials spent a lot of state money to prop up the business, only to switch sides when suing seemed more profitable.

Although they have almost no accountability for the consequences, lawyers and judges are determining our social and economic future. I'll talk a bit more about class actions in a moment, but anyone who thinks big corporate targets are selected by attorneys to address consumer needs is naive or crazy. Tobacco is still heavily subsidized. Our government now partners in its profits. Billions of dollars in legal fees have been paid to private attorneys, and most of the dollars paid as damages are going not toward the health problems smoking causes or to smoking reduction programs that allegedly justified the suits. Some states, like Florida, are reinvesting state pension funds in the tobacco companies, confident that the profits will be there for years to come.

Big problems in many industries need addressing, but the trial court is not the place to do this. Tort lawyers argue that our officials haven't the political gumption to legislate. Wendell Gauthier, a big antitobacco lawyer, told the *Washington Post,* "Where lobbying has gotten so intense and money has gotten so great that they can't legislate, I think legislatures need our help." Who elected these guys? As a *Detroit News* editorial responded: "This administration is using the court system to extract money from the industry that it couldn't obtain politically. Who are the real racketeers here? If the government wants more revenue and tighter regulations on the companies, it should try to get legislation passed—not pervert the justice system."

Money and influence regularly buy silence from our legislators on many controversial issues, but aren't we trading one curse for another? Ralph Nader wrote way back in 1976, "There is something profoundly undemocratic about a 'corporate' state run by only a few without the informed consent and participation of the many." That is exactly what is happening today with the powerful trial lawyers. We are permitting the plaintiffs' bar to determine state and national policy. Its motives are no purer than those of corporate special interest groups, and its tactics are the same. These legal groups contribute millions of dollars to those officials who can assist in their schemes, and billions are returned back to them as contingency fees.

According to Alabama's attorney general, Bill Pryor, "The use of contingency-fee contracts allows government lawyers to avoid the appropriation process; it creates the illusion that the lawsuits are being pursued at no cost to the taxpayers. These contracts also create the potential for outrageous windfalls or even outright corruption for political supporters of the officials who negotiated the contracts." We are way past the point of "potential." The future is here.

From the first national suit, when Richard Scruggs teamed up with his college buddy, Mississippi's attorney general, Michael Moore, the relationships between officials and counsel have been . . . unique. Hiring friends may not seem so bad, but your former law firm? Kansas attorney general Carla Stovall saw no problem with that. The state legislature tried to pass a cap on any fees earned in the Kansas tobacco case but weren't quick enough. The contingency contracts had already been signed.

Stovall has company all over the country as friends and contributors are tossed these absolute gold mines. The *St. Louis Dispatch* described Missouri's cozy confab as "an unholy alliance between the state and tobacco interests . . . a political gravy train [as] the five law firms involved in the case donated a total of more than $500,000 in campaign contributions over the past eight years, mostly to Democrats." About one-quarter of this sum, $139,000, went to the state attorney general, Jay Nixon, who was responsible for hiring and managing the private lawyers. Those attorneys may garner as much as $100 million for representing the state in the Medicaid-tobacco litigation.

Attorney Peter Angelos is apparently a god of sorts to the Maryland legislature. Walter Olson described his connections in a piece for *Reason*: "Among the nation's most munificent Democratic donors, Angelos is, per the *Washington Post* account, 'viewed by many political insiders as the most powerful private citizen in Maryland.' He sports his own personal lobbyist, glove-close relations with Gov. Parris Glendening, and a host of statehouse connections, such as with the president pro tem of the state Senate, who happens to be a lawyer with his firm."

The asbestos cases really put Angelos on the map. At one point he decided that the state needed more judges to hear these asbestos cases, so he proposed a bill to increase their numbers. Although never elected, he said, "Who's going to do it but me? I don't want to be the author of the bill. But I have to be." He got the judges. More than that, he pushed the legislature to essentially change the tobacco rules in the middle of the state lawsuit when he wanted to introduce certain evidence. Retroactive lawmaking was improper the last time I checked. Angelos submitted a bill for $1 *billion* for his tobacco work. The *Washington Post* reported that his billing records revealed that Angelos "had used $12-an-hour lawyers from a temp agency for nearly 25 percent of the hours he billed. From $12 to $15,000 is [quite] a markup."

In December 1998 the five law firms hired by then attorney general Dan Morales to handle Texas tobacco litigation were awarded $3.3 billion in legal fees. Allegations soon were made that Morales had solicited large sums of money from those lawyers. According to the *Houston Chronicle,* local attorney Joe Jamail, who did not participate in the tobacco litigation, said, "Morales solicited $1 million from each of several lawyers he considered hiring." The paper also reported that the ex-wife of one of the lawyers, John Eddie Williams, gave sworn testimony that "Williams had told her that Morales wanted $1 million from one or more of the lawyers that were hired for the tobacco case." These lawyers responded to inquiries by arguing that taxpayers had no business investigating their fees because their monies ultimately were paid by the cigarette companies and not the state.

This story is repeated in state after state. In the spring of 2001, a San Francisco firm launched what it termed the first "affirmative litigation" office. The intent is apparently to partner regularly with the city in profitable suits against various businesses. By 2001 the relationship between the big tort firms and their patrons in the state houses became so blatantly obvious that the American Bar Association (ABA) decided to act.

ABA's House of Delegates indirectly acknowledging this "appearance of impropriety," the BA, after many attempts, finally passed a new ethics rule in 2000 that would bar attorneys from making political contributions if the money is intended to get government work. The practice, commonly known as "pay to play," is prevalent enough to call for action, but I could drive an eighteen-wheeler through this standard. I can hear it now.

"Mr. X, when you gave the $300,000 contribution to Senator Y, did you intend to influence the award of that $20 million contract from the government."

"Oh, heavens, no, sir."

"Well, then, case dismissed!"

While still chairman of the Securities and Exchange Commission, Arthur Levitt testified for the passage of this rule. Not considered particularly naive, Levitt said with a straight face that "this would insure that competence not connections would be the basis for awarding government legal work." Whom was he kidding?

Lawyers will have no more fear of this new ethics rule than politicians have of bribery statutes. Such efforts are not even Band-Aids on the seeping wounds of corruption in our political system. Favors are bought and sold like commodities. For the SEC commissioner or the ABA to pretend that passage of such a rule will accomplish anything is insulting.

On both the state and national level, gifts are delivered to the plaintiffs' bar simply by adding attorney's fees as an element of damages in major legislation. The Americans with Disabilities Act and the Civil Rights Act of 1991 are just two of the countless statutes that promote litigation. All you had to do was watch the lawsuits skyrocket when attorney fees were included in the legislation to see the correlation.

Contrary to British law, we have no "loser pays" provision wherein the plaintiff must pay the cost of litigation if he or she loses. England has instituted this practice with great success. Many variations still encourage representation of needy clients, such as partial payment of plaintiff's fees on settlement, but the fact that there is a cost to frivolous or bad-faith litigation is sobering. Think of all those ridiculous suits that may seem entertaining but are actually clogging the courts and costing money to pursue. If plaintiffs had to pay the other side's fees upon losing, a large number of these cases would disappear—and rightfully so—from the docket. Additionally, some reform plans also deduct a portion of attorney fees from the winning party if that side turned down a settlement offer that exceeded the final trial award. These provisions encourage resolution, not prolonged litigation. In this country we simply sue. Why not? There's no downside.

England has another policy that should be adopted in this country. It does not permit contingency fee contracts. Here in the United States, this practice began as a means of obtaining payment from poor clients in worthwhile cases. Now almost every form of litigation uses this fee structure. This arrangement has become a form of high-stakes gambling for the legal community. While the cost of challenging a major industry can be astronomical, so are the rewards. In a speech last summer, Justice Sandra Day O'Connor noted that lawyers become "business partners of plaintiffs in seeking large-dollar recoveries rather than act as objective servants of the law." She continued: "Such arrangements have made more overnight millionaires than almost any other businesses and the perverse incentives and the untoward consequences they are creating within our profession are many."

Trial work has become a major stand-alone business within the legal community. What was once the place for good advice about the worthiness of a claim has become a gristmill for expanding rights and remedies. To enterprising attorneys, there are few unmerited lawsuits. Traditionally, lawyers were officers of the court who zealously represented clients within legal and ethical boundaries. The interests of justice were paramount, such that intentionally misleading a jury or using discovery simply to wear down an opponent or drain his pocketbook was degrading to the practitioner and unethical as well. Using court pleadings or the media as a litigation tactic to destroy an opponent was unacceptable. Attorneys now regularly solicit clients, conjure up creative and nuisance filings, and delay the trial process, all to line their own pockets.

Even former New York governor and once likely Supreme Court appointee Mario Cuomo succumbed to modern reality in a 2000 commencement address to young lawyers entitled "The Soul of the Profession." In describing the personal meaning of the practice of law, he focused not on the more noble aspects but instead on "putting food on the table . . . and getting the bills paid." He went on to say "Billions of human beings have come and gone, and only an infinitesimal number of them have succeeded in making a difference in the development of this planet." So, why bother? Do your time and cash your checks.

Litigation firms are clearly bent on winning at all costs. They have experts in various fields on staff to help evaluate new cases. Mock courtrooms are built into their office space where they can coach witnesses and even conduct full rehearsals complete with real citizens in the jury box. "Shadow jurors" are hired to sit in the pews during actual trials, watch the day's proceedings, and then critique counselors and witnesses each evening.

In a small midwestern town in 1974, a jury consultant helped select a panel of twelve that, surprisingly, refused to convict several antiwar protestors. Attorneys around the country took notice. Since then some practitioners brag that they can predict "with 96 percent accuracy" what a given jury will do, member by member. This so-called science consists of the ability to recognize and manipulate public opinion about an event, law enforcement, the court process, and the justice system as a whole. Jo Ellen Dimitrius, the jury consultant made famous by the O. J. Simpson case, was credited with empanelling the twelve citizens who bought the defense strategy that produced an acquittal. More than the facts in a case, it is the weighing of attitudes, often fostered by the media, that becomes integral to jury selection.

In 1994 we were treated to tips on how to manipulate the media. Author Robert Weider collected pointers from the likes of Robert Shapiro, Steve Lerman, and Howard Weitzman, attorneys for O. J. Simpson, Rodney King, and Michael Jackson, respectively. "Trial balloons" are floated to test acceptable (not necessarily truthful) theories long before the case reaches the courthouse. The famous "race card" in the Simpson case was played first in the New York press. Attorneys analyzed the ensuing media debate before refining their in-court presentation. It worked.

When the Paula Jones story broke in the *Washington Post,* President Clinton retained attorney Bob Bennett as "part of an aggressive public relations and legal strategy aimed at fighting" these allegations. One White House official was quoted as saying "Bennett is savvy about both the law, as well as the ways of Washington and the press. He brings a lot of assets to this type of case." What followed was an amazing political struggle that only peripherally acknowledged the relevant legal issues of perjury and obstruction of justice.

Whether personal injury suits, class actions, or high-profile criminal cases, the trial process is now a game rather than a search for truth and justice. Rules are thwarted, abuses are tolerated, juries are manipulated, all in the name of winning rather than seeking the truth or doing justice. Each time this occurs, new case law emerges, becoming precedent for further perversion of long-standing legal principles.

Of course, none of this could happen without the help of the judges. Maybe this group is misnamed; today more and more jurists refuse actually to judge by taking a stand on worthless lawsuits or attorney misconduct. It doesn't help when courts are on the ballot, as they are in Texas.

My general election opponent in 1984 was a twenty-two-year incumbent. Despite his regular place at the bottom of the annual bar poll, attorneys kept reelecting him because they "knew" what they were getting. His court was a good place to go for a temporary restraining order at four-thirty on a Friday afternoon when opposing counsel "couldn't be reached." I decided to challenge this judge after my first experience in his court.

I was there seeking a default judgment. To accomplish this, I had to establish certain uncontested facts on the record. The judge would then peruse my paperwork and usually sign it. This process is relatively perfunctory, but a judge is supposed to listen and review the evidence to ensure that all hurdles have been crossed before approving the judgment. After all, I could ask for the moon and get a signature if no one bothered to check. When I approached the bench, the judge told me to start talking; he'd be back in a moment. I did my "prove-up" to the court reporter. When the judge returned, he immediately signed my judgment and moved on. He hadn't a clue whether my allegations and documents were correct.

Despite this judge's legal reputation, attorneys were quite concerned about publicly supporting any opponent. During the election contest, they had to appear before the sitting judge, who might know which candidate they were supporting. It took a lot of work and initially anonymous endorsements from various bar associations and newspapers before attorneys publicly rallied to my campaign. I won the election, was unopposed for my second term in 1988, and then moved on to CNN without having to confront the corrupting influence of money in judicial campaigns. Whether I would have kept my idealistic naiveté is anyone's guess. I like to think I would have.

The trial courts have a case-by-case effect on citizens, but corruption is most worrisome at the appellate level, where rulings become codified and truly affect future cases. The Texas Supreme Court has been infamous for years and relentlessly cited by legal reformers for the influence of money on justice. My apologies to the several friends now sitting on this court, but its history is well known.

In the late 1990s, an organization calling itself Texans for Public Justice began tracking political contributions to the high court to look for any correlation with outcomes. It didn't prove that money purchased results, but it did make a convincing case that it bought access. Only 11 percent of all appeals presented to the court were accepted for review, but your chances quadrupled if you were a contributor. In fact, the justices "were ten times more likely to accept petitions filed by contributors of more than $250,000 than petitions filed by non-contributors," according to the study. "The Court was more receptive to petitions filed by Chief Justice Tom Phillips' old firm than any other major appellate firm." That firm, Baker Botts, was one of just two that contributed more than $250,000 to the justices. It enjoyed an astonishing petition-acceptance rate of 74 percent. These statistics may mean nothing. Very high-profile firms may have more cases of first impression, unique circumstances, or simply the money to pursue lengthy appeals. Then again . . .

The big institutional givers also fared well. While accounting for only 19 percent of all contributions, these corporations still had a 20 percent acceptance rate for petitions. Those giving over $10,000 saw their chances increase to 33 percent. Before its downfall, Enron was the biggest player in this group.

It is also disconcerting that nine sitting members of the state's highest court raised $11 million in the general election campaigns between 1994 and 1998, mostly from firms and big-money interests. It is worth noting that a 1999 Supreme Court survey found that 48 percent of the state's *judges* say that campaign contributions have "a significant influence on the outcome of judicial decisions." The plaintiffs' lawyers were the big contributors to these races in the 1980s when the Democrats ran the high court. As the state came under Republican control in the 1990s, corporate interests and the big defense firms took over as the largest contributors. I wonder why.

Texas is one of eight states that hold partisan elections for their high courts, and its fund-raising is by no means the tops. It has been far surpassed by that of the Michigan judges. Three candidates for that high court spent a total of $16 million in the last election. A total of thirty-nine states elect some of their judiciary. Thankfully fourteen states now look, at least in part, to public funding for these races. The

American Bar Association finally stepped up to the plate in July 2001 and recommended that states fund judicial campaigns to limit the influence of money in our courts. According to ABA president Martha Barnett, "There has been an alarming increase in attempts by special interests to influence judicial elections through financial contributions and attack campaigning." This is not a revelation.

As if direct contributions weren't enough, how about the fact that big firms often subsidize judicial law clerks? In Texas, top firms recruit young lawyers before they begin a judicial internship by paying them large bonuses, sometimes even before the clerkship begins. A 2001 study by Texans for Public Justice reported that "Just four firms hired 33 of the 76 clerks and accounted for 70% of the potential conflicts of interest at the court." Since the court doesn't reveal future employment status or keep records of which clerks are recused from what cases, no one can track actual ethics violations. We are supposed to accept that no clerk would draft an opinion that might benefit his or her future employer. There should be a multiyear ban on appearing before a judge someone clerked for. At least this would give the appearance of propriety. However, the real cure, public funding of all judicial elections, should be mandated immediately.

With the aid of lenient judges, lawyers are now perpetrating a fraud upon the country under the guise of helping the masses. Let's take a closer look at class action lawsuits. Once prohibited under common law, this category attempts to efficiently litigate a large number of identical claims to reduce the effort and costs for all involved. The parties had to agree to participate and be notified about the action as it proceeded. Today nothing of the kind takes place.

Groups of lawyers regularly meet to peruse newspapers, the *Federal Register,* and other publications for ideas. When they find a "wrong," they then troll for plaintiffs, particularly in communities known to favor large awards against the evils of corporate America. Notices go out, sometimes to millions of people, telling them they can "opt out" of a class. If recipients ignore the notice (as most do), they are part of the group. Their "rights" are being litigated whether they want them pursued or not. They rarely learn more until some newspaper reports a settlement or they receive some discount coupon in the mail as their "award." The defendants may never get off the hook now that the Supreme Court has decided an injured party may sue over any settlement even if he or she was *not* a member of the plaintiff class.

Using attorneys' fees earned in similar litigation, these industrious "tort kings" bankroll the next generation of class action lawsuits. Given the recoveries in recent years, their pockets are as deep as many corporations'. As lawyer Richard Scruggs said, "Asbestos gave us a war chest for tobacco"; now tobacco fees will finance "more daunting cases." The very act of targeting an industry can wreak havoc. Upon announcing an attack on HMOs, those businesses experienced a $12 billion stock drop in a single day. Attorneys have gleefully noted that suits against six of these industry leaders could reach 100 million enrollees. Whatever the merits of the action, the effect is to bring an industry to its knees before a lawsuit is ever filed.

Settlement conferences effectively rewrite the rules for a business's operations without elected lawmakers even entering the picture. More than that, such agreements between attorneys are literally setting our national agenda, as they target (read blame) businesses for race relations, accidents, injuries of every kind, and even the health effects of the foods and drinks we ingest. These cases and lawyers have completely circumvented our constitutional process by creating new laws in the courts instead of Congress. As Lester Brickman from the Benjamin N. Cardozo School of Law says, "They have invented a formula where they get megabucks . . . for being a super legislature and creating policy to their liking without regard to the right of the electorate to make the ultimate decisions about public policy."

In much of this class action litigation, the only real beneficiaries are the lawyers. In June 2000 newspapers across the country heralded the settlement of the Publisher's Clearing House suit. All those poor, elderly people who were tragically duped into believing "You're a winner!" by failing to read the rest of the material that clearly stated "if your name is drawn" would now be compensated for their "damages," right? Wrong. The breakdown was as follows: $19 million for consumer refunds, $14 million for attorney fees and administrative costs, and $1 million in civil penalties. The consumer refunds went to twenty-six states, which works out to less than $800,000 per state. Divide that by the population and you have pennies for each complainant. The winners were the lawyers. Of course, Publisher's Clearing House is out a big sum and must now refrain from its "deceptive practices." There will be no more heart-thumping declarations on those envelopes.

In one airlines price-fixing suit, the plaintiffs received a discount coupon for a future flight. Of course, they still had to buy the next ticket, subject to strict blackout periods. As you can imagine, and as the airlines expected, few coupons were redeemed. However, the plaintiff attorneys pocketed $14 million for their efforts.

It is often hard to determine how many class members ever use the token "coupons" that emerge from much of the class actions today. In one case against ITT Financial Corporation, records showed that only two of 96,754 coupons were ever redeemed, a rate of .002 percent. Blockbuster Video settled such a suit over late rental fees with coupons. Class members get a free rental, but the attorneys rake in a bundle.

Sometimes the plaintiffs are actually *out* money despite a victory. In a settlement for overcharging on mortgage fees, some class members "won" about $10, only to have their escrow account docked for eight or nine times that amount to cover attorneys' fees. The lawyers walked away with about $8 million on that one. One class member sued over that settlement only to be countersued by the lawyers for $25 million. Take that!

Even worse, defendants often collude with the other side to avoid future liability. Once a suit is settled, they're off the hook for that entire class of plaintiffs. Even if they'd rather fight what seems to be a nuisance suit, a settlement that disposes of thousands, even millions, of potential lawsuits can be very appealing. This is particularly true when several states have competing lawsuits. If defendants have to throw in a hefty sum for the class attorney to buy them off, so be it. It is a cheaper exit strategy.

In search of the best deal, defendants play one group of plaintiffs' attorneys off the other. This "race to settlement" will mean big money for some lawyers and nothing for others. Attorneys understand this and may substantially water down their demands to get those fees. Their clients never learn about this. A recent RAND study proclaimed, "It is generally agreed that fees drive plaintiffs' attorney's filing behavior, that defendants' risk aversion in the face of large aggregate exposures drives their settlement behavior . . . In other words, the problems with class actions flow from incentives which are embedded in the process itself."

Courts are even permitting lawsuits when no problem has occurred yet! In 1999 Toshiba settled a class action at a cost of $1 to $2 billion for alleged laptop defects that *might* cause users to lose data while saving files to their floppy drives. As the *Los Angeles Times* reported, "no consumer ever complained of losing data as a result of the glitch." Nevertheless, lab experiments showed that under rare circumstances, a user might lose data if trying to save files while doing other "intensive" tasks simultaneously, like playing computer games or watching videos. The company posted software on the Internet that would fix the problem, set up rebate and coupon programs for the 5.5 million laptop owners, made donations of older equipment to charity, *and* paid $147 million to the attorneys.

Within days of the settlement, Hewlett-Packard, Compaq, NEC Packard Bell, and e-Machine, Inc., were under siege. In the wake of the federal antitrust action against Microsoft, private suits were coming in at a record pace. The *Washington Post* reported that this company would be "the next Philip Morris."

I noted earlier the "tort tax" that goes along with these actions. Remember this as your auto insurance rates rise. An Illinois jury decided it was improper for insurance companies to repair cars with generic rather than brand-name parts, despite the approval of the state insurance commissioners and consumer groups. The verdict may cost billions to implement, which will be passed on directly to you and me.

Where is this movement going next? The list of industry targets is endless. Interestingly, some attorneys are beginning to tone down their rhetoric. While some still threaten to destroy a defendant industry, others are becoming more cautious. A few lawyers are publicly supporting some caps on damage payouts, so that "one or two ruinous judgments won't bankrupt the industry." You surely don't want them to run out of money before getting your share of the pie!

Wal-Mart is targeted so often that there are research websites devoted entirely to different kinds of lawsuits against the company. One current suit accuses it of maintaining a "cultlike" atmosphere that encourages employees to put in unpaid overtime. An action suggested by tobacco king Richard Scruggs would allege that Wal-Mart engaged in a national scheme to put small companies out of business! "They've damaged the fabric of American life," Scruggs says. "It offends me." Wal-Mart and other retailers also are being sued as vicariously liable for working conditions in foreign-owned factories. Please note that these American companies do not own, manage, or direct these factories. They simply buy from other companies that happen to acquire products from these places.

Do you have silver fillings in your teeth? Then never fear, Erin

Brockovich's law firm is looking out for you. Attorney Allan Siegel has filed an action against dentists, alleging a "right of patients to know if a well-known toxic substance [his words] is being put into the mouth." Although there has been no flood of illnesses from this practice, Siegel is still trolling for victims. Similar actions are planned against manufacturers, associations, and dental licensing boards, with experts predicting claims in the billions of dollars on the "silver filling informed consent issue" alone.

My current favorite in the class action parade is the proposed litigation against the terrible toothbrush. An enterprising attorney has been using the Internet through his site, *toothbrushlitigation.com,* to search for citizens suffering from "toothbrush abrasion." He wants to sue every dentist, manufacturer, and association that advocates brushing with these dangerous instruments for the failure to warn of potential hazards. All toothbrushes, natural, artificial, and synthetic, apparently are the source of this injury. The attorney notes that studies support his assertions. Those who do not brush their teeth have no abrasion problems. Those with the best oral hygiene may suffer the most!

Not only has the subject matter in such cases entered the Twilight Zone, but so have the damage theories. Persons should be compensated for their actual or "compensatory" damages, not what might have happened or could possibly occur in the future. Yet it is the punitive damages that really get attention on both sides of the legal aisle. This type of recovery was not designed to enrich a plaintiff but to "teach a lesson" by penalizing the defendant for grossly negligent or intentional misconduct. The monies assessed should give the violators pause and encourage a change in behavior so as to avoid repeating such a financial disaster. There are many examples of lawsuits that have encouraged major changes in the way business is conducted and products are manufactured, from bank lending practices to the location of gas tanks in cars.

Unfortunately, the punitive damages tool has become a sledgehammer in the hands of many attorneys. When punitive damages come into play, receiving honest compensation for an injury may not be the goal. The case becomes all about the money. In one Louisiana case, Joseph Grefer, a former state district judge, and his family alleged corporate pollution of their property. Despite Exxon's offer to provide a cash settlement as well as clean up the land (at an estimated cost of $46,000), the plaintiffs pressed on. While the owners themselves valued the property only at $1.5 million, the jury awarded $56 million specifically for the cleanup. The total award with punitive damages was $1 billion. While many of these enormous recoveries are later reduced or negotiated down, the final amounts are still hefty and serve to increase a sense of entitlement by future claimants and their attorneys.

Today many companies are sued repeatedly for the same act in individual and multiple class action suits. Each award of punitive damages becomes essentially a case of double jeopardy. Firestone failed to recall and correct a tire problem. It should be seriously punished for that corporate decision, if, as alleged, it was grossly negligent or intentional in its behavior. However, hundreds of lawsuits now seek that same punitive jackpot for the same corporate decision as a means of enriching claimants and their counsel.

Additionally, why should an enormous recovery in one of these cases go to that single plaintiff or even a group, when the punitive damages are meant as punishment for a greater social wrong? The "lucky" or persistent party that sues for the exploding gas tank or collapsing baby carriage is, in a very real sense, representing *all* consumers who may have faulty equipment. The victim of police brutality is a stand-in for all those existing or potential victims who may suffer from negligent or nonexistent police policies and training. Columbia Law School professor John Coffee summed up my reaction when he said that "the ultimate question is if the punitive damages should go to a few individuals who have a lucky windfall in a legal lottery or to some broader social purpose."

Instead of artificially limiting or capping punitive damages, as some have called for, why not allocate those awards to the state or to federal agencies responsible for the oversight of the product's safety or industry compliance? By stocking campaign coffers, corporate lobbyists can and do discourage the funding, staffing, and monitoring of important agencies. Some of this influence could be countered by mandating that the government's recovery in a tort suit along with any punitive damages from civilian litigation be assigned to remedy the subject problem, such as pollution or consumer safety. While agencies are certainly capable of misusing their own funds, at least a good portion of the awards would be directed at enforcement and protection efforts.

Furthermore, the taxpayers might actually get a break. As society ultimately pays for most tort damages through both price increases and corporate tax deductions, we might as well try to eliminate the double dipping. By funneling litigation recoveries into enforcement agencies, we could reduce the amount of up-front tax dollars needed to fund this work. That way we're not being taxed on both ends of the bargain. This result would be no different from what occurs when an agency like the EPA sues on behalf of the country. Those fines go into government coffers but, once collected, must be used to address the original problems. This was the intent with the state and federal tobacco awards (although, unless mandated in the settlement documents, few states have actually put the money where they promised). If the awards were mandated to go to healthcare or to reducing teen smoking, then the legislature couldn't slip the money into the general revenues. Then the money would benefit the very citizens and consumers who have been endangered by the violations.

Finally, the intimidation factor might be increased. If corporations realized that society (including the jurors hearing a case) would benefit directly from punitive recoveries, they might be less inclined to violate regulations or behave negligently. The government, as well, could best serve their big corporate contributors by stringently enforcing regulations to protect them from large punishment awards from citizen juries.

Attorneys will scream that such potential recoveries are the motivation for private firms to spend the time and money to pursue big cases. O.K., let the plaintiff, as the representative of the people, recover, say, the lesser of 10 percent of any punitive damage award or $10 million. Acting as surrogates for fellow citizens, plaintiffs still would benefit through limited participation in punitive damages, but most of that recovery would go to protecting society at large.

Remember when Shakespeare honored lawyers as the sentries of freedom in *Henry VI*? Only death could dissuade their mission. Properly armed with the sword of justice, attorneys would insure that the rule of law served the people. While dedicated to their clients, each member of the "disinterested class" would first remain loyal to our magnificent legal system. All I can say is we've come a long way, baby.

On September 11, I was sitting on the tarmac at Newark Airport, waiting to fly to the West Coast. I watched out an airplane window as the Twin Towers disappeared in smoke and flames. One of my most precious mantras from anthropologist Margaret Mead kept swirling in my brain: "Never doubt that a few people can change the world. In fact, that's the only way it ever has." That beautiful fall morning, nineteen hijackers turned the world upside down. A handful of men managed to kill thousands, cost us hundreds of billions of dollars, halt our national transportation system, and strike fear into the heart of every American.

In that horrifying moment, where were the rules and laws to protect us? All of our systems and institutions—our government, military and corporate structures—could do nothing to save the day. Federal Aviation Administration regulations proved worthless as did security measures in the airports. No engineering code had calculated the effect of a jumbo jet full of fuel on a steel structure. Evacuation manuals never thought to address whether a plane crash into one building should trigger evacuation from another. As the smoke billowed and the towers came thundering down, people had only their courage and instinct to see them through.

It was the firefighters and cops, the emergency medical service workers and volunteers who restored some semblance of order and unity amid the chaos. It was the hearts and souls of thousands of individuals who were willing to pitch in to help. Organizational charts and assignments went out the window as people simply acted in the best ways they knew how. Some carried water or collected food, blankets, and flashlights. Others opened their homes to strangers they might never see again. Still more lined up for hours to give the only thing they might have, their precious blood. It was black kids in

Harlem donning tricolor doo-rags and neighbors rallying behind some frightened Pakistani or Iraqi shop owner that brought out the best in each of us. It was the National Anthem and Pledge of Allegiance that rang out over the airways in a crescendo unmatched in years that made us all believe we would get through this, bruised but intact.

As the chaos diminished, systems fell back into place. Volunteers were sent home as the professionals steeled their nerves for the long task ahead, but even then, things were not the same. Weeks into the tragedy, New York mayor Rudy Giuliani ordered most of the firefighters back to normal duty while some of their brethren remained under tons of rubble. Apparently union and employment rules defined such activities as beyond the appropriate scope of duty. New York's bravest didn't give a rat's ass for the rules. Many refused to leave and even scuffled with the cops who tried to enforce the order.

I sympathized with the firefighters, although the regulations were quite clear. Those men and women might be needed elsewhere. They also could get injured while outside their designated functions, permitting some insurance company to refuse coverage. But my hat was off to those who cared so much that the system just didn't matter anymore. Their sweat and determination would retrieve those seemingly buried forever. They would show the families grieving at home that loved ones were not forgotten.

In those initial hours, certain rules that did exist were simply ignored. Civilians with no particular training or any liability coverage were clambering over the site to aid in rescue efforts. There was no time for studies on relocating the rubble. The EPA had no chance to examine the immediate or long-term effects of particulate matter. OSHA couldn't scream about the lack of safety rails around the gapping holes emitting fire and fumes. Due process requirements for bidding the excavation job were ignored. All of these rules and procedures took a backseat to the exigencies of the rescue and cleanup operation.

Like the reconstruction of Highway 880 after the 1989 San Francisco earthquake, this removal project would violate many of the legal niceties imposed on such undertakings. Yet the California roadway was restored in record time and below cost estimates, thanks to the emergency conditions. New York taxpayers will likely reap similar benefits as this site is reclaimed.

The companies actually performing this work may not be so

lucky. Some contractors now fear they might go bankrupt from expected lawsuits over the release of toxic substances like asbestos or damage to surrounding buildings from the excavation work. In a *New York Times* piece, Peter K. Tully, president of Tully Construction Company, said, "We've faced a real financial risk. If this had been a normal job, we would have bought insurance ahead of time. But under the circumstances, we couldn't do that. We were here on Sept. 11. No questions asked." It looks like the federal government will pony up coverage for these companies to protect them from financial ruin.

Other agencies had to backpedal on some of their favorite politically correct principles after September 11. Remember that the Justice Department backed away from its support of a plaintiff's suit that was seeking to weaken fitness standards for employment as a police officer. The EEOC now permits previously illegal questions about someone's health "for the purpose of formulating plans for emergency building evacuations." The Americans with Disabilities Act has long been interpreted to require employers to ignore such conditions as extreme obesity, asthma, and poor eyesight. Apparently you may now ask about such problems for this limited purpose although the employee doesn't have to answer. I still recommend employers make contingency plans for every malady and disaster, even the inconceivable. Otherwise you'll probably get sued.

But the insanity that defines so many of our rules remains the norm. The general public understood the need to profile passengers at the airport. In fact, African and Arab Americans topped the list of those who supported selective security checks after the attacks. Unfortunately, our officials were so fearful of appearing to discriminate that such rational behavior was rejected in favor of mass searches of everyone, from infants to the infirm.

Columnist Charles Krauthammer wrote a wonderful piece for *Time* magazine stating the obvious: "Random passenger checks at airports are completely useless. We've all been there in the waiting lounge, rolling our eyes in disbelief as the 80-year-old Irish nun, the Hispanic mother of two, the Japanese-American businessman, the House committee chairman with the titanium hip are randomly chosen and subjected to head-to-toe searching for . . . what? Not for security—these people are hardly candidates for suicide terrorism—but for political correctness. We are engaged in a daily and ostentatious rehearsal of the officially sanctioned proposition that suicide terrorists come from anywhere, without regard to gender, ethnicity, age or religious affiliation."

Things really got interesting as citizens realized how little had been done to prepare for terror in the homeland. We pay plenty of tax dollars for state and federal agencies to protect us, right? True, but remember, the big airlines pay protection money as well. Between January 1999 and January 2001, they coughed up about $8.4 million to federal candidates and the two political parties, according to Associated Press writer Jonathan Salant. He noted this figure in a piece about the annual confab between members of Congress and the big aviation associations that took place in Hawaii in 2002.

For well over a decade the warning signs were building. We had been through several airline hijackings and bombings, and the World Trade Center was attacked in 1993. Osama bin Laden and his cohorts were well known to authorities as the major suspects in the bombing of the USS *Cole,* and our intelligence services had intercepted plans by radical Muslim fundamentalists to "do something big" in the United States around September 2001. Government agencies did not know what would occur or exactly when, but they were on notice to shore up our more obvious weak spots.

So how did they do? They certainly failed Airport Security 101. Most international airlines secured their cockpit doors years ago, but not us. That seems a no-brainer. Before September 11, FAA rules actually permitted box cutters and four-inch knife blades onto airplanes, but things they disallowed made it on board anyway. One undercover examiner conducting a random security test described to me how he walked unmolested through metal detectors with an assault rifle strapped under his jacket.

Guns have been found on passengers numerous times since September 11, but very few nail clippers and eyelash curlers have made it on board. I stabbed myself in grade school with a pencil and still carry the lead in my hand, but no one has taken my writing tools yet. After Richard Reid, the alleged "shoe bomber," was caught, everyone had to take off his or her shoes. A lot of good that did. In January of 2002, security devices at the San Francisco airport detected military explosives residue on a passenger's shoes, then guards promptly let the suspect disappear into the crowd.

Why have these airliners and government agencies been so lax? Well, for one thing, improved security costs more money. The airlines and private security firms wanted no interference with their minimum-wage workers, so Congress and the FAA left them alone. No criminal background checks of airport employees were required. Security screeners could be noncitizens, no high school diploma was necessary, and a few hours of training would get you posted. Often workers scribbled access codes next to the alarmed keypad so the forgetful screeners could access secure sites. This practice was still being reported *after* September 11.

While every human crevice is now examined for errant nose scissors, most checked luggage passes through without a glance. Pan Am 103 blew up over Lockerbie, Scotland, in 1988, so that airline has had a fifteen-year head start on the need for such screening. Nevertheless, the airlines kept complaining that examining all luggage was just too slow and expensive. Congress adopted a few measures before this latest tragedy. Why did they get through? Well, thanks to a sweetheart deal helped along by Senator Tom Daschle's wife, Linda, the airline lobbyist, one company's baggage-scanning machine became a mandated government purchase. Unfortunately, her client's product was deemed substandard by the Department of Transportation. That didn't matter because these machines were written into law. Our tax dollars paid for them although most were never installed.

Now transportation secretary Norman Minetta is scrambling to fulfill congressional promises about checking all luggage. Watch the semantics. Remember, it's all in the way the rules are written. You might think "check" means look at, examine, or screen. Not necessarily. The debate between the airlines and Congress came down to whether the airlines could use a computerized profiling system to identify potentially threatening passengers, then screen just their bags, or whether they would have to match all checked bags to all boarding passengers on each flight. The airlines screamed that the matching takes too long, although they have been doing this on international flights for several years. All this consternation helped deflect attention from the fact that *neither* position requires that all checked luggage actually will be screened.

To improve the quality of security agents, some bright sparks in Congress decided to make them federal employees. There's a joke in there somewhere, but these guys were serious. A few representatives in the know said this move would make it almost impossible to fire the incompetent ones, thanks to our absurd government employment laws. They were assured that this would not be a problem since all new hires would be highly qualified through rigid selection and improved training standards. The former head of security for Israel's El Al airline, Isaac Yeffet, told us exactly what we need: "People who understand how terrorists work, who can spot a false passport, who can ask the right questions of the right people. Every screener is holding on his shoulders a 747 full of passengers. It is impossible to imagine that they would have dropped out of high school."

But as soon as the subject disappeared from the news headlines, politicians gave in to the cost-cutting airlines and security companies that didn't want to replace at least a quarter of their employees. Noncitizens and those without a high school education could still work as screeners. Jim Hall, former head of the National Transportation Safety Board, summed it up when he said, "If all we're doing is recycling the existing screeners, why have we made the tremendous investment in creating a federal workforce?" Here's an obvious reason. Besides the big government bailout of the airline industry, which I'll get to in a moment, the airlines also were relieved of the cost of these employees as the screeners moved onto the federal—taxpayers'—payroll. By March of 2002, the American Federation of Government Employees had already approached the Department of Transportation about collective-bargaining rights for these 28,000 new federal screeners. It's already time for a raise?

Even the most dedicated screeners were getting no help from law enforcement before the attacks. Privacy considerations kept the FAA from sharing computer assisted screening systems with the FBI or the Immigration and Naturalization Service (INS). If one of these agencies issued a terror alert about someone (as occurred for two of the hijackers before September 11), airline personnel would not know to look for or detain the person. In 1996 then vice president Al Gore headed a commission on Aviation Safety and Security. His final report in February 1997 put this weakness among the top concerns to be addressed immediately. Nothing happened. The FBI also had been begging for new computer equipment that could process and analyze all the bits of information from around the world about terror organizations, but Congress didn't want to spend our money there. Guess what? They're spending it now.

The INS remains even less informed. After the 1993 World Trade Center bombing, Congress passed a law requiring that the INS track

foreigners here on student visas. There are over 300,000 people floating around the country who have violated the terms of their visas.
Nine years later, the INS *still* has no way of tracking them. When violators are brought in, they get lots of due process. Their first hearing
may actually produce an order to leave, but there are still options. De-
tainees usually get out on bail while awaiting an appeal, then just disappear again.

Following the terror attacks, you would think the INS would be
examining its records. Not closely enough. The Florida flight school
where Mohammed Atta trained finally got the proper paperwork and
permission from the INS to train Atta and his cohort . . . six months
after September 11. In the meantime, people are calling for the depor-
tation of those who are here illegally. It seems that the rational place
to start would be those young males from nations we know are har-
boring terrorists. Once again, however, political correctness and discrimination laws are thwarting this logical approach.

After the outbreak of anthrax in the mail system, the Centers for
Disease Control (CDC) wisely suggested that the U.S. Postal Service
buy protective masks for its workers. The agency did just that, obtaining almost 5 million "spore-proof masks" by the end of October. But
here's the catch. Employees couldn't use the masks until completing
appropriate OSHA training and passing a "fit test."

The fear of a major bioterroristic attack had members of the medical community calling for the reintroduction of the smallpox vaccine.
Historically a small number of recipients suffered adverse side effects,
but the overwhelming majority handled the treatment just fine. Today, however, the smallest risk is intolerable. President Bush actually
discussed the concern over rare complications as a reason for post-
poning any large-scale distribution. Trial lawyers salivated over potential lawsuits. One multimillion-dollar class action by a handful of
injured people could ruin the pharmaceutical manufacturer. Do we
ban all access because of this small risk? Should lawmakers limit potential lawsuits, or impose an "assumption of the risk" provision, so
that people can decide for themselves whether to chance it? Wouldn't
you like the opportunity to decide for yourself?

We have also learned that our supply of anthrax vaccine, even for
the military, is quite limited. Why? The FDA wouldn't approve the
manufacturing practices of the only company producing this vaccine.
The end product was perfectly fine, but the agency said certain rules

were being ignored during assembly. Finally in February of 2002, the FDA relented and production got under way.

Here is my favorite political abuse emerging from the tragedy of September 11. I firmly believe that the ability to write and manipulate laws is the real currency in elected politics. Even if you eliminated big contributions, this powerful quid pro quo remains. Sure enough, the events of September 11 offered an excuse for an extraordinary jumble of favors and concessions to big business, most arising out of preexisting conditions having *no* relationship to the attacks. Note how many politicians, long opposed to any sort of tort reform, have quickly rallied to protect their favorite corporations. No friends of, say, an asbestos company or old lead paint maker, liberal members of Congress were falling over themselves to protect hometown businesses and big contributors from the wrath of the trial lawyers. Washington senator Patty Murray (who was in Hawaii for the industry's Aviation Issues Conference this year) was working to limit Boeing's exposure while New Yorkers Chuck Schumer and Hillary Rodham Clinton pushed for legislation to protect the leaseholder of the World Trade Center, the Port Authority, the City of New York, airport operators, and the makers of certain aircraft from overwhelming and possibly devastating lawsuits. These same legislators would scream if anyone tried to limit the number of cases or restrict recovery by citizens in other circumstances.

Despite the fact that we entered a recession around March 2000, every struggling industry blamed its troubles on September 11. The insurance market was already facing huge premium increases, especially in the transportation area, by early summer. Our airlines were all in financial trouble long before September 11. Nevertheless, the attacks became an excuse for subsidies, grants, and bailouts for industries experiencing this general loss of earnings.

First Congress passed a bailout worth $15 billion for our "essential air service." Stephanie Mencimer was kind enough to clarify Washington's definition of "essential" in a report for the *Washington Monthly*. Warbelow's Air Ventures of Alaska "is a charter service that, among other things, delivers mail to remote Alaskan villages and takes hunters and fishermen on guided trips into the Alaskan bush." Warbelow's local industry group suggested he file for help, and "Warbelow says he wasn't even required to submit any documentation with the seven page form." While he was only grounded for two days and lost a maximum of $40,000, he has collected $95,000 so far. Helicopter companies that conduct tours and work "for film and video companies, aerial photography for real-estate surveys, as well as some corporate charters" are all collecting. "Casino Express Airlines flies tourists from around the country to exactly one place, The Red Lion Inn in Reno, Nevada. But Casino Express was grounded just like American Airlines, so it received $829,389 from the bailout fund." The reason is obvious: "No airline bailout bill as going to make it through committee without taking care of constituents back home, including every little puddle jumper flying the Alaskan bush."

Best of all, in the terror aftermath, the Bush administration patriotically attempted to eliminate Reagan's Alternative Minimum Tax for corporations, complete with a rebate on all such taxes paid since 1986. I wish I could have heard the executives at places like General Motors absolutely howling with laughter at this scam. The terror attack would provide brilliant cover for this tremendous giveaway.

The horrible day of September 11 was an oddly reinforcing moment for me. To paraphrase Secretary of Defense Donald Rumsfeld, "We need more human intelligence . . . people who speak Farsi, who can infiltrate the streets of Cairo or Baghdad." His point was simply that our politically correct rules and laws had castrated the Central Intelligence Agency and other intelligence agencies. Heaven forbid our agents associate with disreputable characters to glean information or permit bribes or deception to achieve important ends.

These few incidents and observations about September 11 I've set out do not begin to cover the dastardly influence that "the system" had on so many elements that converged on that tragic day. Bad laws, good laws with no enforcement, needed rules that were too costly or time consuming to require: The list is long. Try this exercise sometime. Pick up your local paper, or the *New York Times* or *Washington Post* if you really want some fun, and circle every story that suggests the various patterns I have discussed, including the selective enforcement of our laws, rule making as political payback, or election fodder and litigation for a lawyer's bottom line not the client's benefit. Some pieces will actually mention lawyers, lobbyists, or politicians, but most will just discuss the creation and enforcement of laws. Ask yourself the questions I've raised: Do we need this law? Is the goal achievable? Who benefits and who pays? What are the ancillary consequences? Would we rather take our chances without the rule or law or regulation than add one more mandate to our crushing load? Rarely will the articles answer even the first few questions; as for the rest, they are almost never addressed. However, we *must* ask, for you and I ultimately will bear the cost, social disruption, and outright corruption that accompany our nation of laws.

It is easy to point fingers and complain about the legal insanity sweeping the country today. It is something else entirely to provide solutions to many of the problems. Some are legal, others are legislative, and the hardest ones are the human changes in attitudes and inclinations. In an attempt to offer some hope, I will take an abbreviated stab at each of these areas.

Civil Litigation

We began this journey by looking at some of our civil laws, primarily in the area of tort liability. Plenty of excellent measures on the books need to be reinstated in pleadings and judicial findings. The reasonable man standard is a good start. Our laws should not compensate every foolish or tragic event if the plaintiff wasn't necessarily at fault. Would a reasonable man have foreseen the tourists from Tampa getting waylaid in Miami or the car rental client flying into a rage and hurting some passenger? Of course not.

When you and I are at fault, no matter how sympathetic our situation or how reprehensible the defendant, there should be no recovery. The evil tobacco companies should have been strung up for deceptive trade practices, fraud, and misrepresentation in decades past, but today no one can reasonably claim ignorance about the dangers of smoking. If the government doesn't want to ban nicotine or cigarettes, then why should it be able to collect reimbursement for related health costs?

Assumption of the risk should be restored in all its logical glory. I want to be able to rent a horse, climb a mountain, go skydiving (well, maybe not), and engage in any other behavior that carries with it certain obvious risks. No one should be responsible if that inherent danger presents itself and I am injured. It is one thing if the parachute packer forgot to put in the ripcord; it is another if I forget to pull the rope or hit the ground a bit harder than I expected.

Joint and several liability is utter nonsense. Defendants should pay for their own conduct, not someone else's. If I sue several people and the least culpable happens to be the richest, that's my tough luck. If the others cannot pay their portion of the judgment, then I'll just have to keep chasing them for the money. The same goes for contributory negligence. If I am deemed to have contributed, say, 25 percent of the negligence that led to my injuries, any award of damages should be reduced proportionately.

All of these commonsense legal principles have been watered down or rejected as we move farther away from the notion of personal responsibility. Today there is a theory to capture almost every peripheral player in an event. If I try to iron my clothes while wearing them (which I have done before), it is not the iron manufacturer's fault if I burn myself. If I eat or drink myself into an early grave, the French fry or whiskey company is not responsible.

Class actions should once again be strictly controlled by the courts so that the current abuses are minimized. People should not have their rights adjudicated because they failed to opt out of some lawsuit. Forum shopping by attorneys—accomplished by rounding up one plaintiff in a community known for big verdicts—should be prohibited. The federal courts should step in when such behavior is used to manipulate the system. And, of course, with contingency fees out, there will be fewer coupon cases where the attorneys are the only ones with money at the end of the day.

Damages must not be paid unless the party actually has suffered some injury. A potential problem with a car or computer should not get you into court. That does not prohibit a plaintiff from presenting evidence, for example, that it is likely that some future problems may occur as a result of an injury, but that testimony should be allowed only if based on a specific standard of reasonable medical probability.

The monetary calculations of injury and loss have orbited out of sight as we now value each human life in the seven- and eight-digit range. Everyone is "priceless." But somewhere between the several dollars' worth of flesh and bone we possess and the immeasurable value of our being, there has to be a more reasonable calculation of damages for the loss of a loved one. As clinical as it sounds, the law must use a victim's economic value, because that is all it can do. Nowadays, to get around that singular calculation, attorneys conjure up exorbitant figures for psychological and other incidental damages. Why should the emotional pain of losing a loved one in a plane crash or even surviving that horror be so much more valuable than the suffering by a war vet or the mother whose child was gunned down in a drive-by shooting? Is it only because there is some defendant capable of paying these enormous sums that we allow such decisions to stand? The area of compensatory damages has expanded well beyond the intended compensation for actual loss. I've already talked about punitive damages. Suffice it to say there should be a reasonable cap on this category or, if not, a place where those awards are assigned to benefit society rather than enrich one lucky plaintiff.

As discussed earlier, we should follow the British example. Contingency fees must go, and the loser pays all costs would be the biggest single change to improve our civil court system today. Indigent plaintiffs can receive aid or legal assistance in many ways without permitting the legal community to partner in the litigation process. The states have plenty of money to hire private attorneys at fair, even generous, hourly rates if they need help beyond their own legal departments. Delivering these huge government cases to lawyer buddies and taking an exorbitant cut of the proceedings is bad enough; seeing that money go back into an official's campaign coffers stinks to high heaven.

Furthermore, judges should be as liberal with their sanctions against unethical or obstreperous lawyers as those attorneys are with the damage figures they request in their pleadings. Assertions in bad faith, discovery abuses, and tactics to delay and harass should all result in monetary sanctions against the attorneys or even dismissal of the case itself in the most flagrant situations. Judges should be willing to grant motions for summary judgment to dispose of frivolous claims as soon as possible in the litigation process. As it is now, they find it easier to push the cases on up to the court of appeals and beyond rather than take responsibility for such decisions. Here is where public funding of judicial elections or the appointment of judges comes into play. Jurists will not impose these various remedies if the lawyers appearing before them are also their cash lifeline to reelection.

Mediation and arbitration are outstanding sources for dispute resolution that need more support from lawyers and judges. There is nothing wrong with mandating certain settlement procedures before a case is actually set for trial as long as the parties have the option of rejecting suggestions. Companies and individuals should be able to contract for truly independent arbitration in lieu of a court proceeding.

Finally, whether by settlement or judgment, the outcome of cases filed in our courts must be accessible to the public. Sealed records do more harm than good as we're seeing in the abuse cases involving Catholic priests. A judge can easily remove the names of parties, any reference to corporate trade secrets or other material that might harm parties to the suit. The practice of sealing settlements was once rare and is now standard operating procedure.

Regulatory Law

With all laws, it is important to remember what they can and cannot do. Whether we're talking about OSHA, the EPA, the FDA, or the IRS, it is virtually impossible for these agencies to check on every business, every problem, every violation. As with criminal laws, we must rely primarily on voluntary cooperation to accomplish the regulatory goals. Therefore, citizens must, first of all, view the laws as rational and necessary. The common man might conclude that defining the size of a warning bell on a boat, in inches no less, may be a bit much, but OSHA has yet to get that message. The activities regulated must truly move us toward an agency's bigger goals.

Right now there is far too much emphasis on the process of writing regulations and not the end product. The obvious reason for this is measurability. We have a compulsion today to record statistics as accomplishments. When it comes time to ask "Have we done better than last year?" few can answer the question without looking at the papers pushed and the number of violations written. Congress must be willing to examine the overall achievement of an agency, rarely measurable using our current statistics, rather than the minutiae to evaluate success.

There are many ways to "encourage" cooperation in these areas, from tax breaks to serious sanctions. Although companies cannot be trusted completely to correct and reform problems, the carrot-and-stick approach has been successful for centuries. Give them the latitude to propose their own solutions and then the chance to implement them. If the goals aren't achieved, then escalating fines without decades of due process should be effective. If anyone screams about cutting off rehearing and review, I'd suggest they look at our changes in the death penalty appellate process. We have no problem calling for a cut on the time it takes to kill someone. Even "evidence of actual innocence," as the high court told us in *Herrera,* may not be enough for another look. Surely we can restrict the endless delay tactics used by businesses to avoid compliance. The idea that seat belts took twenty years to be mandated or that GE could fight a determination about the Hudson River made in the 1970s right on into the twenty-first century is more an indictment of our process and politicians than the particular laws. If necessary, shut the slaughterhouse for an extended interval, close down the industrial plant, or deny that defense contractor further government contracts for a meaningful period of time. Unemployment compensation exists for a reason. That action *will* get a company's attention. Up to now, politics and procedure have been tools of the lawyers and lobbyists to avoid any legitimate punishment for serious violations.

Realistically, most of these operations should be concentrated in the states. The closer to the ground an agency is, like the community cop on the beat, the more likely it will see problems or, better yet, be able to help remedy them. This is a no-brainer.

Criminal Laws

The criminal justice system is in need of a serious house cleaning. We should start with the drug laws. Our approach is not working. How many people, conservative and liberal, must scream this out before the government will react? Marijuana possession should be a misdemeanor and a fine, period. The idea that we're spending fortunes to capture and lock up pot smokers is ridiculous. For more serious narcotics, we should expand the drug courts that route defendants into treatment several times before we resort to jail or prison. If that person is committing other crimes, our response may change, but simple use, even addiction, should be treated as a health problem.

Mandatory minimum sentences must be abandoned. Why have judges if we don't trust them to make judgments? They usually know who is really bad and who is more pathetic. To require a magistrate to give some welfare mom twenty years for carrying a few rocks of crack or grams of cocaine for a boyfriend is obscene. The same holds true for any determinative sentencing. If you think some commission can devise the right punishment for every criminal by putting points on a chart, your perception of justice is very different from mine. A range of punishment that includes the option of probation should be afforded to the one in charge of sentencing. Our fear of "discrimination" or unfairness has led to the knee-jerk reliance on absolutely objective standards, which are, one, impossible and, two, unjust.

We should tell juries about parole laws. They should know what happens to people found not guilty by reason of insanity. It is ridiculous that we expect these people to make life-and-death decisions but are afraid to give them all the facts. And of course, the death penalty is out. I will not argue morality or retribution. Life without parole will insure that the offender is never released. Restrictions on access and movement can eliminate any perceived danger from an inmate. But there is nothing that we can do to bring back an innocent person killed in the name of the state.

Juvenile offenders should be tried in juvenile courts. For serious crimes like robbery and murder, the dual system of punishment I discussed earlier should become the national model. The idea of sentencing a twelve-year-old to life behind bars with no parole is horrifying.

One area where serious enforcement might really deter criminal behavior is that of white-collar crime. Businesspeople are more likely to calculate the cost-benefit aspects of crime than someone burglarizing a home for living expenses. However, this is the area most susceptible to political pressure and selective enforcement. Rarely do major frauds or regulatory violations result in swift, meaningful punishment.

Political Lawmaking

In all areas of the law, but particularly in the criminal system, we allow politicians to grandstand, promising things to appease or win support. We must demand that they give a full accounting of the costs, the effects, and of whether the legislation can accomplish the intended goal. Don't ask us to pay for things that only look good on paper. Put more cops on the street without providing for future salaries or expanding the rest of the criminal justice process, and the result is a one-year dog-and-pony show that at best creates a nationwide logjam. Promise a war on drugs and flood the prison system with low-level dope smokers, then realize we must release truly violent felons to make room for these inmates. Ignore the need for drug treatment and rehabilitation, and we end up simply warehousing then recycling the same people through our prisons. Rule makers also completely disregard the intangible costs of the rules they establish. Police become villains as they do our legislative bidding by the book rather than based on a community's needs. Social workers and probation officers haven't the time for personalized assistance and are judged on the number of cases they close, so they simply process their clients. Expenditures for foster care and welfare for the families of inmates are overlooked, as are the psychic costs to the next generation as families begin to view jail time as a right of passage.

Politicians want tangible results to thrust at their constituents. Unfortunately, social change cannot always be measured in numbers. Even worse, the pressure to make everything equal and fair has made us rely even more on rules and manuals. Do things by the book and no one can accuse you of discrimination. Sadly, the more that rules and laws bind our decision making, the less we rely on our critical faculties to do a good job. Cops know they're being judged not on general crime reduction but on arrest numbers. Just as courts and prosecutors tally their disposition numbers.

Federal agencies know they are judged on the numbers as well. However, they must also keep their fingers in the wind to enforce or regulate in a manner consistent with the prevailing mood. The attitudes of the current administration are more important than the laws that are supposed to be enforced. The Republican administration wants less from the bureaucrats who might rein in business. They might make a show of applauding the work of those bureaucrats, but behind the scenes, they are staffing the agencies with the very people who should be regulated. If all else fails, they simply cut the budget.

The Democrats meanwhile are hand in hand with Republicans on much of the financial legislation. They were on the front lines of deregulation when accountants wanted to consult for and audit their clients despite political handwringing when Enron fell. They subsidize big agriculture and the rust-belt industries along with the best of them. They do tend to step up the environmental, safety, and social welfare activity but in a way that attempts unsuccessfully to micromanage our lives. They have little faith in people, whether individual or corporate citizens, to put their best foot forward for the country. With heavy hands they demand legal proceedings over progress and seem satisfied if the courts come to a standstill in the name of due process.

Our efforts at campaign reform are certainly steps in the right direction to limit the natural tendencies to favor those who favor you. But as I said early on, money is not as corrupting as the ability to write the rules. We must reform the way legislation is passed. The practice of slipping last-minute provisions into bills without notice to fellow members of Congress should be outlawed. I support the line-item veto as a means of removing at least some of the more egregious giveaways. It is easier for the press and public to learn about and attack a provision within a bill than to digest thousands of pages, some of which might actually be worthwhile. Failing that, I would require that each piece of legislation be restricted to the dominant subject of the bill. To attach pork-barrel domestic riders to an emergency defense measure is corrupt on its face, no matter how worthwhile the home project might be. There is no legitimate reason other than subterfuge.

Critically, the five-year ban on lobbying the government after service therein should be reinstated for both domestic and foreign matters. This period should span at least one presidential election cycle to allow for a possible turn over in the administration.

These legal and political suggestions represent substantive change, but they are not enough. The most necessary and most difficult change comes from outside the system. As our laws reflect much about our modern society, we must take a look at ourselves.

Why should you and I care about any of this? What does it matter if we are "benevolently" ruled by an enclave on Capitol Hill that enriches itself while anesthetizing the rest of us? So what if our every step is regulated and supervised by lawyers and judges? Our economy looks pretty good. Most people are busy at something. We listen to nightly political debates on a dozen different shows. We are a righteous bunch, whether from the right or the left, and appear to be moving very fast—toward what doesn't seem to matter.

Actually, because this discussion is a bit philosophical, it may not matter to most people. If few people care about the kind of government or the quality of our citizenry, then all my words are for naught. If we think that pouring more money into schools simply to turn out mediocre consumers is a valid goal, then I should be quiet. If equality is the end all for this society, such that talent, ambition, and excellence are no longer valued, then my ideals are sorely out of step.

Unfortunately, if this is so, there are very real consequences. They just take time to manifest. The loss of our collective vigor and spark may be irreversible. We call out for boldness yet show none ourselves. We proclaim that our mission is to encourage and truly educate our children, yet our example is pathetic and the standards we design are worse. To the world, we are the reigning republic, but upon close examination, the description doesn't fit. We bemoan the state of politics, but democracy is a contact sport, and most of us are sitting on the sidelines. As Henry Grumwald said in his article "The Second American Century," "Sometimes the cry for leadership is a sign of civic laziness." We have been asleep at the switch for decades. Soon there will be no one left to awaken us.

We devote ourselves first and foremost to the almighty dollar and have more in common with fellow employees than with our neighbors. The decisions we make often are defined by an employer's needs, not the interests of community or even family. As Wall Street applauds mergers, downsizing, and relocations, the once-secure American worker is told to develop flexibility and learn to adapt. We are shown statistics that the average worker will change jobs four or five times in a lifetime and told simply to "get used to it."

The mantra of political correctness has become codified into law. We fear saying not just blatantly offensive words but anything that might affect another's sensibilities. Schools prohibit touching of any sort, universities dismiss teachers who cause controversy, the lazy and incompetent can whine about rights and protections in the face of their inadequacies, and in the face of all this we tremble. The sameness we encourage in the name of tolerance or equality leaves me cold, yet as a nation we seem to applaud this direction.

Ervin Duggan, in a speech to the Aspen Institute a few years ago, described the United States as a "culture in chaos" and talked of the Balkanization of America. We are no longer a nation of Americans, he said, but instead just a collection of groups that reside in this country. Today we define ourselves as black, white, Hispanic, gay, straight, fundamentalist, Muslim, or Jew. We no longer agree on a fundamental set of principles and ideals that united our forefathers and defined this nation. Instead, we quarrel endlessly over who has what right, who has the political or legal clout to assert dominance over others. The conversation is not about Right and Wrong but about Rights and Laws, about process. With no agreed social norm, we follow the existentialist Martin Heidigger, who suggested that "to make one's own rules is the highest freedom."

This Balkan pluralism, wherein our differences are utmost and our unity almost nonexistent, is now our national character. Certainly our diversity should be applauded, but there must be an overriding desire to retain a public philosophy that preserves and protects what is special about this country. Walter Lippmann warned back in 1955, "If what is good, what is right, what is true is only what the individual chooses to invent, then we are outside the tradition of civility. We are back in the war of all against all."

Pope John Paul II made this the subject of his 1998 encyclical. I am a bit of a heathen, but I was fascinated with his philosophical plea for a rejection of nihilism and relativism in favor of some universal recognition of truth. Interestingly, he accepted that people may reject a faith-based truth but felt that they must see that there are universal truths that have been judged to be so over time. He lamented the notion that "a legitimate plurality of positions has yielded to an undifferentiated pluralism, based upon the assumption that all positions are equally valid." This result has been inevitable as we promote sameness and equality as our highest goal.

According to the Reverend Richard John Neuhaus, editor of *First Things,* "the basic message is that philosophers have to regain their nerve to trust in the use of human reason. It does seem intellectually dishonest, even cowardly, to refuse to make distinctions in the name of tolerance. While accepting that people may disagree, we need not treat every position as equal, every argument as valid."

This shift away from reason and judgment, encouraged by lawyers, politicians, and the media, makes me fear for our system of government. The individual is now supreme, well armed with rights and process but with virtually no social or public responsibility. We are living in Duggan's "culture of chaos," characterized by "moral relativism and self-invented rules." Particularly in the moral and political realms, especially in the highly visible world of television, we witness that Hobbesian conflict.

Deborah Tanner recognized this in her book *The Argument Culture.* Everything we report must be presented as a battle between opposing sides. There is little attempt to discover any truth but only to win the argument. I have had guests come on the set of my show and ask, before we begin how much fighting I want. As Tanner says, "In the argument culture, the quality of information we receive is compromised, and our spirits are corroded by living in an atmosphere of unrelenting contention."

Sadly, the debates are further degraded by the ad hominem attacks on various positions. One cannot proclaim a belief for fear of being labeled a racist or bigot, of being declared intolerant or somehow perverse. Disagreement becomes personal rather than productive, and legitimate dialogue is suppressed.

Politicians encourage this to sustain a loyal and divided constituency; but sadly, the media does it for ratings. The news community must now battle with the entertainment world for viewers. It is not enough to engage in solid reporting. That, my friends, is simply too boring in this fast-paced, competitive world. If a story doesn't sizzle, it doesn't get much play. Balance is achieved by pitting the loudest voices from the left and the right against one another. Conciliation or resolution is not exciting; we need a fight. The word "infotainment" was coined to describe this phenomenon.

After all, television is a medium that tends to portray the world as left and right, good and bad, black and white. There is little time for the all-important grays where real life exists. If television were strictly an entertainment vehicle, this might not be so bad. However, it is our primary arena for public debate, and the effect is devastating.

The litigious behavior that we identify with attorneys has infected our political debate, news programming, and society at large. This gladiator style may bolster ratings in a world where wrestling and *Survivor* are our premier entertainments, but it is damaging our form of government and way of life. Today people fight constantly over who has the "right" or legal clout to behave in a certain fashion. We now have layers of protection for every powerful or vocal segment of society. Our increasing diversity has produced no shared acceptance of right and wrong, yet agreed goals and responsibilities are essential to a free but ordered society.

I believe that principles and ideals, not the rule of law, are the true underpinnings of a viable republic. Law is a necessary adjunct to a free society, but it cannot replace shared values and community as the ultimate control. The real essence of American law is the codification of social norms that encourage voluntary compliance. Whether civil or criminal, people obey laws in a democracy primarily because of personal morality and social pressure. The threat of punishment carries great weight, but countless studies have concluded that the social and moral motivators are more powerful in guiding human behavior.

The notion of community standards might conjure up the public stockade of centuries past. I hope we are well beyond such horrors. However, the underlying theory is still valuable as a means of resolving disputes and transgressions without the need for so many formal rules. These methods have been labeled the "hidden laws" that allow a society to self-regulate through moral and psychological motivators, such as ostracizing or shame. These factors are far less invasive than legal restrictions or law enforcement. With them our rights to privacy and discretion are retained.

However, to achieve voluntary compliance, there must be a shared sense of right and wrong among the citizenry. Without unifying principles and ideals, the law must step in to fill to vacuum and make those determinations, and it has. We are willingly abdicating social control to "the law" and substituting rules and process for voluntary agreement about how we live our lives. We have exchanged personal responsibility for legal, institutional, and bureaucratic control. We fly the banner of capitalism and democracy while succumbing to the seductive benevolence of government. Have we forgotten that it was the lack of personal autonomy and innovation that led to the demise of communism? Can't we see the social disaster in countries like France where government largess has replaced human initiative? Conceding personal responsibility may seem attractive, but the consequences are devastating for the nation.

Remember Dworkin's words? "Any genuine contest between liberty and equality is a contest liberty must lose." I hope they are not true. Liberty and equality are not the same. One does not give rise to the other. Choices must be made when pursuing one so as not to destroy the other. Compromise must occur to encourage both, but they will never exist in perfect balance. Recognizing the chaos that comes with freedom, Tocqueville warned that while we cannot be completely equal without being completely free, we can be completely free without perfect equality.

The Frenchman wrote one of the saddest passages I've ever read about this condition: "By hatred of privilege and embarrassment over choosing, one comes to compel all men, whatever their stature might be, to pass through the same filter, and one subjects them all indiscriminately to a multitude of little preliminary exercises in the midst of which their youth is lost and their imagination extinguished; so they despair of ever being able to enjoy fully the goods that are offered to them; and when they finally come to be able to do extraordinary things, they have lost the taste for them."

Insisting on absolute equality of results is a stultifying thought. It is the death knell for competition, innovation, and creativity. Accomplishment is rejected in favor of a bland commonality. Instead of embracing the wonderful notion that equal at birth we can make our own way and achieve our own status by hard work and wiles, we lower all standards in an attempt to obtain an equality of outcome. We so fear inequality that our greatest assets, judgment and reason, are denounced as evidence of prejudice. Any distinction based on merit, talent, or, heaven forbid, personal preference is either unacceptable or illegal. We respond to this slow enslavement like Tocqueville's sheep.

This destructive evolution can be changed but *not* by rules or laws. Only a change of heart will do. We must see where all this nonsense has taken us. We must first recognize that a collection of words on a page alone will not abolish crime, improve reading scores, or better the life of one impoverished inner-city mom or child. Regulations alone do not prevent corporate pollution or ensure workers' safety. Problems require people for solutions, people who actually do their jobs, help others, and care about the quality of their work. Police who walk their beats and know their communities will do more to reduce crime than all the laws on the books. Teachers who personalize their instruction and are valued for their excellence will do more for students than standardized testing.

This was always Thomas Jefferson's plan. In *American Sphinx,* Ellis highlighted Jefferson's idealistic vision of certain societies. The European structure was seen as the wolves over sheep; the Americans, and to an extent the British, devised a "precious degree of liberty and happiness." But Jefferson's real acclaim was saved for the American Indians, "where without formal government, society was managed by remaining small and assuring the internalization of common values among all members." He actually believed that free men would naturally interact in harmony, exercising social responsibility as dictated by a shared moral sense.

John Adams, Alexander Hamilton, and James Madison strongly disagreed. They did not trust in man's good nature. Government would determine the needs of the whole, granting only as much freedom as was compatible with a structured society. It seems that Jefferson won the battle but his opponents won the war.

Decisions that should be made in smaller groups have become the province of our federal leadership. Our social disputes, oneupmanship, and moral and ethnic contests are an inappropriate but convenient distraction on the national stage. In the meantime, the real economic and political issues are left to those with money, power, and influence. They proceed to direct the government, unencumbered by a preoccupied citizenry.

We bemoan the influence of big money but fail to use our votes or manpower during elections to regain legitimate representation. Most of us are too disillusioned with "the system" or too focused on our personal well-being and our retirement portfolio to participate. If interest rates and unemployment are down and the markets are up, we simply tune out further responsibility as participants in the republic. We abdicate our future well-being to the residents of Capitol Hill. Empowered by rules and laws, emboldened by our acquiescence, the business of government has become a government of business.

For years we have looked outward for solutions: to our local and state governments or to Washington to solve issues of crime, education, poverty, or homelessness; to churches and synagogues to restore moral values and spiritual meaning in our lives; to conglomerates on Wall Street or the Federal Reserve to secure our financial well-being; and always to the "other guy" to make the sacrifices that will clean up and preserve our glorious home, Mother Earth. But it is not the other guy; it is neither the rules nor the institutions that create and implement change. That privilege belongs to you and me. We have the ability to respond to these circumstances and thereby create the world we desire *if* we choose to reclaim it.

Victor Frankl realized this during the most extraordinary circumstances and delivered his conclusions in *Man's Search for Meaning*. This Jewish psychiatrist discovered at a most opportune moment, while imprisoned by the Nazis, that between stimulus from the world and any response by him, he had the freedom to choose his response. His choice to survive made all the difference in the world, literally between life and death. He writes of the notion that "responsibility" is actually just the ability to respond. Rather than a burden or obligation, Frankl explains that accepting responsibility is the key to acquiring power and instigating change.

This concept applies to every aspect of our lives, but it is our national soul that concerns me now. If we care to throw off the tyranny of law and take back our country, if the prospect of a slightly more dangerous but certainly more rewarding environment is one you would relish, then we have all the tools it takes. Our founders knew a thing or two when they drafted our Constitution. Absent a literal coup by those holding power, we can regain control overnight.

We witnessed this once in the last ten years. Back in 1992, the national debate went something like this: "Which Jennifer goes with which candidate?" Or maybe: "Who should debate the draft, Dan Quayle or Bill Clinton?" Very little was being discussed that seemed to rally our interests until this little fellow with big ears stepped forward on *Larry King Live*. Ross Perot threw down the gauntlet to the American people. He said, If you will be the masters, I will be your servant. Okay, I can't see Ross as anyone's servant, either, but the meaning was clear. He proposed that we take back the country.

In many ways, we did that year. Perot bought time on NBC and, with his charts and pointer, actually discussed the budget and the deficit. He told us what it would mean to balance one and pay down the other. He moved a nation from its Pavlovian response to tax cuts, to a people committed to fiscal responsibility. He changed the debate overnight from one of personality to one of policy.

Regardless of whom you supported, Ross Perot altered the tenor of that campaign. He told us we made a difference, and overnight we did just that by responding vigorously with our interest and our votes. Upon election, Bill Clinton did what most politicians do when he delivered a message that essentially said "Thanks for playing. Now you can go home." We trickled away, once again relegating our governance to the fiefdom in Washington.

Yet independent individuals have always been the strength of this nation long motivated by grassroots movements. From the suffragettes' fight for a woman's right to vote, to a national movement to ban racial discrimination spurred on by a single rider refusing to give up her seat on a bus, to the Ralph Naders who created consumer awareness, to the many today taking up the banner for environmental awareness, it has been one person here and one there who have shaped this country.

If we can, through individual effort, elevate racial equality and the

224 I CATHERINE CRIER

environment to a national cause, so can we unite to fight for education or drug prevention or crime reduction. We can fight for a nation of principles and values that exact the best from each of us for ourselves, for the country, and for generations to come. To accomplish this takes people—people who believe in the power we possess, the power to take responsibility and refuse simply to delegate our deliverance into the hands of "others": the government, the lawyers, the corporations. We are those institutions. We are the cogs in the wheels that drive this civilization.

In response to the September 11 attack, a television public service announcement was aired that depicted people of every stripe proclaiming "I am an American." It was heartening to see, but I question what they meant. We have lived so long as a nation of hyphenated allegiances that I wonder what it is we truly share.

Within hours of the horror, New York City was draped in red, white, and blue. Flags flew in every ethnic neighborhood in the city. Tattoo parlors were doing land-office business in Old Glory body art. Yet, if asked, how would citizens describe this community? Is it just our common land, Western culture, or the shared tragedy and loss? How many would verbalize the ideals and principles that nurture this extraordinary experiment?

Making value judgments about different attitudes or philosophies has become politically incorrect. It is unacceptable to make universal proclamations in favor of relative tolerance. A friend of mine called a few days after the tragedy to angrily relate that his children had never been taught the Pledge of Allegiance at school. "It is too controversial," the principal told him. American history is now portrayed as a patchwork, with no focus on the events and players that truly shaped our national philosophy. Recent polls for the Freedom Forum First Amendment Center showed that nearly half the respondents couldn't name a single freedom embodied in the First Amendment.

In this era of globalization, many groups are becoming more tribal. They are fervently proclaiming unique truths by which to live. They recognize that internal unity is a means of self-preservation. In recent years we have faltered in our civic role and have forgotten our communal dreams. Yet values and principles are not the stuff of history books that can be dusted off and waived when needed. They must be lived each day and taught to each succeeding generation.

Learning about the honor in our heritage is no longer in vogue. Understanding the true nature of an active democracy and the responsibilities of citizenship is rare. However, being an American is not common blood, origin, or upbringing. It is primarily a state of mind wherein liberty, equality, and justice under the rule of law is the human ideal. A republic requires a knowledgeable, active body politic to survive.

Mine is not a call for political indoctrination or unquestioned support for policies or administrations. We have freely debated our future at every turn and should continue to do so. But that debate must emerge from a common set of principles and ideals. Our founders were not relativists. They did not equivocate on underlying values. They took a stand on the kind of government and nation that was intended.

Despite the horror, September 11 was an amazing example of the best we can be. It was not rules or regulations that made us great that day. It certainly wasn't lawyers or lawsuits. It was just an emotion and feeling of unity that gave us strength in the face of such tragedy. It is time to do more than fly the flag. We must understand and proclaim the American principles that have given life to hopes and dreams around the world. We must actively rescue our liberties from those who would tyrannize us. Finally, we must restore the rule of law to its proper place as our safeguard in a government created of and by and for the American people.

Acknowledgments

This book has been many years in the making. The writing was just the final step in what has been formulated through countless speeches and interviews over the last fifteen years. I'll keep it short, but there are many people who encouraged, debated, and taunted me into completing this work. I want to reach back over a decade and thank Jim Logan for the riverside debate that helped crystallize my take on the law, Pat Pearson for pushing me to speak out, and the fabulous Gail Evans for opening the door to a new career and guiding me through with patience and support. Despite my procrastination, Jan Miller, my literary agent, and Bob Asahina, literary provocateur, kept the faith for so many years. Heidi Krupp never quit tugging on my sleeve and making me laugh each time I would retreat. I must single out the team at Court TV for tolerating my final push to complete this book: Rita Barry; Emily Barsh; all my wonderful producers and bookers; the amazing Jennifer Kahn, who kept me grounded throughout the chaos; and my chief, Henry Schleiff. Many thanks to my wonderful editor, Gerry Howard, who coaxed this book from my scribbled rants and raves; and finally to Christopher Wilson, who carried on with tolerance, humor, and understanding throughout this long process.

Author's Note

By its release date, this book will contain cases and political debates that have either shifted or crystallized. Such is the risk of writing about the present. However, I suggest the underlying circumstances will most often remain true to my arguments. Also, I do not pretend this to be an exhaustive or scholastic examination of these subjects, but simply certain observations from one of Lady Liberty's faithful followers.

I am an inveterate newspaper clipper. Many of the references are from news accounts in newspapers and magazines, particularly the *New York Times, Wall Street Journal, Washington Post, Los Angeles Times, USA Today, Washington Monthly, Atlantic Monthly, Harper's, Reason, The Weekly Standard, National Review, New Republic, The Nation, Mother Jones,* and *The Week.*

The Internet is a truly extraordinary tool. One particular site has proved absolutely invaluable (and infuriating): Walter Olson's *overlawyered.com* is the definitive source for daily updates on the struggle against legal insanity. Walter, please accept my admiration and thanks for your dedication to the cause.

As this book goes to press, Philip K. Howard is expanding the fight for legal reform through his organization, Common Good. His bipartisan assemblage of idealists hopes to create a grassroots movement to demand action from our officials on Capitol Hill. I intend to participate to the fullest extent and would encourage anyone so inclined to log on to *www.ourcommongood.com* for your marching orders.

The literature I reviewed covers a vast spectrum from law and politics to American history, government, and various social and philosophical looks at this subject. The following bibliography reflects the principal sources I relied on.

Selected Bibliography

Barlett, Donald L., and James B. Steele. *The Great American Tax Dodge*. New York: Little, Brown, 2000.

Carrington, Paul D., and Marshall D. Price. *Law and Contemporary Problems*. Durham, NC: Duke University School of Law, 1998.

Dershowitz, Alan M. *Shouting Fire*. New York: Little, Brown and Co., 2002

Ellis, Joseph P. *American Sphinx*. New York: Alfred A. Knopf, 1997.

Fletcher, George P. *With Justice for Some*. Reading, MA: Addison-Wesley Publishing Co., 1995.

Friedman, David M. *Law's Order*. Princeton, NJ: Princeton University Press, 2000.

Fukuyama, Francis. *The Great Disruption*. New York: The Free Press, 1999.

Glassner, Barry. *The Culture of Fear*. New York: Basic Books, 1999.

Goldberg, Bernard. *Bias*. Washington, DC: Regnery Publishing, Inc., 2002.

Greider, William. *Who Will Tell the People*. New York: Simon & Schuster, 1992.

Hall, Kermit L., ed. *The Oxford Companion to the Supreme Court*. New York: Oxford Press, 1992.

Hitchens, Christopher. *Letters to a Young Contrarian*. Cambridge, MA: Basic Books, 2001.

Howard, Philip K. *The Death of Common Sense*. New York: Random House, 1994.
———. *The Lost Art of Drawing the Line*. New York: Random House, 2001.

Huffington, Arianna. *How to Overthrow the Government*. New York: HarperCollins Publishers, 2000.

Johnson, Paul A. *History of the American People*. New York: HarperCollins Publishers, 1997

Judis, John J. *The Paradox of American Democracy*. New York: Pantheon Books, 2000.

Ledeen, Michael A., *Tocqueville on American Character*. New York: St. Martin's Press, 2000.

Mansfield, Harvey C., and Delba Winthrop, eds. *Alexis de Tocqueville, Democracy in America*. Chicago: University of Chicago Press, 2000.

Olson, Walter K. *The Excuse Factory, How Employment Law Is Paralyzing the American Workplace*. New York: The Free Press, 1997.

Osborne, David, and Peter Plastrik. *Banishing Bureaucracy: The Five Strategies for Reinventing Government*. Reading, MA: Addison-Wesley Publishing Co., 1997.

Pizzi, William T. *Trials Without Truth*. New York: New York University Press, 1999.

Robinson, Matthew B. *Justice Blind?* Englewood Cliffs, NJ: Prentice-Hall, 2002.

Rothwax, Harold J. *Guilty: The Collapse of Criminal Justice*. New York: Random House, 1996.

Sandel, Michael J. *Democracy's Discontent*. Cambridge, MA: Belknap Press, 1996.

Schlag, Pierre. *Laying Down the Law*. New York: New York University Press, 1996.

Schlosser, Eric. *Fast Food Nation*. New York: Houghton Mifflin, 2001.

Stith, Kate, and José A. Cabranes. *Fear of Judging: Sentencing Guidelines in the Federal Courts*. Chicago: University of Chicago Press, 1998.

Tannen, Deborah. *The Argument Culture*. New York: Random House, 1998.

Vidal, Gore. *Perpetual War for Perpetual Peace*. New York: Thunder's Mouth Press/Nations Books, 2002.

Wilson, James Q. *Moral Judgment*. New York: Basic Books, 1997.

Index

About the Author

CATHERINE CRIER is the host of *Crier Live* on Court TV and is a former news anchor and host on CNN, the former host of *The Crier Report* on Fox News, as well as an Emmy Award–winning correspondent for *20/20* and substitute host for ABC's *World News Tonight* and *Nightline*. A former lawyer and judge from Dallas, she lives in Westchester County, New York.